JOHN HOLMWOOD
THERESE O'TOOLE

C000185685

COUNTER....
EXTREMISM IN
BRITISH SCHOOLS?

The truth about the Birmingham
Trojan Horse affair

First published in Great Britain in 2018 by

Policy Press
University of Bristol
1-9 Old Park Hill
Bristol
BS2 8BB
UK
t: +44 (0)117 954 5940
pp-info@bristol.ac.uk
www.policypress.co.uk

North America office:
Policy Press
c/o The University of Chicago Press
1427 East 60th Street
Chicago, IL 60637, USA
t: +1 773 702 7700
f: +1 773 702 9756
sales@press.uchicago.edu
www.press.uchicago.edu

British Library Cataloguing in Publication Data
A catalogue record for this book is available from the British Library.

Library of Congress Cataloging-in-Publication Data
A catalog record for this book has been requested.

ISBN 978-1-4473-4413-1 (paperback)
ISBN 978-1-4473-4415-5 (ePub)
ISBN 978-1-4473-4416-2 (Mobi)
ISBN 978-1-4473-4414-8 (ePDF)

Cover design by Policy Press
Front cover: image kindly supplied by Alamy
Printed and bound in Great Britain by CMP, Poole
Policy Press uses environmentally responsible print partners

Contents

Preface and acknowledgements

This book is a detailed examination of what came to be known as the 'Trojan Horse affair' involving a claimed plot to 'Islamicise' schools in Birmingham, UK. The affair first hit the headlines in March 2014 and was subject to intense media reporting, as well as government action through a number of different agencies and inquiries. School governors and teachers lost their positions and disciplinary proceedings were later brought against teachers with the possibility that they could be banned from teaching for life. The hearings were conducted through the National College for Teaching and Leadership (NCTL), an executive agency of the Department for Education (DfE), and they dragged on until July 2017, with sporadic media reporting unfavourable to the teachers.

Early on a narrative was established that the affair represented a failure of multiculturalism, where conservative and religiously motivated individuals took advantage of a situation in which local politicians and other authorities were unwilling to challenge ethnic minority representatives, even where those individuals were acting in direct contradiction of dominant values of democracy, pluralism and tolerance. The affair, it was argued, represented the failure of some Muslims to integrate and instead to pursue a hardline agenda of separation.

From the outset, it seemed to us that there was no basis at all to this narrative and, indeed, that the school at the centre of the affair, Park View (and its multi-academy trust, Park View Educational Trust), was the opposite of how it was described. It was a highly successful school, expanding the opportunities for its pupils and preparing them very well for life in modern Britain. The puzzle is how it came to be understood otherwise. This book is an answer to that puzzle. Equally importantly, it also seeks to redress a serious injustice, that of the arbitrary and severe consequences that followed for the governors and teachers who were caught up in it and were widely vilified in the press. A significant number of teachers and school governors have had their careers and reputations ruined. And children at the schools have had their life chances seriously diminished as examination results have declined.

Matters took a dramatic turn when the NCTL case against senior teachers at Park View Educational Trust (PVET) was discontinued at the end of May 2017. This was associated with the failure of the NCTL to disclose documents[1] (approximately 1600 pages of them) that were relevant to the case and, it transpired, familiar to solicitors acting for the NCTL since October 2014. Indeed, it also transpired, after initial denials, that these documents had formed part of their preparation of the case against the teachers and should, therefore, have been disclosed to lawyers for the defence. Failure to disclose them was initially presented as a 'departmental misunderstanding', implying that they had not formed part of the preparations. However, it emerged in early May 2017 that the Professional Conduct Panel had been deliberately misled about their role. In discontinuing the case, the Panel judgement stated: 'there has been an abuse of the process which is of such seriousness that it offends the Panel's sense of justice and propriety. What has happened has brought the integrity of the process into disrepute'.

In reaching the judgement the Panel also commented on 'the investment in these proceedings, in terms of time, emotion and

[1] NCTL, May 2017, 'Monzoor Hussain, Hardeep Saini, Arshad Hussain, Razwan Faraz, Lyndsey Clark. Professional conduct panel outcome: Panel decision and reasons on behalf of the Secretary of State for Education in respect of applications for the proceedings to be discontinued', paragraph 174. Available at: www.gov. uk/government/publications/teacher-misconduct-panel-outcome-mr-monzoor-hussain-mr-hardeep-saini-mr-arshad-hussain-mr-razwan-faraz-ms-lyndsey-clark.

money and the genuine public interest and importance in knowing the findings of the Panel in respect of the allegations which have been made'.[2] In part, the public interest in the affair was a product of the media reporting that followed the actions of the government and its willingness to use the affair to promote new counter-extremism policies. It was also a product of the long-drawn-out nature of the proceedings initiated by the NCTL. At the end of July all outstanding cases were dropped.[3]

However, the teachers themselves have been left in limbo, with no opportunity to clear their names of the serious allegations that have been made against them, allegations that are repeated in media reports notwithstanding the gravity of the charges against the Department for Education and its agency, the NCTL, for abuse of process. We will show that individuals who should have been celebrated for their dedicated professionalism and contribution to equal opportunities and community cohesion in Birmingham have been subjected to an unconscionable abuse of power.

Our view that the Trojan Horse affair was radically different to how it appeared in the media and in government statements derives from our long association with the city of Birmingham. John Holmwood, currently professor of sociology at the University of Nottingham, was previously employed at the University of Birmingham, where he organised international summer schools on religion and public life in 2007 and 2008, using Birmingham as a 'laboratory' for living together with difference. Therese O'Toole is reader in sociology at the University of Bristol and a member of the Centre for the Study of Ethnicity and Citizenship, where she works on ethnicity, religion, governance and political participation. She led a major ESRC/ AHRC (Economic and Social Research Council/Arts and Humanities Research Council) study of *Muslim Participation in Contemporary*

---

[2] Ibid

[3] See the report by Richard Adams, 'Trojan Horse affair: remaining proceedings dropped', the *Guardian*, 28 July 2017. Available at: https://amp.theguardian.com/education/2017/jul/28/trojan-horse-affair-remaining-disciplinary-proceedings-dropped-teachers-birmingham-schools.

Governance that examined the impact of the Prevent agenda on state–Muslim engagement in the UK at the national level and in three case study areas: Birmingham, Leicester and Tower Hamlets, and an ESRC/AHRC Connected Communities study of the local implementation of Prevent in Bristol.

All the documents discussed in our book are publicly available. These include evidence and transcripts from the proceedings of the NCTL hearings. Although some individuals are named in the book, their names are in the public domain through media reporting of the hearings. John Holmwood acted as an expert witness for the defence in the hearing involving senior teachers at PVET. Although instructed by the defence (or prosecution), an expert witness has an obligation to the court to provide well-founded opinion. In the words of the Crown Prosecution Service, 'Expert witnesses are under a duty to the court to provide an objective and independent opinion on matters outside the experience or knowledge of a jury irrespective of any obligations owed to the party instructing them.'[4]

This is the spirit in which this book is written for its intended 'jury': a public interested in the case and in wider issues of multiculturalism and community integration and willing to entertain the idea that, for all the media- and government-sponsored smoke, there was, in fact, no fire.

★★★

We would like to thank Gurminder K. Bhambra, Marius Felderhof, Desmond King, Shirin Rai, Andy Wells and two anonymous reviewers of the manuscript for their helpful comments.

This book is dedicated to the senior teachers at Park View Educational Trust – Lindsey Clark, Razwan Faraz, Arshad Hussain, Monzoor Hussain and Hardeep Saini – and to the lawyers who represented them – Claire Darwin, Andrew Faux, Katie Langdon and Melanie McDonald. It is also dedicated to Tahir Alam, head of the Board of Governors of Park View Educational Trust, and to the other teachers caught up in the affair.

---

[4]   See Crown Prosecution Service (2014) 'Expert evidence'. Available at: www.cps.gov.uk/legal/assets/uploads/files/expert_evidence_first_edition_2014.pdf.

INTRODUCTION

A plot to Islamicise schools?

This is a book about multicultural Britain and its discontents. Some of the issues it raises were recently highlighted in the independent review by Dame Louise Casey into Opportunity and Integration. 'Discrimination and disadvantage', she wrote, is 'feeding a sense of grievance and unfairness, isolating communities from modern British society and all it has to offer'.[5] This is the general context for more specific concerns about underachievement in schools – most recently expressed about white working class boys, but also associated with ethnic minority pupils, especially those from Muslim religious backgrounds. Indeed, Dame Louise connected the issues, writing that she also found other, equally worrying things, 'including high levels of social and economic isolation in some places and cultural and religious practices in communities that are not only holding some of our citizens back but run contrary to British values and sometimes our laws'.[6]

This narrative about disadvantage being self-produced within some communities has grown over the last decade. It is argued to derive from

---

[5]   *The Casey Review: a review into opportunity and integration.* An independent report for the Department of Communities and Local Government, 5 December 2016. Available at: www.gov.uk/government/publications/the-casey-review-a-review-into-opportunity-and-integration, page 4.

[6]   Ibid, page 4.

COUNTERING EXTREMISM IN BRITISH SCHOOLS?

segregation and a lack of commitment to 'British values' of opportunity, democracy, the rule of law and religious tolerance. It is a criticism that has been directed at Muslim communities, notwithstanding that they show a higher degree of commitment to those values than do other minorities, as we shall see in the next chapter. In part, this follows from a general anxiety following the 9/11 and 7/7 terror attacks in New York in 2001 and London in 2005, and increased emphasis on countering violent extremism, especially from groups operating in the name of Islam.

However, this narrative also received further impetus from events in Birmingham that came to the public attention in March 2014 involving an alleged plot by conservative and hardline Sunnis – 'men of Pakistani heritage', as one report put it[7] – to Islamicise a number of state-funded schools where there were significant numbers of Muslim pupils. Attention was focused on one particular school, Park View Academy, and its associated Park View Educational Trust (PVET), incorporating two other schools, Nansen Primary and Golden Hillock secondary. The affair also drew in many others who were suspected of extremist activity – with 21 schools in Birmingham subjected to snap Office for Standards in Education (Ofsted) inspections and included in the various inquiries into the affair. The government, as we shall see, cites the 'plot' in its argument about the need to develop a new counter-extremism strategy that confronts extremist ideology and not just threats of violence.[8] Yet we will also see that the Kershaw Report and some other commentators argue that there was, in fact, no evidence of extremism. This was also the conclusion of the Parliamentary select committee that reviewed the different reports. It concluded: 'we note once again that no evidence of extremism or radicalisation, apart from a single isolated incident, was found and

---

[7]   Ian Kershaw (2014) *Investigation Report: Trojan Horse Letter* (Kershaw Report). Prepared for Birmingham City Council and published by Eversheds LIP, page 9. Available at: www.birmingham.gov.uk/downloads/file/1579/investigation_report_trojan_horse_letter_the_kershaw_report.

[8]   Home Office (2015) *Counter-Extremism Strategy*, 19 October 2015. Available at: www.gov.uk/government/publications/counter-extremism-strategy.

that there is no evidence of a sustained plot nor of a similar situation pertaining elsewhere in the country'.[9]

Tim Boyes, CEO of Birmingham Education Partnership, appointed by Birmingham City Council to oversee schools after the Trojan Horse affair, is similarly clear. He had expressed his concerns about possible extremism in Birmingham schools in 2010,[10] but his later view is a little different. He writes, 'the problem that sits behind Trojan Horse is not about Islamic extremism, it's about schools unhelpfully locked into the closest parameters of their neighbourhoods'.[11] On this alternative account, the problems are attributed to poor governance at schools and failure to follow regulatory requirements, rather than extremism, albeit that it is the latter that grabbed the headlines.[12]

From the outset, however, there was an anomaly that disrupted both these narratives of 'extremism' and 'poor governance'. Park View had been a failing school as recently as 1996, but, over a short period of time, it had been transformed. Indeed, in 2006 it was deemed one of the most improving schools in England. By 2012, when it moved out of Local Education Authority (LEA) control to become an academy, it had examination results that placed it in the top 14% of schools in

[9] Education Select Committee (2015) 'Extremism in schools: the Trojan Horse affair'. Available at: www.publications.parliament.uk/pa/cm201415/cmselect/cmeduc/473/47302.htm.

[10] Report by the Permanent Secretary at the DfE, Chris Wormald (January 2015), *Review into Possible Warnings to DfE relating to Extremism in Birmingham School*. Available at: www.gov.uk/government/uploads/system/uploads/attachment_data/file/396211/Review_into_possible_warnings_to_DfE_relating_to_extremism_in_Birmingham_schools.pdf.

[11] See 'Trojan Horse one year on: headteacher who warned the government five years ago reveals plans to create "families" of schools', *Birmingham Mail*, 23 April 2015. Available at: www.birminghammail.co.uk/news/trojan-horse-one-year-on-9095037.

[12] Sara Cannizzaro and Reza Gholami conducted a content analysis of media reports on the Trojan Horse affair between March and August 2014 and discovered that a significantly higher proportion were focused on 'Islamist ideology', rather than 'poor governance' at the schools. Sara Cannizzaro and Reza Gholami (2016) 'The devil is not in the detail: representational absence and stereotyping in the "Trojan Horse" news story', *Race, Ethnicity and Education*. First online, 19 July 2016. Available at: http://dx.doi.org/10.1080/13613324.2016.1195350.

England. At the time, Park View was a small, mixed gender, secondary school for pupils aged 11–16. It had a school roll of approximately 600 pupils. The community in which it was located – Alum Rock – was, in Dame Louise's terms, deprived and segregated, with a high proportion of Muslims, but its school was providing an exemplary education. Its pupils, including girls, were well prepared for life in modern Britain, in particular for jobs and for further and higher education. We will also see that Ofsted, in its January 2012 report, had judged its students to be 'very thoughtful, independent and confident young people'.[13] It is hard to see that these outcomes could have been achieved in a school with poor leadership.

It is worth emphasising the context of this success. According to data presented in the Clarke Report,[14] Park View Academy had a pupil intake that was 98.8% Muslim, with 72.7% on free school meals (an indicator of social deprivation) and just 7.5% of pupils with English as a first language. There are no separate data on the proportion of Muslim pupils in Birmingham schools, but the BME (Black and minority ethnic) school population in Birmingham is 66.6%, compared with 28.9% nationally, while the proportion with English as a first language in Birmingham is 64.2% and 82.7% nationally, and the figure for free school meals is 28.9% in Birmingham and 15.2% nationally.[15] In addition, the school had a higher than average number of pupils with special needs. Moreover, its 'feeder' primary school, Nansen – a school directly across the road from Park View – was a failing school,

---

[13] Park View Business and Enterprise School Inspection report, reference number 105324 (January 2012), page 4. The Office for Standards in Education, Children's Services and Skills is a non-ministerial department of government reporting to the DfE. Inspection reports since 2014 are available from the Ofsted website: *https://reports.ofsted.gov.uk/*. Rockwood Academy is the successor school to Park View. Earlier reports for schools at the centre of the Trojan Horse affair are no longer available online.

[14] Peter Clarke (2014) *Report into Allegations concerning Birmingham Schools arising from the 'Trojan Horse' Letter.* London, House of Commons. HC 576 (Clarke Report). Available at: www.gov.uk/government/uploads/system/uploads/attachment_data/file/340526/HC_576_accessible_-.pdf.

[15] Information provided by Education Service, Birmingham.

so that the pupils entering Park View had attainments that were well below the national average. At the same time, the Ofsted report of 2012 described Park View Academy as, 'a truly inclusive school in which there is no evidence of discrimination and students, sometimes with major disabilities, are welcomed as members of the school community'.[16] Rather than being a school 'unhelpfully locked into the closest parameters of their neighbourhoods', it would seem to be a school that transcended those parameters. Its place in the top 14% of schools nationally was in the context of 'parameters' that make such success highly unusual.

Unsurprisingly, the school's success had earlier been taken up by politicians and by the Chief Inspector of Ofsted, Sir Michael Wilshaw, who affirmed that all schools should be like it.[17] Its head teacher, Lindsey Clarke, was awarded an OBE for services to education in January 2014, and its chair of governors, Tahir Alam, was equally celebrated. Park View Academy was designated as a 'National Support School'.[18] How it had achieved its success was of particular interest to other schools with a high proportion of Muslim pupils, an interest that would later be seen as an indication of suspicious links and a wish to 'Islamicise' them. More significantly, its 'takeover' of other (underperforming) schools – Golden Hillock and Nansen – was at the behest of the Department of Education (DfE) together with the Birmingham Education Services department as part of its school improvement programme.

In February 2014, the situation changed dramatically. This was when an anonymous letter – the so-called 'Trojan Horse letter' – sent to Birmingham City Council in November 2013 was leaked to the press. The letter enclosed a document, 'found when clearing my bosses

---

[16] Park View Ofsted Report, 2012.

[17] See the report by Jeevan Vasagar, 'An Inspector calls: the day the Head of Ofsted visited one school', *The Guardian*, 27 March 2012. Available at:www.theguardian.com/education/2012/mar/27/michael-wilshaw-ofsted-school-inspector.

[18] See the article by Dorothy Lepkowska, 'First "outstanding" school of 2012 reveals all', *The Guardian*, 13 February 2012. Available here: www.theguardian.com/education/2012/feb/13/outstanding-osted-for-birmingham-school.

[sic] files', concerning a plot to 'Islamicise' schools in Birmingham and purportedly addressed to others similarly engaged.[19] It outlined a five-step plan to take over schools by dominating governing bodies, ousting head teachers, organising the recruitment of sympathetic teachers, and the establishment of a curriculum and practices based on Sunni Islamic principles. The story first appeared in an article by Richard Kerbaj and Sian Griffiths, in the *Sunday Times* on 2 March 2014, outlining an 'Islamist plot to take over schools'.[20] Further press stories discovered anonymous witnesses who 'confirmed' the seeming malpractices. Various inquiries were set up by Birmingham City Council and the Department for Education, with one journalist, Andrew Gilligan, developing his own inquiry in *The Telegraph* focused on Park View Academy and the 'dramatic changes that had taken place since 2012' (when it became an academy),[21] notwithstanding that the letter, and the subsequent Kershaw and Clarke Reports, suggested that the process had been taking place for over a decade: that is, over the period of Park View's improvement and not just since it became an academy.

The school that had brought about such a major improvement in pupil performance was now claimed to be betraying 'British values' and promoting an Islamic religious agenda.[22] As the story gathered pace, its achievements were omitted and its practices deemed to be both contrary to 'British values' and unlawful. Part of the difficulty is to understand how a school – and set of schools – could be advocated by Ofsted and the DfE and, within a short space of time, subjected to such misunderstanding and repudiation by erstwhile supporters.

Part of the explanation is the political climate in which the events took place. There had been a recent shift in public policy

---

[19] The letter and document is appended to the Clarke Report.

[20] Richard Kerbaj and Sian Griffiths, 'Islamist plot to takeover schools', *Sunday Times*, 2 March 2014. Available at:www.thesundaytimes.co.uk/sto/news/uk_news/Education/article1382105.ece.

[21] Andrew Gilligan, 'Trojan Horse: how we revealed the truth behind the plot', *The Telegraph*, 15 June 2014. Available at: www.telegraph.co.uk/education/educationnews/10899804/Trojan-Horse-how-we-revealed-the-truth-behind-the-plot.html.

[22] Cannizzaro and Gholami (2016) 'The devil is not in the detail'.

concerning 'British values' and a turn against what was called 'state multiculturalism'. This became evident in a speech on security given by then Prime Minister, David Cameron, in Munich in February 2011. The speech indicated the need for a strong national identity and a requirement to engage robustly with the agendas of different organisations before extending public support, whether by national or local government: 'Do they believe in universal human rights – including for women and people of other faiths? Do they believe in equality of all before the law? Do they believe in democracy and the right of people to elect their own government? Do they encourage integration or separatism?'[23]

As with Dame Louise later, there was an easy (and, as we shall see, false) assumption that areas with a high density of Muslim residents are self-segregated, motivated by different values, and that these values are implicated in the radicalisation of young Muslims. In this way, the very context of disadvantage in which the school had achieved its academic success became an indication of vulnerability to extremism and a presumed lack of integration of the community from which it drew its pupils.[24] The Prime Minister's call for a more 'muscular liberalism' was also taken up within different departments of state, giving rise to a high-level conflict between the then Home Secretary, Theresa May, and Secretary for State for Education, Michael Gove, over the Prevent strategy and the role of schools.

Prevent is one strand of the government's CONTEST counter-terrorism strategy that was launched in 2003. It was directed at stopping

---

[23] David Cameron, 'PM's speech at Munich Security Conference', 5 February 2011. Available at: www.gov.uk/government/speeches/pms-speech-at-munich-security-conference.

[24] Andrew Gilligan's approach was a little different. He regarded the 'hardline Islamist' teachers and governors as being out of touch with their communities and the problem lay with the attitudes of officials: 'the almost mono-racial nature of Alum Rock and its schools made it easier for the plot to remain under the radar. Many council officers and journalists mistakenly saw Alum Rock as monolithically conservative and religious, and wrongly took self-appointed representatives such as Mr Alam as a true reflection of his community.' Gilligan, 'Trojan Horse'.

people from becoming terrorists or supporting violent extremism.[25] Theresa May, as then Home Secretary, published the review of Prevent in 2011. Although she did not identify any problems with publicly funded schools, she did suggest that there was regulatory confusion at the DfE which could cause problems in the future

Notwithstanding the Conservative-led coalition government's commitment to reducing and simplifying regulation, it was certainly the case that policies toward schooling (in particular, the programme to increase the number of academies and free schools) had increased in complexity and had created confusion over responsibilities. For example, schools might be publicly funded and under LEA control and scrutiny. This would involve a requirement to follow the National Curriculum, including a locally agreed curriculum for religious education, developed by local Standing Advisory Councils on Religious Education (SACREs). We will address the significance of the latter in a later chapter. Or schools might be academies (or free schools), publicly funded, but under the direct authority of the DfE with no obligation to follow the National Curriculum and outside LEA control. There remained a requirement for religious education in such schools, but this need not be the locally agreed curriculum under the auspices of the relevant SACRE. In addition, schools could be designated as 'faith schools' – 'schools with a religious character', as they are more properly called – or as local community schools. However, as we shall see, it would be wrong to suggest that schools that were not designated as faith schools, should, by that token, be understood as 'secular'.

---

[25] CONTEST comprises 'Prevent', 'Protect', 'Prepare' and 'Pursue'. In 2007, following the 7/7 attacks, Prevent was relaunched by the DCLG as a 'hearts and minds' approach to 'preventing violent extremism'. It was subsequently revised by the coalition government in 2011. See DCLG (2007) *Preventing Violent Extremism: Winning Hearts and Minds*. London: DCLG, and Home Office (2011) *Prevent Strategy*. Presented to Parliament by the Secretary of State for the Home Department by Command of Her Majesty. London: Cm8092. Available at: www.gov.uk/government/uploads/system/uploads/attachment_data/file/97976/prevent-strategy-review.pdf.

All schools in England, Wales and Northern Ireland are required to have a daily act of collective worship, which frames the school day, and to provide religious education, regardless of school type.[26] Collective worship for faith schools will be the religion of that faith, but for other schools it must be 'wholly or mainly, of a broadly Christian character', as the legal regulation puts it. This latter requirement can be varied if the nature of their pupil intake warrants it. In other words, collective worship can reflect other faiths, such as Islam. Determination for 'other faith' worship is overseen by the SACRE for LEA schools and by the DfE for academies and free schools. Religious education, for its part, is required to be, 'in the main, Christian', while taking into account the presence of the principal religious traditions represented in Great Britain. We will examine these issues and how they bear upon the Trojan Horse affair more fully in a later chapter.

When academy schools outside LEA control were first introduced in July 2000 by the then Labour government of Tony Blair, as a development of an earlier City Technology Colleges programme, they were designed to reinvigorate failing schools and tackle low expectations. After the Conservative–Liberal Democrat coalition was elected in 2010, the policy shifted to encouraging all schools to become academies, using a variety of financial inducements, as well as compulsion for failing schools. It is in this context that Ofsted began to be criticised for its lack of independence and the use of failure at inspections to compel local authority schools to become academies against the wishes of parents and school governors.[27] This involved two

[26] This requirement is set by the 1944 Education Act. In Scotland, the Education (Scotland) Act 1872 allows discontinuation of religious education by decision from a local electorate. Post-devolution, education policy is a devolved matter. For details of the specific requirements across England, Scotland, Northern Ireland and Wales, see Peter Cumper and Alison Mawhinney (eds) (2015) *Collective Worship and Religious Observance in Schools: An Evaluation of Law and Policy in the UK* (AHRC Network report). In that report, they note evidence of very high levels of non-compliance with this duty across schools in England – and particularly in secondary schools. See page 8.

[27] See, for example, Richard Garner, 'Teachers urge boycott of new Ofsted regime', *Independent*, 31 March 2013. Available at: www.independent.

categories of academies: (willing, though not always unanimously so) 'convertor' academies and (failing) 'sponsored' academies. The latter were sponsored under the tutelage of a successful academy which was expected to engage with staff (including governors), as well as the existing practices and structures of the schools to bring about change. Park View became a convertor academy in April 2012 and, between that time and its dissolution in 2014, was sponsoring two other schools within its Park View Educational Trust – Nansen Primary school and Golden Hillock secondary school – with the support of Birmingham City Council and the DfE.

What should be evident is that the process of transforming schools into academies is potentially a conflictual one, with disagreements among teachers, governors and parents about the reorganisation of their schools, and also potential conflicts with new senior management teams from a sponsoring academy. Moreover, Sir Michael Wilshaw, Chief Inspector at Ofsted, had made several high-profile statements about the need to challenge underperforming teachers and governing bodies. Indeed, in an interview in 2012 with Andrew Marr, he had commented that, 'it's about good performance management in schools, and up to now I don't think it's been robust enough and that's something we're going to look at much more carefully'.[28]

The precise circumstances surrounding the emergence of the letter outlining the 'Trojan Horse plot' are unclear. It was sent anonymously to Birmingham City Council in November 2013. The letter and document are widely viewed as a hoax. More precisely, they are viewed as written by someone knowledgeable of Birmingham schools and of specific conflicts between governors and head teachers, but not written by someone with an 'insider's' knowledge of a plot; that is, they are not from the Trojan Horse's mouth. The initial response of

co.uk/news/education/education-news/teachers-urge-boycott-of-new-ofsted-regime-8555233.html. See also Jacqueline Baxter (2016) *School Governance: Policy, Politics and Practices*, Bristol: Policy Press.

[28] Andrew Marr, 'Interview with Sir Michael Wilshaw, Ofsted's Chief Inspector', *The Andrew Marr Show*, 2 September 2012. London: BBC. Transcript available at:http://news.bbc.co.uk/2/shared/bsp/hi/pdfs/0209122.pdf.

the council was to dismiss it. At around the same time, the British Humanist Association had been forwarding to the DfE material from 'whistleblowers' about the transformation of 'secular state schools' into 'strict, conservative faith schools'. It would emerge subsequently that evangelical Christians had raised concerns about pressure from Muslim parents on schools a year earlier. The original letter and document outlining the 'plot' had also been forwarded to the DfE by West Midlands Police via the Home Office, although they also investigated the matter and had no concerns.

In the face of growing media concern – the story was taken up by *The Telegraph, Express* and *Daily Mail*, as well as *The Sunday Times* (and *The Times*), in which it was first reported, and also in the *Guardian* – the DfE took peremptory action, with Sir Michael Wilshaw ordering special snap Ofsted inspections of the schools against which allegations had been made. There were reports on 21 schools, all with significant numbers of Muslim pupils. The inspection reports were published between March and June and, in the case of Park View, serious grounds for concern were found with regard to the 'Behaviour and safety of pupils' and 'Leadership and management', two of the four criteria against which school performance is evaluated. The rating of the school was downgraded from 'outstanding' to 'inadequate'. A report in May 2014 by the Education Funding Agency (EFA) into the PVET ended its funding and sought new trusts to take over Park View Academy and its other schools.[29]

Alongside the Ofsted reports, the then Secretary of State, Michael Gove, also commissioned a separate report into the allegations about Birmingham schools that arose from the Trojan Horse letter. This report was conducted under the auspices of Peter Clarke, the former Metropolitan Police head of Counter-Terrorism. At the same time, Birmingham City Council set up an inquiry under Ian Kershaw of the Northern Education Trust into the culpability of the council (which

---

[29] Education Funding Agency, *Review of Park View Education Trust*, 9 June 2014. Available at: www.gov.uk/government/publications/review-of-park-view-educational-trust.

was also under separate investigation for failures in its child services department).[30] Both reports were published at about the same time in July 2014.[31] The Clarke Report found that there was an 'organised campaign to target certain schools' and 'an intolerant and aggressive Islamic ethos'.[32] In the light of this and the Ofsted reports, Sir Michael Wilshaw also declared that there had been an 'organised campaign' targeting schools in Birmingham to impose a 'narrow, faith-based ideology', with the same people 'highly influential across several of the schools'.[33] The findings of the Kershaw Report were similar. The council, it argued, had failed to act on reported concerns and Ofsted had previously failed to identify the 'dysfunctions' evident within the schools. Having initially resisted the criticisms, Sir Albert Bore, leader of the council, apologised, with a statement that, 'we have previously shied away from tackling this problem out of a misguided fear of being accused of racism'.[34]

---

[30] Kershaw Report; *A Report to the Secretary of State for Education and the Minister for Children and Families on Ways Forward for Children's Social Care Services in Birmingham*, chaired by Professor Julian Le Grand, February 2014. Available at: www.gov.uk/government/uploads/system/uploads/attachment_data/file/297748/Birmingham_report_25.03.14.pdf; while a wider *Report on Birmingham City Council's Governance and Organisational Capabilities: An Independent Review under Sir Bob Kerslake* was published in December 2014. Available at: ,www.gov.uk/government/publications/birmingham-city-councils-governance-and-organisational-capabilities-an-independent-review.

[31] A third report by the Permanent Secretary at the DfE was published in January 2015 (Wormald, *Review into Possible Warnings*). However, it had a very narrow frame of reference, just addressing whether allegations had been raised with the department and not examining its engagement with Park View Education Trust through the Academy process.

[32] Clarke Report, page 14.

[33] Sir Michael Wilshaw, Speech, 9 June 2014. Available at:www.birminghammail.co.uk/news/midlands-news/trojan-horse-sir-michael-wilshaws-7240705.

[34] As reported in *the Birmingham Mail*, 15 July 2014. Available at:www.birminghammail.co.uk/news/midlands-news/birmingham-mail-trojan-horse-investigation-7456936.

This was now seen as confirming earlier newspaper reports. *The Telegraph*, in particular, regarded its own investigation as vindicated and its reporter, Andrew Gilligan, wrote that:[35]

> there are, as our reporting has made clear, three separate strands of wrongdoing. There is clearly extremism in some of these schools, as Ofsted and the DfE found, but it is not the most important strand. The employment of relatives, the bullying and other dubious practices show another strand is simple, old-fashioned power-grabbing and nepotism.
>
> But the most significant and worrying aspect is the promotion of an isolationist ideology. The problem highlighted by Trojan Horse is not really a security one, but a deep concern for community cohesion.

The *Guardian*, for its part, headlined its story on the Clarke Report as a 'co-ordinated agenda to impose hardline Sunni Islam', writing that there was an attempt to 'impose and promote a narrow faith-based ideology' and quoting the Clarke Report that it was 'a deliberate attempt to convert secular state schools into exclusive faith schools in all but name'.[36]

By now, a particular form of the narrative had been established. The practices put in place in Park View might have been acceptable had it been a 'faith school', but were not appropriate for what the Clarke Report, and the press more widely, described as a 'secular' school, notwithstanding, as we have observed, that non-faith schools in England are not secular and have a requirement for daily collective worship and compulsory religious education. Particular 'facts' had

---

[35] Andrew Gilligan, 'Trojan Horse: how we revealed the truth behind the plot', *The Telegraph*, 15 June 2014. Available at: www.telegraph.co.uk/education/educationnews/10899804/Trojan-Horse-how-we-revealed-the-truth-behind-the-plot.html.

[36] Patrick Wintour reporting in *The Guardian*, 17 July 2014. Available at: www.theguardian.com/uk-news/2014/jul/17/birmingham-schools-inquiry-hardline-sunni-islam-trojan-horse.

been reported in the press and had been highlighted in the reports – for example, the recording of a jihadi video in the school media centre, handouts proclaiming that it is a wife's duty to consent to sex, the invitation of a radical preacher to speak at a school assembly, the 'banning' of Christmas celebrations. They were used to give credence to the wrongdoing, alongside complaints by teachers of discrimination and favouritism in appointments and promotions.

However, none of these 'facts' had been properly tested. The Clarke Report and the Kershaw Report took many witness statements, including from those teachers and governors who were held to be culpable, but there was no attempt to reconcile different accounts. Peter Clarke's status as a former police officer probably gave credence to his report as being established in well-grounded complaints, but with the exception of the chair of PVET and former chair of governors at Park View, Tahir Alam, whom he regarded as untrustworthy, the responses of those who were criticised went unreported.

In this context, the reports (including those of Ofsted) are taken as establishing the 'evidence' and yet the reports are themselves deeply unsatisfactory and, as we shall see, fail to provide any context about the requirements of religious education in British schools. For example, the role of Birmingham SACRE was not discussed in the Clarke Report. Nor do the reports discuss the requirements on the teaching of health and personal relations, the guidelines for schools on promoting community cohesion, and the specific nature of the obligations on schools under the Prevent agenda. In the absence of a proper treatment of these issues, there is no clear benchmark against which the schools were judged. Did the schools act differently from other schools, and did they act unlawfully? The presumption of the reports is that they did. But, as we shall see, the reports are ill-informed and frequently erroneous. Indeed, it is hard to avoid the conclusion that they represent the improper exercise of arbitrary authority by the DfE and a breach of due process.

Equally important, the Birmingham 'Trojan Horse affair' is used by the government to indicate the need for its new counter-extremism strategy. The Clarke Report, for example, is cited as revealing 'extremists gaining positions on governing bodies and joining the staff, unequal treatment and segregation of boys and girls, extremist speakers making presentations to pupils, and bullying and intimidation of staff who refused to support extremist views. In total around 5,000 children were in institutions affected'.[37] It further states that, 'as Trojan Horse demonstrated, children can be vulnerable to purposeful efforts by extremists to take control of their schools and create a space where extremist ideologies can be spread unchallenged'.[38] In fact, many of the reports – for example, the Kershaw Report, and one by the House of Commons Select Committee for Education, as we have seen – stop short of the accusation of extremism, though they do criticise the schools for an intolerant and conservative religious ethos.[39]

The purpose of this short book is to address multicultural Britain, educational (and other) disadvantage and the experience of British Muslims in the context of the promotion of 'British values'. But it is also about a serious miscarriage of justice, similar in character to that of the Hillsborough affair, where it took a prolonged campaign to dislodge the false narrative established by the collusion of police and media in the immediate aftermath of the disaster at the football match between Liverpool and Nottingham Forest in April 1989. In the Trojan Horse affair, a group of teachers and governors whose achievements in raising educational standards should have been celebrated (indeed, for a time they were) have been vilified in the national press and have been accused of imposing an Islamic agenda in schools with little opportunity to counter the claims in the face of an overwhelmingly hostile media.

The first opportunity for teachers to challenge the claims came when hearings against them for professional misconduct were begun over a year after the publication of the reports by the designated body, the National College for Teaching and Learning (NCTL), an independent agency of the DfE, in September 2015. Teachers were informed that

[37] Home Office (2015) *Counter-Extremism Strategy*, paragraph 20.
[38] Ibid, paragraph 70.
[39] Education Select Committee (2015) *Extremism in Schools*.

hearings were being planned a little earlier with Case Management Hearings in July and August 2015 to establish the nature of charges and evidence to be submitted (the evidence file expanded from around 1000 pages to 6000 pages between the two meetings). This was *after* the government had cited the Trojan Horse affair as justification for its new plans to counter extremism. The hearings derived from the Clarke Report and its recommendation 3, 'that the DfE should consider taking action against teachers who may have breached the teacher standards'.[40] They were expected to be concluded quickly, but continued through until May 2017. The rush to set up the hearings in July and August 2015 providing little time for the preparation of the case for the defence prior to the start of the hearings contrasts with the long-drawn-out nature of the proceedings once they had started.

The hearings were convened with the purpose of determining whether the teachers at the schools should be permanently disbarred from teaching. However, the arrangements for the hearings were deeply unsatisfactory, with four separate cases brought against different groups of teachers associated with PVET and one other school, Oldknow Academy (involving teachers previously employed at PVET). The cases against junior teachers were heard separately from that against the senior leadership team at PVET. Once again, there has been misreporting of the evidence and little coverage of the detailed rebuttal of claims indicated above, for example of banning Christmas celebrations, or handouts promoting the obligations on wives to consent to sex with their husbands.

The Birmingham Trojan Horse affair dramatically came back into media attention in October 2016 after one of the hearings that had concluded went to the High Court on appeal. The findings were quashed on grounds of serious procedural irregularities. Mr Justice Phillips declared that evidence for the defence presented in the hearing against the senior leadership team should have been made available to the defendants in the other case.[41]

[40] Clarke Report, page 98.
[41] *In the High Court of Justice, Queen's Bench Division Administrative Court. In the Matter of an Appeal Under The Teachers' Disciplinary (England) Regulations*

A further comment by Mr Justice Phillips is noteworthy. At paragraph 37 of his judgement, he writes that:

> the Panel expressly stated in each decision, when pronounced on 9 February 2016, that the allegations were 'in no way concerned with extremism'. It appears that this wording troubled the Head of the Department for Education's Due Diligence and Counter Extremism Group, Hardip Begol. He asked for publication to be delayed pending 'clarification'. With the apparent agreement of the Chair of the Panel, the decisions were amended prior to publication so as to state that the allegations against Mr Anwar and Mr Ahmed were 'in no way concerned with violent extremism'.

The government's wish to act against a much broader remit of extremist ideology and have the Birmingham Trojan Horse case as a justification for this extension shines through.

The charge of failure to disclose documents from the main hearing against senior teachers in other hearings, however, indicated a possibility of a similar failure on the part of NCTL to fulfil its obligations of disclosure in the hearing against senior leaders. The Panel had been ready to announce its decision in the case on 23 December 2016, but an urgent application for disclosure, relating, in part, to transcripts associated with the Clarke Report, was made by defence lawyers on 24 November.[42] At the time, media reporting expressed alarm that the transcripts were those of 'whistleblowers' who had provided statements under terms of confidentiality.[43] However,

---

2012. Birmingham Civil Justice Centre, 13 October 2016. Neutral Citation Number: [2016] EWHC 2507 (Admin). Available at: www.bailii.org/ew/cases/EWHC/Admin/2016/2507.html.

[42] NCTL, May 2017, 'Professional conduct panel outcome', paragraph 16.

[43] See, for example, Camilla Turner, 'Alarm at move to reveal identity of whistleblowers who exposed Trojan Horse scandal', *The Telegraph,* 4 January 2017. Available at: www.telegraph.co.uk/education/2017/01/04/alarm-move-reveal-identity-whistleblowers-exposed-trojan-horse/.

what was at issue also included other documents outside the Clarke Report that had potentially been relevant to the case. Altogether the documents that were deemed to be relevant amounted to about 1600 pages.[44] However, what came to be the main matter of concern was whether transcripts from evidence submitted to the Clarke Report had been used in the preparation of the NCTL case.

Initially, the failure to disclose the transcripts was explained as a 'departmental misunderstanding', albeit one, according to the Panel, where, 'even on that basis such failure was simply unacceptable'. However, it transpired that, just before the Panel was due to rule on 3 May 2017 on an application by the defence lawyers to discontinue, the NCTL presented a note from their solicitors. This stated that, on 14 October 2014, they had received, '25 of the Clarke transcripts to include transcripts of 10 interviewees who went on to be witnesses for the NCTL in these proceedings. This pre-dated by approximately 3½ months the date on which the witness statements were signed and finalised'. This led the Panel to conclude that the matter had not been a 'misunderstanding', but that the transcripts were 'deliberately withheld from disclosure'. In consequence, the Panel judged that the matter was 'an abuse of the process which is of such seriousness that it offends the Panel's sense of justice and propriety. What has happened has brought the integrity of the process into disrepute'.[45] The case against the senior leaders was discontinued, as were the remaining cases in July.[46] The Trojan Horse affair had come to an abrupt end, albeit one that was deeply unsatisfactory.

Teachers had faced lifetime exclusions from teaching. However, the possible consequences would have been more serious for the individuals concerned if the government's plans for its counter-extremism strategy were to proceed, since, under those plans,

[44] NCTL, May 2017, 'Professional conduct panel outcome', paragraph 110.
[45] Ibid, paragraphs 86, 102, 107, 174.
[46] Richard Adams, 'Trojan Horse affair: remaining disciplinary proceedings dropped', *The Guardian*, 28 July. 2017. Available here: amp.theguardian.com/education/2017/jul/28/trojan-horse-affair-remaining-disciplinary-proceedings-dropped-teachers-birmingham-schools.

exclusions could be extended to employment in the public sector and by any charity or non-governmental organisation (NGO) in receipt of public funding. In the meantime, their lives have been severely disrupted and they have been denied the pursuit of their careers for the last three years. Equally importantly, they have been denied the opportunity to clear their names from the charges made against them and widely promoted in the media and to have their achievements in advancing the educational prospects of their pupils in a disadvantaged area properly celebrated and recognised. Counsel for Lindsey Clark, executive head of PVET and former head teacher of Park View, stated, 'today's victory is a hollow one. She had very much fought for, and sought to obtain, a verdict clearing her of any wrong doing. This, now, is no longer possible'.[47]

Indeed, a special adviser at the DfE at the time of the Trojan Horse affair, Jaimie Martin, has specifically linked the case to the Manchester Arena bombing of May 2017, arguing that a problem of extremism remains and writing that, 'it is important to note as they were not tried for the charges, they were therefore not cleared of them', and, further, that, 'people who downplay the seriousness of Trojan Horse, claiming those involved exhibited "mainstream" Islamic views, are guilty not only of stunning naivety, but of a dangerous error'.[48] A similar claim was made by the conservative think tank Policy Exchange, which had previously advised on Michael Gove's schools programme. The co-head of its Security and Extremism Unit, Hannah Stuart, and its head of education, John David Blake, proposed that 'non-disclosure of anonymous witness statements from the Clarke inquiry was described as an "abuse of process", and that is deeply unfortunate, but this falls short of an exoneration. The decision to discontinue disciplinary proceedings was based on procedural grounds – not on a shortage of

---

[47] As reported by Richard Adams, 'Five teachers in Trojan Horse affair free to return to classroom', *The Guardian*, 30 April 2017. Available at: www.theguardian.com/education/2017/may/30/trojan-horse-tribunal-five-birmingham-teachers-islam.

[48] Jamie Martin, 'Schools must be more vigilant on Islamism than ever', *Schoolweek*, 11 June 2017. Available at: http://schoolsweek.co.uk/schools-must-be-more-vigilant-on-islamism-than-ever/.

evidence'.[49] As evidence, they cite the Ofsted inspection reports and the Clarke Report, which, as we shall show, are deeply flawed. Perhaps most importantly of all, the Queen's Speech setting out the legislative programme of Theresa May's new minority government included measures for combatting non-violent extremism and the setting up of a new commission for countering extremism.[50]

In what follows, we will seek to show that there was, in fact, no extremism and no conservative religious ideology promoted at the schools in question. Park View was both mainstream and exemplary. It followed regulatory requirements and guidelines and the Islamic practices in the school were subject to proper scrutiny and approval by the local SACRE. Indeed, they facilitated the school's achievements and its relationships with the local community in a manner previously commented on directly and commended by Ofsted. We will also set out the broader context of the affair in order to demonstrate its significance for all of those who believe in equal opportunities and addressing inequalities in pupil achievement. But the case also matters because it is indicative of a wider populism that scapegoats fellow citizens who are Muslims and promotes a disregard for due process and rights; that is, it is a betrayal of the very values that the teachers in the Birmingham case are held to have disavowed.

We have divided the book into two parts. The second part – Chapters Six to Nine – sets out the details of the Trojan Horse affair and provides an examination of the charges made against the schools and the evidence underpinning them. In these chapters, we show that the allegations made against the schools and teachers were based on errors and poor investigatory processes. However, we also wanted to understand how the affair could have been so misrepresented. The first

---

[49] See Hannah Stuart and John David Blake, 'Trojan Horse: "If anyone is still in any doubt that the practices uncovered were inappropriate, just listen to the pupils"', *TES*, 16 June 2017. Available at: www.tes.com/news/school-news/breaking-views/trojan-horse-if-anyone-still-any-doubt-practices-uncovered-were?platform=hootsuite.

[50] Queen's Speech, 21 June 2017. Available at: www.gov.uk/government/speeches/queens-speech-2017.

part of the book – Chapters One to Five – explains the wider context of schooling in England, religious education and collective worship and the obligations placed upon schools with regard to the promotion of community cohesion and preventing violent extremism. This context indicates gross negligence on the part of various authorities charged with reviewing what happened at the schools in question; in particular, negligence associated with their failure to understand the specific policies and guidelines that had been issued to schools and the requirements for religious education and collective worship. The second part, focusing on the case, can be read without the first part explaining the policy context, but our intention is to draw broader conclusions about policies for life in multicultural Britain than simply pointing out the injustices visited upon the teachers and governors involved in the schools. In that way, their experiences might also provide the way to better policies and of ensuring that others are not subjected to similar arbitrary and unjustified actions.

PART 1

Context

ONE

'British values' and community cohesion

The Trojan Horse affair has shaped subsequent debates on community cohesion and the counter-extremism agenda, but it was, in its turn, shaped by preceding events. These earlier events – urban disturbances, claims that communities are self-segregating, perceived threats of terrorism, and specific acts of terrorism themselves – have produced a variety of political interventions. These have included policies designed to mitigate what were understood to be problems of community cohesion, threatening the social fabric and security. The interventions helped to create the narratives that were drawn upon in interpretations of the Trojan Horse affair, just as the latter has been taken as evidence of the veracity of those concerns and as a motivation for further interventions.

The importance of promoting 'British values' is a recurrent theme, and is frequently reasserted as a new necessity, notwithstanding that policies reflecting this imperative have been in place for some considerable time. To some extent, this may appear to exemplify the claim of French social theorist Michel Foucault that modern neoliberalism 'governs through failure'. That is, interventions produce unintended effects and problems – 'failures' – which in turn give rise to renewed exhortation and interventions.[51] We will propose something a little different, arguing that policies and interventions – especially those associated with community cohesion and schooling – have *actually been successful*, but are, notwithstanding, represented as failing. This is particularly poignant with regard to the Trojan Horse affair. Park View school was an example of that success, yet it has come to represent failure and, in the process, its pupils (or, more precisely, those of its successor school, Rockwood Academy) have had their life chances severely diminished.

Securing the community

For our purposes, the emphasis on British values and community cohesion as an object of public policy can be traced to public debates after the summer 2001 urban unrest in Bradford, Oldham, Burnley and other northern towns. Of course, there had been similar disturbances in previous decades, as well as concerns over Irish republican terrorism, especially in Birmingham. Nonetheless, the unrest in 2001 gave rise to a wave of debate and subsequent policy interventions. There were two government reports, one interdepartmental, the other from the Home Office – the Denham Report and the Cantle Report, respectively – which focused on issues of ethnic difference and the 'separate lives' of ethnic minorities and local (similarly disadvantaged) white people.[52] Middle class people, of course, also lived separate lives, but this was not a matter of concern. Spatial segregation and limited social relations

---

[51] See, for example, Michel Foucault (1991) 'Governmentality', in Graham Burchell, Colin Gordon and Peter Miller (eds), *The Foucault Effect: Studies in Governmentality*, Hemel Hempstead: Harvester Wheatsheaf, pages 87–104.

[52] John Denham (2001) *Building Cohesive Communities: A Report on the Ministerial Group on Public Order and Community Cohesion*, London: Home Office. Available at: www.tedcantle.co.uk/publications/005%20Building%20 Cohesive%20Communities%20(The%20Denham%20Report)%202001.pdf; Ted Cantle (2001) *Community Cohesion: A Report of the Independent Review Team*, London: Home Office. Available at: http://resources.cohesioninstitute.org. uk/Publications/Documents/Document/DownloadDocumentsFile.aspx?recordId= 96&file=PDFversion.

among groups were seen to be the main issues, including 'self-segregation' by some ethnic minorities deriving from their supposed different cultural values. Among other recommendations, the Cantle Report called for an oath of national allegiance from immigrants and proposed that politicians, community leaders and the media should promote 'a meaningful concept of citizenship'. The Denham Report, for its part, called for a debate about identity, shared values and citizenship.

These reports came shortly after the Runnymede Trust's Commission on the Future of Multi-Ethnic Britain and the publication of the Parekh Report in 2000.[53] The latter advocated a form of multiculturalism in which national identity was understood as inclusive of minorities and expressive of their right to co-determine the political community to which they belonged. The report elicited a strongly negative reaction from some sections of the media,[54] but it articulated the idea that multiculturalism was part of a shared conception of citizenship rather than the expression of multiple separate communities with different values. However, the idea that multiculturalism reinforces separatism has been a persistent criticism.

These warnings have sometimes come from unexpected sources. For example, Trevor Phillips, then chair of the Commission of Racial Equality and its successor organisation (in 2006) the Equality and Human Rights Commission, was among the first of major public figures to argue that multiculturalism had failed and that there was a need for an emphasis on 'core British values' to mitigate separation.[55]

---

[53] Runnymede Trust (2000) *The Future of Multi-Ethnic Britain. The Parekh Report*, London: Profile Books.

[54] See, for example, Philip Johnston, 'Straw wants to rewrite our history', *The Telegraph*, 10 October 2000. Available at: www.telegraph.co.uk/news/uknews/1369663/Straw-wants-to-rewrite-our-history.html.

[55] The context was a speech on 22 September 2005, 'Sleep-walking to segregation' delivered after Hurricane Katrina in New Orleans and reflecting on US experience. The text of the speech is available at: www.jiscmail.ac.uk/cgi-bin/webadmin?A3=ind0509&L=CRONEM&E=quoted-printable&P=60513&B=%E2%80%94%E2%80%94_%3D_NextPart_001_01C5C28A.09501783&T=text%2Fhtml;%20charset=iso-8859%E2%80%931&pending=.

This is an argument he has repeated, as we will see, with increasing emphasis on perceived problems within Muslim communities.[56]

The focus on Muslims as a 'special problem', of course, has been further reinforced by the threat of terrorism deriving from radical Islamism and especially the risk of 'home grown' terrorism 'incubated' within 'separate' communities. The urban unrest in 2001 as well as the threat of terrorism since the 7/7 bombings in London in 2005 and the killing of Private Rigby in London in May 2013 have all elicited crisis narratives on the claimed problem of self-segregation and failed integration as a result of what Prime Minister David Cameron called 'state multiculturalism'.[57]

As with later commentators, Phillips' core argument was that multiculturalism is a form of identity politics, which, in embracing difference, had failed to address the systematic inequalities faced by ethnic minorities.[58] However, while he has continued to maintain that addressing inequalities is the solution, he has also suggested that Muslims may be an exception and that Muslim communities are 'unlike others in Britain' and 'will not integrate in the same way'.[59]

The idea that there is a failure to accept 'British values' among Muslims in Britain has increasingly drowned out explanations of ethnic community alienation that might arise from a failure to fulfil British values by securing equality of treatment within British institutions. Indeed, in this context, it is significant that the success of Park View

---

[56] For example, he returned to this in his Channel 4 documentary, 'What do British Muslims really think?', broadcast in April 2016, in which he claimed many British Muslims 'do not accept the values and behaviours that make Britain what it is' and were forming a 'nation-within-a-nation'. Available at: www.dailymail.co.uk/news/article-3533041/Warning-UK-Muslim-ghettoes-Nation-nation-developing-says-former-equalities-watchdog.html.

[57] Cameron, 'PM's speech at Munich Security Conference'.

[58] The Parekh Report, in fact, was explicit on the need to address inequalities systematically and that this should be done across all groups, devoting one section of the report to the topic.

[59] The context was a speech given at the Policy Exchange, right of centre think tank, on 27 January 2016 and widely reported, for example in 'Muslims are not like us, race equality chief says', The Times, 27 January 2016. Available at: www.thetimes.co.uk/tto/news/politics/article4675392.ece.

Academy in turning around a failing school and producing results in the top 14% of all schools in England has been largely elided in accounts of the Trojan Horse affair.

The critique of multiculturalism has increasingly turned on the assertion that, in the concern to address inequalities experienced by ethnic minorities, the white working class have been neglected. Trevor Phillips' arguments have been used to suggest that in focusing on addressing educational disadvantages among ethnic minority pupils, the government has ignored under-attainment among white working class boys.[60] Alongside increased immigration, the financial crisis and the economic restructuring that has accompanied globalisation, multiculturalism, it is claimed, has led to the white working class being 'left behind'. Notwithstanding the evidence that ethnic minorities in Britain have similarly been 'left behind' by the economic downturn, the backlash against multiculturalism, particularly in the context of the recent referendum on leaving the European Union, has given rise not to a retreat from, but an intensification of, identity politics – although one that often posits diversity and inclusivity as an existential threat, and which focuses on the need to re-assert 'British values', now provided with a 'particularist' construal.[61]

The 'populism' that is evident in the Brexit calls to 'take back our country' is a form of 'nativism' that denies the differentiation and pluralism that is the positive substance of multiculturalism. It expresses hostility not only to external powers that might limit the scope of national action, but also to those within the nation who are not seen as properly part of it. Those who are not part of the 'we' are racialised minorities, immigrants and what Enoch Powell once chillingly called,

---

[60] See the editorial 'Britain is no place for the white, working-class male', *The Telegraph*, 14 January 2010. Available at: www.telegraph.co.uk/news/politics/labour/6990777/Britain-is-no-place-for-the-white-working-class-male.html.

[61] See, for example, Ed West (2013) *The Diversity Illusion: What we Got Wrong about Immigration and How to Set it Right*, London: Gibson Square; David Goodhart (2017) *The Road to Somewhere: The Populist Revolt and the Future of Politics*, London: Hurst and Company.

the 'immigrant descended'.[62] Significantly, in the wake of Brexit, the 'legitimacy' of racialised particularism and opposition to immigration has been argued forcefully by David Goodhart, most recently to claim that white 'racial self-interest' should not be seen as 'racism'.[63]

'British values'

Much contemporary political debate has become preoccupied with 'national identity' as something that should bring people together and provide a sense of common purpose and social cohesion. Yet, as much scholarly literature on national identity observes, this is frequently achieved by defining others as not part of that identity. It is also clear that this concern with national identity is associated with anxieties, especially that others are a potential threat, or, at best, people with whom we are in competition.

This dynamic was evident in the UK in the debate over leaving the European Union and the referendum in June 2016. For those who sought to leave, the desire to 'take back control' had underlying it a 'we' who would take back control from 'them' in the exercise of 'our' sovereignty. Apparently, sovereignty was not something that could be shared and differentiated. It was not something that could also sometimes be exercised together with 'them' as part of an expanded 'us'. That division between 'them' and 'us' was also offered as a division within the political community, between 'elites' and the 'people' (or 'decent, respectable people', 'ordinary people' – 'people like us'). 'They', 'elites', promote shared sovereignty because it benefits them at the expense of 'us'.

As we have also seen, 'taking back control' has been interpreted as meaning taking back control over borders, essentially of the movement

---

[62] In his notorious 'Rivers of Blood' speech delivered to a Conservative association meeting in Birmingham on 20 April 1968. Available at: www.telegraph.co.uk/comment/3643823/Enoch-Powells-Rivers-of-Blood-speech.html.

[63] See, most recently, David Goodhart endorsing a publication by Eric Kaufmann (2017) 'Racial self-interest is not racism', *Policy Exchange*, 3 March. Available at: https://policyexchange.org.uk/publication/racial-self-interest-is-not-racism/.

of people not like 'us'. How, then, are resident migrants to be counted within the political community and what is the status of post-migration ethnic minorities within it? Just as Muslims feel that they are the particular focus of public debates about Prevent, as we shall see in the next chapter, so ethnic minorities feel they are the particular focus of debates about immigration.[64]

The discussion of 'Britishness' and national identity is fraught, not least because the United Kingdom is a political cluster of nations, with separate political institutions, also expressing devolved and differentiated sovereignties – as indicated by the separate Scottish, Welsh and Northern Irish Assemblies. The referendum on Britain's membership of the EU was preceded by the Scottish referendum on continued membership in the United Kingdom in September 2014. This was also a referendum about the nature of sovereignty and the extent to which that was better articulated directly through Holyrood and Brussels, or mediated by Westminster with Scotland a part of Britain. It could hardly be argued that 'Britishness' did not include Scottish identity, and the problem for those arguing that Scotland should remain within the United Kingdom was how to present a positive version of British identity that couldn't also be seen as integral to a Scottish identity legitimately expressed through separation. Scotland voted (more narrowly than had been expected) to remain in the United Kingdom, but (along with Northern Ireland) voted later to remain in the European Union. The fact that the wider United Kingdom voted to leave has created further problems to which the response – for example, by the Prime Minister, Theresa May – has been to argue that, in pursuing Brexit, there is a need to overcome divisions and 'pull together' as 'a nation'.

Of course, the idea that 'Britishness' signifies a 'nation' in the conventional sense is problematic for other reasons. The UK was

---

[64] See Omar Khan and Debbie Weekes Bernard (2015) *This is Still About Us: Why Ethnic Minorities See Immigration Differently*, Runnymede Report on Race and Immigration. Available at: www.runnymedetrust.org/uploads/Race%20and%20 Immigration%20Report%20v2.pdf.

previously an empire and its population 'British subjects'.[65] As an empire, it was a multicultural political community, albeit organised through relations of domination and subordination rather than equality. However, British rule was predicated on movement of populations across empire. As Gurminder K. Bhambra has argued,[66] in the post–war period Britain came to define subjects as citizens and limit citizenship in various Acts of Parliament, but, in so doing, it turned some who previously had claims within the wider political community into migrants and restricted their freedoms (for example, their rights of entry, as well as the rights of entry of family members, such as non–British spouses).[67]

How should we make sense of all this? On the one hand, there is some notion of 'Britishness' that resides in 'traditions', common 'histories' and common ways of life, albeit that these may also be differentiated by regions – for example, the different nations of the UK, but also of the different regions of those nations. Others also have their different national identities, which are, in turn, internally differentiated. However, in the case of the UK, some of those others were made 'British' as a consequence of Britain's long history of empire. That empire was a diverse one, differentiated by other traditions and practices, including those of different religions. The multiculturalism of empire, then, is an integral part of 'Britishness'.

On the other hand, in current political debates, emphasis on 'British values' are also designed to specify principles of democracy, the rule

---

[65] See Runnymede Trust (2000) *The Parekh Report*.

[66] Gurminder K. Bhambra (2017) 'Locating Brexit in the pragmatics of race, citizenship and empire', in William Outhwaite (ed) *Brexit: Sociological Responses*, London: Anthem Press.

[67] These were introduced in June 2012 by then Home Office minister, Theresa May. They involved that 'sponsors' of visas for their spouses should have a minimum income (independent of the spouse's own earnings) and that spouses should pass a stringent earnings test. Immigration groups estimated that up to two-thirds of British people would fail to meet the earnings test. For a report, see the 'Stark choice under new immigration rules: exile or family breakup', *The Guardian*, 8 June 2012. Available at: www.theguardian.com/uk/2012/jun/08/immigration-rules-couples-stark-choice.

of law and religious tolerance. These are only contingently 'British', in the sense that they are of relatively recent origin and, therefore, 'Britishness' – historically – also includes their repudiation as well as affirmation. For example, when the Secretary of State for Education, Michael Gove, proposed a revision of the history curriculum in schools, as a version of 'our Island story', he was roundly criticised, not just for eliding the violence of empire, but also struggles for democracy associated with class domination and women's rights.[68] But they are contingently British in another sense, namely that they are affirmed by other political communities as also being *their* values and the governing principles of their institutions. As Christian Joppke has argued, there is nothing particularly 'national' about these liberal civic values.[69]

It seems that there are two kinds of 'Britishness' that are being utilised. We suggest that the first kind resides in different forms of particularism embodying the practices of daily interaction and common life; it is these, and a respect for their diversity, that are properly represented by the term 'multiculturalism', whether fostered by institutional policies or expressed in more bottom-up practices of 'everyday multiculturalism' that arise in areas characterised by cultural diversity.[70] Recognition of the practices of others and their rights of expression as integral to 'Britishness' has been a slow development, however. For example, at different points in the debate over religious education in schools, especially from the 1970s to the 1990s, there have been arguments against 'multi-faith' education as being a form of 'relativism' and that Christianity is an essential part of 'Britishness' that should be recognised and affirmed by everyone, at least as a matter

---

[68] See David Priestland, Margaret Reynolds, Richard Wentworth, Matt Parker, Yvonne Baker, Chris Hamnett and Nick Byrne, 'Michael Gove's new curriculum: what the experts say', *The Guardian*, 12 February 2013. Available at: www.theguardian.com/commentisfree/2013/feb/12/round-table-draft-national-curriculum.

[69] Christian Joppke (2008) 'Immigration and the identity of citizenship: the paradox of universalism', *Citizenship Studies*, 12(6): 533–546.

[70] See, for example, A. Wise and S. Velayutham (eds) (2009) *Everyday Multiculturalism*, Basingstoke: Palgrave Macmillan.

of national heritage.[71] This was a view that was resurrected by David Cameron in his speech to commemorate the 400th anniversary of the completion of the King James Bible in 2011, when he declared: "we are a Christian country. And we should not be afraid to say so".[72]

A second kind of 'Britishness' – the 'British values' of democracy, the rule of law and religious tolerance most explicitly promoted by government as 'fundamental' – represents a set of transcending principles which facilitate cooperation across particularities. This was indeed the version of Britishness that was espoused by the Parekh Report. It is because these values are shared that sovereignty can also be differentiated and shared, whether across the different assemblies of the UK, or in cooperative agreements across nations (for example, as in the EU).

This has been a lengthy preamble, but it has been necessary to unpick the meaning of 'British values' and the way in which their invocation can act as a shifting signifier in public debate. On the analysis presented, it is a 'category error' to place multiculturalism in conflict with values of democracy, the rule of law and tolerance of religious diversity. However, it is one that politicians and journalists have frequently made. For example, David Cameron's speech at Munich in 2011 argued that:

> we have allowed the weakening of our collective identity. Under the doctrine of state multiculturalism, we have encouraged different cultures to live separate lives, apart from each other and apart from the mainstream. We've failed to provide a vision of society to which they feel they want to belong. We've even tolerated these segregated communities behaving in ways that run completely counter to our values.[73]

[71] S.G. Parker and R.J.K. Freathy (2011) 'Ethnic diversity, Christian hegemony and the emergence of multi-faith religious education in the 1970s', *History of Education*, 41(3): 381–404.

[72] See David Cameron, the Prime Minister's King James Bible Speech, 16 December 2011. Available at: www.gov.uk/government/news/prime-ministers-king-james-bible-speech.

[73] Cameron, 'PM's speech at Munich Security Conference'.

Similar elisions were evident in the then Chancellor of the Exchequer Gordon Brown's attempt to initiate a debate on British identity in February 2007. Significantly, this took place at the Commonwealth Club (a venue redolent of the multiculturalism of the former empire). He began with setting out a range of areas where such a debate mattered:

> whether all the different countries of the union – Scotland, Wales, England and Northern Ireland – all want to stay together, part of the union; how we better integrate our ethnic communities and respond to migration; how we respond to Muslim fundamentalism; what is our role in Europe and the European constitution. And whether facing global challenges we need a stronger sense of national purpose.[74]

Paradoxically, given that his concern was to argue for the need for a debate on Britishness, he also cited opinion poll findings that, over the last few years, those who identified with being British had risen from 46% to 65% and that more people in Britain felt patriotic than in almost any other country. It is unlikely, though, that this rise reflected the affirmation of general values, but was rather about affirming an exclusive 'particularistic' Britishness through those values, against other particularistic identities which were imputed to deny them. After all, that was the context in which general values were being articulated as a solution.

As the Chancellor warmed to his theme, he elaborated how common values of tolerance, liberty and fair play arose from the need to live together in a multinational state. Yet, as we have suggested, these are the values embedded in common democratic institutions which are the proper object of 'internationalism', rather than 'patriotism'. If there is a British history of their invention then that, too, has its darker side. The invocation of the abolition of the slave trade as a 'British' contribution

---

[74] Full text of Gordon Brown's speech, *The Guardian*, 27 February 2007. Available at: www.theguardian.com/politics/2007/feb/27/immigrationpolicy.race.

neglects the fact that the trade itself was also 'British'. The changing status of 'subjects' of empire, to 'subjects' of Commonwealth, and from citizens to migrants, as well as the different treatment of the white 'Dominions' are also part of the national tradition and divide as well as unite. It is one thing to invoke values of democracy, the rule of law and religious tolerance and expect them to be shared, but it is quite another to expect a common understanding of their history and their relation to the British state. Inequalities in the present are likely to be understood in relation to inequalities in the past.

The political philosopher Danielle Allen has written powerfully of the dangerous aspects of the idea of popular sovereignty – intolerance of difference – that is frequently represented as a democratic ideal.[75] For example, incorporated in the US Declaration of Independence, and reproduced daily in US schools, is the 'pledge of allegiance' to 'one Nation indivisible with liberty and justice for all'. The idea of 'one Nation indivisible', she argues, implicitly passes all voices into one. What would happen, Allen asks, were we to propose instead an allegiance to the 'whole Nation indivisible'? The whole Nation would be understood as a Nation of parts – that is, as differentiated – where an obligation towards indivisibility would be an obligation towards difference and its recognition. A commitment to the *whole* nation would require an obligation toward multicultural equality. It is precisely that commitment that now appears fragile, in part as a consequence of proposing that the particular traditions of some members of the political community entails them being hostile to general 'British values'.

Muslims and 'British values'

In a context where a 'particularism' of practices and a 'generality' of values are presented as in tension (although we argue they need not be), Muslims have come to be regarded as irreconcilably different

[75] D.S. Allen (2004) 'Invisible citizens: on exclusion and domination in Ralph Ellison and Hannah Arendt', in M. Williams and S. Macedo (eds) *Nomos XLVI: Political Exclusion and Domination*, New York: NYU Press.

from other citizens in some particular respects, especially with regard to religion and its practices. These differences are visible in the architecture of towns – the presence of mosques and specialist food and other businesses – and is embodied on the streets – in the language spoken amongst each other, differences in clothing, or in gendered practices of covering. But these differences need not be understood as oppositional. What is at stake here is well represented in the comment by former chair of the Conservative Party, Baroness Sayeeda Warsi, that:

> my faith is about who I am and not about who you are. It's a rule-book for me, not a forced lecture series for you. Its strength is a source of peace for me not ammunition with which to fight you. It's a ruler I have chosen to measure myself against, not a stick with which to beat you. It allows me to question myself, not to judge you. And recognizing myself, being sure of who I am, being comfortable in my identity, does not mean having to downgrade, erase or reject who you are.[76]

Notwithstanding, it is clear that, for some, the visibility of difference represents an 'alien presence' and even an affront, and an indication that those who are different do not 'belong'. Such a view was put forward by Nigel Farage at a UKIP (UK Independence Party) conference in February 2014.[77] It was also bound up in Enoch Powell's opposition to non-white 'Commonwealth immigration' in the 1960s and 1970s. Significantly, Powell's 'Rivers of Blood' speech, delivered in Birmingham in April 1968, challenged the 'steady progress towards a multi-cultural society'. However, this nativist particularism is, ostensibly, not what governments, whether, Labour, Conservative-led coalition, or the Conservative government, have meant by 'Britishness'

---

[76] Sayeeda Warsi (2017) *The Enemy Within: A Tale of Muslim Britain*, London: Allen Lane, page 270.

[77] 'Nigel Farage: Parts of Britain are like a foreign land', *The Guardian*, 28 February 2014. Available at: www.theguardian.com/politics/2014/feb/28/nigel-farage-ukip-immigration-speech.

– at least in the values they have promoted in public policy declarations, even if criticisms of multiculturalism have risked that interpretation.

The explicit focus of government concern has been that there is a failure on the part of Muslims to identify with values of democracy, the rule of law and religious tolerance. As we have seen, the main reasons for this failure have been attributed to the segregation and isolation of Muslim communities, and thus a failure to engage with such values, especially where 'British values' may contradict what are perceived to be local cultural traditions (for example, of arranged marriages and other perceived patriarchal practices). 'Multiculturalism' has been seen to be part of the problem, in so far as it has meant that local authorities and politicians have been unwilling to promote more general values for fear of being seen as 'racist'. This is a theme that is used to explain 'inaction' on the part of the authorities with regard to the early indications of a Trojan Horse 'plot'. But is it correct?

As the public policy debate has taken this turn, so it has been subject to scrutiny in academic research seeking to test the underlying framing in terms of segregation and disassociation from general British values. For example, Ludi Simpson of the ESRC-funded Centre on Dynamics of Ethnicity at the University of Manchester has demonstrated that segregation declined over the period from 2001 to 2011.[78] Richard Gale records similar findings when looking at religious segregation, rather than ethnic segregation in Birmingham.[79] The widely reported

[78] See Ludi Simpson (2012) 'More segregation or more mixing?', Manchester: Centre on Dynamics of Ethnicity. Available at: www.ethnicity.ac.uk/medialibrary/briefingsupdated/more-segregation-or-more-mixing.pdf; Ludi Simpson (2013) 'Has neigbourhood ethnic segregation decreased?', Manchester: Centre on Dynamics of Ethnicity. Available at: www.ethnicity.ac.uk/medialibrary/briefingsupdated/has-neighbourhood-ethnic-segregation-decreased.pdf; Nissa Finney and Ludi Simpson (2009) *Sleepwalking to Segregation? Challenging Myths about Race and Migration*, Bristol. Policy Press.

[79] R.T. Gale (2013) 'Religious residential segregation and internal migration: the British Muslim case', *Environment and Planning A*, 45: 872–891.

idea that England is increasingly segregated, or that it is 'sleep-walking' to segregation, as Trevor Phillips put it, is false.[80]

Saffron Karlsen and James Nazroo, for their part, have used the Citizenship Survey to address attitudes to Britishness among different ethnic and faith communities. This showed that 90% of Muslims, Hindus, Sikhs and Christians felt part of Britain. In particular, Muslims were more likely than Caribbean Christians to report a strong British identification and (along with Hindus and Sikhs) to recognise potential compatibility between this and other aspects of identity. As they put it, 'many Muslims, and those with other minority ethnicities and religions, do not see a contradiction between being British and maintaining a separate cultural or religious identity',[81] and they cite similar findings from other studies which have also identified a positive association between Muslim affiliation and positive national identities. Nor are the outcomes affected by the intensity of religious commitments. There is a positive correlation between British identification and higher religiosity.[82] These associations have remained strong across the period since 2001.

In other words, the public discourse on 'British values', and the urgency with which it is expressed, does not seem to be a response to increased segregation, or declining identification with Britishness,

---

[80] Trevor Phillips, speech to the Manchester Council for Community Relations, 22 September 2005. Available at: /www.jiscmail.ac.uk/cgi-bin/webadmin?A3=ind0509&L=CRONEM&E=quoted-printable&P=60513&B=%E2%80%94%E2%80%94_%3D_NextPart_001_01C5C28A.09501783&T=text%2Fhtml;%20charset=iso-8859%E2%80%931&pending=. The speech was given in the immediate aftermath of the 7/7 bombings and reflections on the aftermath of Hurricane Katrina in New Orleans and the mistreatment of poor African Americans.

[81] Saffron Karlsen and James Y. Nazroo (2015) 'Ethnic and religious differences in the attitudes of people towards being "British"', *Sociological Review*, 63(4): 774.

[82] See A. Guveli and L. Platt (2011) 'Understanding the religious behaviour of Muslims in the Netherlands and the UK', *Sociology*, 45: 1008–1027; N. Foner and R. Alba (2008) 'Immigrant religion in the US and Western Europe: bridge or barrier to inclusion?', *International Migration Review*, 42: 360–392; A. Manning and S. Roy (2010) 'Culture clash or culture club? National identity in Britain', *The Economics Journal*, 120(542): F72–F100.

or with any secure basis in other kinds of evidence. Rather, each public intervention appears to be based on a 'snapshot' of current levels of population concentration independently of the trends that are associated with those concentrations. These concerns came to the fore again with Dame Louise Casey's report on opportunity and integration, mentioned in the introduction to this book.[83] This was followed by another report on segregation and schooling, presented by Ted Cantle on behalf of one of the bodies involved in the research, in which it was asserted that, while neighbourhoods were becoming less segregated, schools were becoming more segregated than their neighbourhoods.[84] This was again argued to be a consequence of 'self-segregation', but the report takes no account of the different age structure of ethnic minority populations compared with the white British population, which means that the former are likely to have a higher proportion of children in school. We will see in Chapter Four that the same issue arises when considering religious belief and secularism and their distribution in the population.

The conclusion of the academic research is that it is precisely multiculturalism that facilitates identification with being British on the part of citizens outside the dominant cultural and religious traditions.[85] This is because ethnic and religious minorities associate 'Britishness' with a commitment to a plurality that recognises their different traditions.[86] Indeed, Yasmin Hussain and Paul Bagguley suggest that where disaffection among Muslim young people exists, it is not because of the attractions of radical Islam, but because of disappointment in the realisation of their *rights as British citizens*, especially in the context

[83] *The Casey Review.*

[84] *Understanding School Segregation in England 2011–2016*, March 2017. Published by SchoolDash, the Challenge and the iCoCo Foundation. Available at: www.schooldash.com/blog.html#20170322.

[85] See Varun Uberoi and Tariq Modood (2013) 'Inclusive Britishness: a multiculturalist advance', *Political Studies*, 61: 23–41.

[86] H. Jayaweera and T. Choudhury (2008) 'Immigration, faith and cohesion: evidence from local areas with significant Muslim populations', York: Joseph Rowntree Foundation. Available at: www.compas.ox.ac.uk/2008/pr-2008-muslims_cohesion_final/.

of unequal opportunities and material disadvantage.[87] In this respect, Trevor Phillips' argument that the key issue is inequality is correct, but he is mistaken to suggest that multiculturalism is a problematic form of identity politics that distracts from this. Inequalities have widened over the last decades and the impact of the politics of austerity in the aftermath of the 2008 financial crisis (if not the longer-term trend of de-industrialisation since the 1980s which has affected traditional working class communities) has hit ethnic minorities particularly hard. Gemma Catney and Albert Sabater, for example, show persistent inequalities in labour market participation and occupational concentration for ethnic minorities nationally, with Birmingham among the top five local authorities for unemployment for several ethnic groups – Indian, Pakistani, Chinese and African.[88]

Hiranthi Jayaweera and Tufyal Choudhury's research also shows that there is an interest in greater participation in civic and political life on the part of ethnic minorities. However, this is seen to be more difficult as opportunities for local involvement are displaced by stronger central direction and by removing local services from the public sector. This has been especially pronounced following the 40% cuts to local authority budgets since the election in 2010 of the Conservative–Liberal Democratic government, and its Conservative successor in 2015. This has also been associated in Birmingham with longstanding problems in governance, especially its children's social care services, which had been subject to interventions by the Department for Health and other government agencies since 2002.[89]

---

[87] Yasmin Hussain and Paul Bagguley (2005) 'Citizenship, ethnicity and identity: British Pakistanis after the 2001 "Riots"', *Sociology*, 39: 407–425.

[88] See Gemma Catney and Albert Sabater (2015) 'Ethnic minority disadvantage in the labour market: participation, skills and geographical inequalities', Report for the Joseph Rowntree Foundation. Available at: https://livrepository.liverpool.ac.uk/2014190/1/ethnic-minority-disadvantage-full.pdf.

[89] See the Report on Birmingham City Council's governance and organisational capabilities: an independent review under Sir Bob Kerslake, December 2014. Available at: www.gov.uk/government/publications/birmingham-city-councils-governance-and-organisational-capabilities-an-independent-review.

Significantly, just as politicians like Gordon Brown argued that a multinational state like Britain is sustained by people recognising separate and complementary loyalties, a similar pattern is evident for ethnic minorities whose attachments are transnational – that is, lying within and outside Britain. Integration is unaffected by continued orientation to country of origin. As Jayaweera and Choudhury put it:

> those with the most transnational attachment and involvement were also most likely to be employed, financially stable, have voted in the general election and to meet more people of different ethnicity and religion and in more places (although least likely to participate in mixed organisations). This evidence shows that continuing transnational attachment does not need to be a barrier to economic and social integration in the UK and thus that initiatives to promote belonging in Britain do not need to challenge a complementary sense of belonging to the country of birth.[90]

Put simply, from the everyday experiences of many ethnic and religious minorities, the issue of integration appears to be less *their* unwillingness to integrate, and more a *failure by others to include*. This is compounded when political discourse seems to stress the incompatibility of their traditions and values with 'Britishness' as the reason for their failure to integrate. This is evident from Jayaweera and Choudhury's interviews with local policy makers and practitioners in three locations – Newham in London, Bradford and Birmingham: 'Many interviewees argued that efforts on improving cohesion issues at the local level can be undermined by national policy and political rhetoric, and by media discourse, particularly around issues of asylum and terrorism.'[91] In Birmingham, the fallout within the local community from the Trojan Horse affair on these issues has been considerable.

---

[90] Jayaweera and Choudhury, 'Immigration, faith and cohesion', page 127.
[91] Ibid, page 117.

Conclusion

Ethnic and religious minorities have a particularly strong commitment to the shared values that we have characterised as 'general', precisely because they perceive themselves to be vulnerable in terms of the everyday particularities that differentiate them from other fellow citizens, a differentiation evident in the language of policy and academic discussion that describes them as 'minorities'. Yet the promotion of 'British values' elides the distinction between general values and particular traditions and 'ways of life' and, in turn, seems to favour those of the white population over non-white others. As we have seen, Enoch Powell coined an ugly turn of phrase to mark the difference when he referred in a speech to the 'immigrant descended', and we have also seen the emergence of an argument that white racial self-interest is not racism. The risk is that inclusion has now become assimilation, where, to paraphrase the poet Daljit Nagra, you can become 'one of us', so long as you 'pass your voice into ours'.[92]

Christian Karner and David Parker (citing Sennett) put the problem of assimilation (as distinct from integration) well, when they write that 'the pressure towards discovering a unified collective identity risks destroying the essence of urban civility "which is that people can act together without the compulsion to be the same"'.[93] It is the ability to act together, while being different, that British Muslims and other ethnic and religious minorities regard as at the heart of 'British values' and a tolerance of plurality. This is a generous and expanded idea of Britishness, and, we will argue, Park View school was part of that vision, albeit that it came to be (mis)represented as Islamic particularism.

---

[92] 'The man who would be English', in Daljit Nagra (2007) *Look We Have Coming to Dover*, London: Faber and Faber.

[93] Christian Karner and David Parker (2011) 'Conviviality and conflict: pluralism, resilience and hope in inner-city Birmingham', *Journal of Ethnic and Migration Studies*, 37: 369.

In the next chapter, we will look at how the idea of community cohesion comes to butt up against the Prevent agenda and the way in which the latter places British Muslims under increasing suspicion. It is this conjunction which helped create the conditions for the Trojan Horse affair to be seen as a threat to 'British values'.

TWO

Prevent: from hearts and minds to muscular liberalism

In this chapter, we set out the 'security' context of the Trojan horse affair in relation to the government's Prevent strategy for addressing extremism and radicalisation. It is noteworthy that at the time that the Ofsted inspections of 21 schools in East Birmingham were being carried out in March–April 2014, guidance to schools on how to implement the 2011 Prevent strategy had not been issued by the DfE. In fact, this guidance was not issued until July 2015 – more than a year after several of the schools had been inspected and downgraded by Ofsted for their failures to address extremism or to implement Prevent.[94] Thus, the schools were penalised for their failure to implement a policy that had not yet received full articulation. It is also

---

[94] See Department for Education, *The Prevent Duty: For Schools and Childcare Providers*, 1 July 2015. Available at: www.gov.uk/government/publications/ protecting-children-from-radicalisation-the-prevent-duty#history. At the time of the inspections, the existing guidance to schools took the form of a toolkit for schools, published in 2008, that embedded Prevent within a framework that focused on democratic engagement, commitment to diversity, promotion of community cohesion and awareness of terrorism. This was, though, non-statutory and as we show in Chapter Three, schools' awareness of Prevent across the sector in this period was relatively low.

unclear, as we shall see in the next chapter, whether the requirement to address extremism and implement Prevent was applied to all schools in this period.

So, why were these schools penalised for an alleged failure to implement a policy agenda that had yet to be fully articulated? To answer this, we need to examine the evolving nature of Prevent in that period – especially in relation to the changes to Prevent that followed the formation of the David Cameron-led coalition government in 2010 that significantly altered its remit and purpose. In particular, the definition of extremism within Prevent shifted towards a much wider focus on countering *extremist attitudes* – broadly defined – rather than preventing *violent extremism*, while its implementation shifted away from engagement with Muslim communities and organisations to a focus on charging personnel in public sector institutions with a responsibility to spot and report on signs of radicalisation.

These changes embedded a significantly expanded approach to the remit and implementation of Prevent, and were, following the passing of the 2015 Counter-Terrorism and Security Act, imposed as a statutory duty across public sector institutions, including schools.[95] As we shall see, at the time of the Trojan Horse episode in 2014, however, the Prevent policy was in flux, and the schools became entangled in an evolving counter-extremism agenda, in which the purported facts of the Trojan Horse affair were used to justify the expansion of the conceptualisation and remit of the government's counter-extremism agenda. Furthermore, Prevent and the subsequent, broadened counter-extremism agenda – pre- and post-2010 – have operated with a spatial logic that has focused on places where Muslims are resident, and this is significant for understanding how the focus of the enquiries and interventions relating to the Trojan Horse affair unfolded.

---

[95] Counter-Terrorism and Security Act, 2015. Available at: www.legislation.gov.uk/ukpga/2015/6/contents/enacted.

Prevent: a 'hearts and minds' approach

The Prevent strategy that was launched by the Department of Communities and Local Government (DCLG) under the New Labour government in 2007 set out a 'hearts and minds' approach to counterterrorism, in which engagement and partnership with British Muslims were seen as key to tackling (the causes of) violent extremism.

The 2007 Prevent strategy set out four key objectives: 'promoting shared values, supporting local solutions, building civic capacity and leadership and strengthening the role of faith institutions and leaders'.[96] Accordingly, 'Preventing Violent Extremism' (PVE) or 'Prevent' initiatives included a raft of youth, women's and faith-based projects, particularly at the local level in areas of Muslim residence. These initiatives focused on disaffected Muslim young people (often taking the form of targeted youth work) who were seen as particularly vulnerable to radicalisation, and mobilising Muslim women, whom government considered to be potential moderating forces on young Muslim men, as well as on modulating expressions and practices of Islam in Britain. Supplementing this, the New Labour government created the National Muslim Women's Advisory Group and the Young Muslims Advisory Group in 2008 to enable government to engage directly with Muslim women and youth. It also set out to develop theologically based counter-narratives to al-Qaeda ideology and foster British-based forms of Islamic religious authority (with funding for the Radical Middle Way project and support for the creation of the Mosques and Imams National Advisory Board (MINAB) to create a UK-based system of mosque regulation). Through such means, as the 2007 Prevent strategy document declared, the government's aim was to 'fundamentally rebalance our engagement'.[97]

---

[96] Department for Communities and Local Government (2007) *Preventing Violent Extremism: Winning Hearts and Minds*, London: DCLG. Available at: http://webarchive.nationalarchives.gov.uk/20070701080545/http:/www.communities.gov.uk/index.asp?id=1509398, page 5.

[97] Ibid, page 9.

The implementation of Prevent began by targeting areas with Muslim populations of 5% or more.[98] This spatial focus problematically constituted Muslim presence itself as a security risk. Following this logic, over 90 local authorities were identified as eligible for PVE funding, which in 2008–9 entailed a budget of over £140 million.[99]

Driven by a concern with tackling 'home-grown terrorism' in the wake of the 2005 London attacks, New Labour aligned its approach to Prevent closely with its community cohesion agenda, which sought to tackle the perceived lack of integration among British Muslims. As we discussed in Chapter One, the community cohesion agenda was framed by the Cantle Report's earlier analysis of the disturbances in Bradford, Burnley and Oldham in 2001, which portrayed these as an outcome of ethnic communities living 'parallel lives'.[100] It is noteworthy that the report makes very little reference to Muslims or religion. After the 9/11 attacks in New York and Washington shortly after the 2001 disturbances, this narrative shifted from a focus on ethnic groups and the failed integration of Pakistani and Bangladeshi communities, to a concern with *Muslim* self-segregation and separation.

The New Labour government viewed community cohesion as essential to realising the goals of Prevent, as a DCLG guide to Prevent in 2008 asserted:

> The Prevent strategy requires a specific response, but we must also make the most of the links with wider community work to reduce inequalities, tackle racism and other forms of extremism (e.g. extreme far right), build cohesion and empower communities … the arguments of violent extremists, which rely on creating a 'them' and 'us', are less likely to find traction in cohesive communities.[101]

[98] Department for Communities and Local Government (2007) *Preventing Violent Extremism Guidance Note for Government Offices and Local Authorities in England*, London, DCLG.

[99] Yahya Birt (2009) 'Promoting virulent envy?', *The RUSI Journal*, 154(4): 52–58.

[100] Cantle (2001) *Community Cohesion*.

[101] Department for Communities and Local Government (2008) *Delivering Prevent – Responding to Learning*. Available at: http://lx.iriss.org.uk/content/delivering-prevent-responding-learning, pages 6–7.

This was reinforced by the involvement of both the DCLG and Home Office in the delivery of Prevent – each with its own, substantial Prevent budget.[102] The overlap in these agendas was also evident in the creation of the 'Cohesion and Extremism Unit' in the DCFS in 2007. According to Paul Thomas, many of the agencies charged with implementing Prevent and community cohesion did not discern any difference between these agendas. For example, the Association of Police Authorities (APA) in 2009 apparently commented that 'many Police Authorities question whether, in practice, there is any real difference between Prevent and community cohesion'.[103] Similarly, research by one of the authors found that cohesion and Prevent tended to be closely entwined in the initiatives that were pursued at the local level.[104]

Prevent came to be widely criticised, with a key charge that it securitised the state's engagement with Muslims, and it was regarded with suspicion by many Muslim organisations that were the putative partners with government in the implementation of Prevent. As several studies have shown, many government and civil society actors were critical of the ways in which Prevent was conceived and implemented, its impact on Muslim communities and the constraints it placed on Muslim civil society organisations' terms of engagement with government.[105]

---

[102] Between 2008 and 2011, the DCLG budget for Prevent was almost £67 million according to a detailed response by the DCLG to a Freedom of Information request in 2011. Available at: www.gov.uk/government/publications/prevent-funding. Between 2009 and 2011, Home Office funding came to £84 million, whilst FCO funding came to £36 million: see Home Office (2011) *Prevent Strategy*.

[103] See Paul Thomas (2010) 'Failed and friendless: the UK's "Preventing Violent Extremism" programme', *British Journal of Politics and International Relations*, 12(3): 453.

[104] Therese O'Toole, Stephen H. Jones, Daniel Nilsson DeHanas and Tariq Modood (2013) 'Prevent after TERFOR: why local contexts still matter', *Public Spirit*, December 2013. Available at: www.publicspirit.org.uk/the-importance-of-local-context-for-preventing-extremism/.

[105] See Therese O'Toole, Daniel Nilsson DeHanas, Tariq Modood, Nasar Meer and Stephen H. Jones (2013) *Taking Part: Muslim Participation in Contemporary Governance*, Bristol: University of Bristol. Available at: www.bristol.ac.uk/media-

The overlap between Prevent and community cohesion became a particular concern, with critics arguing that this overlap diluted the objectives of Prevent and securitised community cohesion initiatives – undermining both. For example, a House of Commons Committee report on *Preventing Violent Extremism* in 2010 concluded:

> we question the appropriateness of the Department of Communities and Local Government – a Government department which has responsibility for promoting cohesive communities – taking a leading role in counter-terrorism initiatives. We agree with the majority of our witnesses that Prevent risks undermining positive cross-cultural work on cohesion and capacity building to combat exclusion and alienation in many communities.[106]

A 'muscular liberal' approach to Prevent

When the coalition government came to power in 2010, it announced an immediate review of Prevent. After much internal wrangling and delays, as reported by Peter Oborne,[107] the revised Prevent strategy that was eventually announced in 2011 marked some key changes to Prevent relative to the approach of New Labour. It included: a separation between Prevent and community cohesion; a focus 'on all forms of terrorism'; reduced, and more tightly and centrally controlled,

library/sites/ethnicity/migrated/documents/mpcgreport.pdf; Charles Husband and Yunis Alam (2011) *Social Cohesion and Counter-Terrorism: A Policy Contradiction?*, Bristol: Policy Press; Arun Kundnani (2009) *Spooked: How not to Prevent Violent Extremism*, London: Institute of Race Relations. Available at: www.irr.org.uk/news/spooked-how-not-to-prevent-violent-extremism/.

[106] House of Commons (2010) *Preventing Violent Extremism: Sixth Report of Session 2009–10*, Communities and Local Government Committee, London: House of Commons. Available at: www.publications.parliament.uk/pa/cm200910/cmselect/cmcomloc/65/65.pdf, page 3. See also Thomas (2010) 'Failed and friendless', and O'Toole et al (2013) *Taking Part.*

[107] See Peter Oborne, 'Where's the divide?', *The Spectator*, 29 January 2011. Available at: www.spectator.co.uk/2011/01/whereandx2019s-the-divide/.

funding; and, in relation to tackling 'the ideological challenge of terrorism', a focus not just on 'vulnerable individuals' who might be drawn into terrorism, but on working with 'sectors and institutions' – in effect mobilising frontline staff in education, health, charities and criminal justice to become actively involved in tackling radicalisation – such that, in the ominous words of the Prevent strategy, 'there will be no ungoverned spaces'.[108] This echoes the analysis put forward by Quilliam in its confidential briefing paper to the Office for Security and Counter-Terrorism in 2010, which argued that universities had become '"ungoverned spaces" in which the Prevent programme has had little impact'.[109] That paper also listed Muslim organisations and individuals that it regarded as holding extremist views, and that government ought not engage with – including those who have been vocal advocates of Muslim democratic engagement. Many of the recommendations of Quilliam's report are evident in the developing strategy since 2011.

The 2011 strategy, furthermore, made clear that pragmatic engagement with Islamist 'extremists' – albeit non-violent – who do not adhere to core British values would not be permitted, in keeping with Cameron's 'muscular liberalism' speech to the Munich security conference earlier in February 2011, in which he called for an end to tolerating 'these segregated communities behaving in ways that run completely counter to our values'.[110] It is noteworthy that, at this stage, the government signalled its unwillingness to change the law to make Prevent a statutory duty.[111]

That position changed in the wake of the murder of Lee Rigby in May 2013. The report of the Task Force on Tackling Radicalisation and Extremism (TERFOR) of 4 December 2013 signalled a hardening of the 'muscular liberal' rhetoric of the 2011 Prevent strategy and a

---

[108] Home Office (2011) *Prevent Strategy*, page 6, para 3.9; page 9, para 3.39.
[109] Quilliam (2010) 'Preventing terrorism: where next For Britain?'. Available at: www.scribd.com/doc/34834977/Secret-Quilliam-Memo-to-government, page 32.
[110] Cameron, 'PM's speech at Munich Security Conference'.
[111] Home Office (2011) *Prevent Strategy*, page 6, para 3.13.

tightening up of implementation at the local level[112] – including the announcement that government would introduce legal requirements for local authorities in priority areas to deliver Prevent and the government's de-radicalisation Channel programme.[113] It did not at this stage seek to make Prevent a statutory duty in schools, but it did announce that it was working to introduce 'even tougher standards from September 2014 to ensure that schools support fundamental British values', whilst signalling the introduction of particular measures by April 2014 for independent schools to 'bar individuals involved or linked with extremism from managing or teaching' at such schools.[114]

From community engagement to public sector monitoring

At the time of the Trojan Horse episode, then, Prevent was in the process of being strengthened and centralised. Its application to schools, universities, local authorities, charities and health services was an element of the government's 2011 Prevent strategy, but it was not yet a statutory duty for these institutions. The government had signalled an intention to prevent extremists from taking up positions in independent schools, but had not applied these to publicly funded schools. As we discuss in further detail in Chapter Three, where the 2011 Prevent strategy did express some concerns about extremists operating in educational settings, these were directed toward madrassahs and the variety of educational arrangements that provide education below the level of hours per week that would make them subject to regulatory frameworks.

---

[112] HM Government (2013) *Tackling Extremism in the UK: Report from the Prime Minister's Task Force on Tackling Radicalisation and Extremism*, December 2013, London: Cabinet Office. Available at: www.gov.uk/government/uploads/system/uploads/attachment_data/file/263181/ETF_FINAL.pdf.

[113] See HM Government (2015) *Channel Duty Guidance*. Available at: www.gov.uk/government/uploads/system/uploads/attachment_data/file/425189/Channel_Duty_Guidance_April_2015.pdf. See O'Toole et al (2013) 'Prevent after TERFOR'.

[114] HM Government (2013) *Tackling Extremism in the UK*, page 5, section 5.1.2.

Following the Trojan Horse affair, the government set in train a series of further measures to widen and enforce the implementation of Prevent. In particular, the Counter-Terrorism and Security Act that received Royal Assent in February 2015 made Prevent a legal duty on public authorities – including schools. Furthermore, the Act strengthened the focus of Prevent on non-violent extremism, making the duty to monitor Muslims for broadly conceived signs of radicalisation statutorily enforceable across a wide range of public sector institutions; in the words of the Home Office, to 'increase the consistency of its delivery across England, Wales and Scotland'.[115] This has entailed mobilising public sector personnel in schools, colleges and the NHS to be vigilant in spotting signs of increased religiosity, or socially conservative views or a failure to comply with 'fundamental British values'. The Act also increased the powers of the police and extended the use of Terrorism Prevention and Investigation Measures (TPIMs).

The Extremism Bill that the incoming Conservative government went on to propose in the Queen's Speech in May 2015 went further, seeking to 'strengthen government and law enforcement powers to stop extremists promoting views and behaviour *that undermine British values*', and to create powers 'to deal with extremism that falls below the thresholds in counter-terrorism legislation'.[116] It included proposals for: Banning Orders for extremist organisations which seek to undermine democracy or use hate speech in public places; 'Extremism Disruption Orders' (the so-called 'extremism ASBOs'), which are court orders to limit harmful activities of extremist individuals (where 'harmful' includes a risk of public disorder, harassment, alarm or distress or a 'threat to the functioning of democracy'); Closure Orders granting

---

[115] See Home Office (2015) *CONTEST: The United Kingdom's Strategy for Countering Terrorism: Annual Report for 2014,* March 2015, London: Home Office. Available at: www.gov.uk/government/uploads/system/uploads/attachment_data/file/415708/contest_annual_report_for_2014.pdf.

[116] HM Government (2015) The Queen's Speech, page 62. Available at: www.gov.uk/government/uploads/system/uploads/attachment_data/file/430149/QS_lobby_pack_FINAL_NEW_2.pdf.

new powers to close premises, including mosques, where extremists seek to influence others; Broadcasting Bans to censor extremist content on mainstream and social media; and Employment Checks to prevent extremists from working with children.

Following from this, the Counter-Extremism Strategy that was unveiled by the Home Office in October 2015 proposed a series of further measures to deal specifically with 'extremist entryism' – citing the claims and conclusions of the Clarke Report on the Trojan Horse affair as evidence of the threat of extremist entryism to public institutions. Referring to events in Birmingham, it argued that 'There is evidence that our institutions are increasingly targeted by extremists, who look to use them to spread their ideology'.[117] That evidence was Clarke's 'detailed report', of 'co-ordinated, deliberate and sustained action … to introduce an intolerant and aggressive Islamic ethos' by 'extremists gaining positions on governing bodies and joining the staff'. The strategy document went on to allege that around 5000 children had been affected. The Counter-Extremism Strategy set out a number of priorities including: measures to prevent extremist entryism (badged as 'safeguarding institutions'); addressing extremist ideologies – particularly in online spaces; disrupting extremists; and a renewed emphasis on cohesion and integration. In relation to the latter, issues such as promoting English, creating a National Citizen Service for young people, and tackling violence against women and 'illegal cultural practices' became objectives within the government's expanding counter-extremism agenda.

In this way, the Trojan Horse affair was both shaped by a changing political agenda and used as justification for those changes.

From 'preventing violent extremism' to 'countering extremism'

The direction of the government's evolving Prevent agenda has been to shift from a focus on 'preventing violent extremism' under New Labour to 'countering extremism' under the coalition onwards.

---

[117] HM Government (2015) *Counter-Extremism Strategy*, page 13.

Under New Labour, Toby Archer argues, an increasingly dominant counterterrorism agenda laid the basis for 'the policy exchange of fears and beliefs' across a range of governance domains, creating 'a patchwork of insecurities' and a generalised 'politics of unease' around Muslims in British society.[118] This was facilitated by the delivery of Prevent across a wide range of policy areas. As Charles Husband and Yunis Alam also point out, the multi-agency nature of its delivery in that period meant that on the ground Prevent came to permeate a wide range of policy areas[119] – including cohesion, equalities, youth and interfaith work. In Birmingham, for instance, the Prevent programme there was led from 2009 to 2011 by a counterterrorism police officer who had been seconded from the regional Counter-Terrorism Unit into the city council's Equalities Division to lead the programme locally.

The evolving counter-extremism agenda since 2011 has greatly intensified this 'politics of unease' through its implementation across an ever wider range of policy domains, and particularly through its conceptually broadened concern with tackling 'extremism' generally, rather than *violent* extremism specifically. This more expansive counter-extremism agenda is underpinned by a pre-emptive approach to addressing attitudes that are deemed to run counter to 'fundamental British values' among what are posited as segregated, poorly integrated Muslim communities. Through the embedding of the so-called 'conveyor belt thesis' in government policy, this approach links conservative or illiberal views with violent political extremism, based on the proposition that non-violent Islamism or conservative Islamic values and practices provide the enabling conditions for terrorism.[120]

---

[118] Toby Archer (2009) 'Welcome to the *Umma*: the British state and its Muslim citizens since 9/11', *Cooperation and Conflict*, 44(3): 332. For a discussion of how Prevent has permeated across policy domains, see Therese O'Toole, Nasar Meer, Daniel Nilsson, Stephen H. Jones and Tariq Modood (2016) 'Governing through Prevent? Regulation and contested practice in state-Muslim engagement', *Sociology*, 50(1): 160–177. Available at: http://journals.sagepub.com/doi/pdf/10.1177/0038038514564437.

[119] Husband and Alam, *Social Cohesion and Counter-Terrorism*.

[120] See Christopher Hope, 'David Cameron: we will "drain the swamp" which allows Muslim extremists to flourish', *Telegraph*, 3 June 2013,. Available at: www.telegraph.co.uk/news/politics/10097006/David-Cameron-We-will-drain-the-swamp-which-allows-Muslim-extremists-to-flourish.html.

A leading terrorism expert, Richard Jackson, has argued that contemporary counterterrorism approaches are increasingly premised on the view 'that we cannot know who, when, where, why and how terrorists might strike and that terrorists are sophisticated, adaptive, and always creatively evolving their tactics',[121] and that there are no clear signs of terror to be identified. Consequently, the focus of counterterrorism strategies in many Western countries is on 'pre-crime', 'risky citizens' and 'efforts to control words and images considered to be capable of infection'. This enlarged focus, he argues, is a manifestation not of an evidence-based understanding of the threat of terrorism, but its opposite. It is a response that is preoccupied by 'symptoms' and 'signs of future threat', rather than 'the deeper roots or causes of terrorism', and it is an indication of a crisis in knowledge and understanding in counterterrorism circles. The Counter-Extremism strategy, like the Clarke Report and the more recent Casey Review, focuses on identifying signs and symptoms of extremism, such as conservative or 'hardline Sunni' values, attitudes supporting gender segregation and inequalities, intolerance of homosexuality, opposition to the UK's foreign policy or attitudes that run counter to 'fundamental British values'. Yet the evidence that these values are indicators of a propensity to engage in terrorism is lacking. The government's preoccupation with ideological causes of terrorism, moreover, has been criticised by many for its insufficient engagement with evidence on the causes of radicalisation.[122]

In making Prevent a legal duty on public sector institutions, the Counter-Terrorism and Security Act 2015 entailed a significant operational expansion of Prevent, facilitated by the rolling out of

---

[121] Richard Jackson (2015) 'The epistemological crisis of counterterrorism', *Critical Studies on Terrorism*, 8(1): 33–54.

[122] See Lynn Davies, Zubeda Limbada, Laura Zahra McDonald, Basia Spalek and Doug Weeks (2015) *Formers and Families: Transitional Journeys in and out of Violent Extremisms in the UK*. Available at: www.connectjustice.org/admin/data/files/UK%20Formers%20&%20Families%20Final.pdf; and Arun Kundnani (2015) *A Decade Lost: Rethinking Radicalisation and Extremism*, London: Claystone. Available at: http://www.claystone.org.uk/wp-content/uploads/2015/01/Claystone-rethinking-radicalisation.pdf.

Prevent training workshops and modules that frontline personnel are required to undertake. Indeed, much of the funding that has been put in to Prevent since 2011 has been expended on Prevent coordinators and Workshop to Raise Awareness of Prevent (WRAP) training[123] – rather than, as was the case under New Labour, on community engagement projects. This training has been criticised, however, for offering a decontextualised reading of radicalisation – presenting radicalisation in terms of symptoms without causes beyond the psychological vulnerability of individuals.[124] This approach requires frontline personnel to be vigilant for signs of increased religiosity or 'religious seeking' – although a leaked MI5 report on the profiles of those who have engaged in jihadi violence found that religiosity is not a particularly strong feature of their biographies.[125] Reflecting on the profiles of European jihadis, Olivier Roy, a French political scientist and scholar of global Islamism, has argued that 'terrorism does not arise from the radicalisation of Islam, but from the Islamisation of radicalism'.[126] Yet the everyday practices of public sector workers are being reorganised to enable them to identify and report on purported signs of radicalisation, involving often cursory training that is itself based on a weak and contested understanding of radicalisation.

One consequence of this expanded vision of extremism is that a larger range of Muslim community organisations and actors fall under the definition of 'extremist' and are no longer eligible for government funding or to be potential partners with government. This has ruled out many Muslim organisations from inclusion within governance

[123] Over 400,000 public sector workers have undergone Prevent training according to the government's annual CONTEST report for 2015: Home Office (2016) *CONTEST*, page 16.

[124] See Leda Blackwood, 'What is wrong with the official "psychological" model of radicalisation?', *Public Spirit,* 23 October 2015. Available at: www.publicspirit.org.uk/what-is-wrong-with-the-official-psychological-model-of-radicalisation/.

[125] See Alan Travis, 'MI5 report challenges views on terrorism in Britain', *The Guardian*, 20 August 2008. Available at: www.theguardian.com/uk/2008/aug/20/uksecurity.terrorism1.

[126] Olivier Roy, 'Who are the new jihadis?', *The Guardian,* 13 April 2017. Available at: www.theguardian.com/news/2017/apr/13/who-are-the-new-jihadis.

initiatives – including groups that are ethically and actively opposed to violent extremism.[127] It also means that previous engagements with such organisations which were once viewed positively, are now viewed with suspicion, a suspicion which, in the Trojan Horse affair, is applied retrospectively.

Spatial logics of Prevent and counter-extremism

We began this chapter with the question of why 21 schools in Birmingham were targeted for special inspections by Ofsted. Among the 21 inspected schools, only 14 had had any allegations made against them according to the Clarke Report. As we discuss in detail in Chapter Three, guidance to schools on implementing the 2011 Prevent strategy at that point had not been issued, and it was not yet a statutory duty for schools either. Nor was there much emphasis on monitoring the implementation of Prevent in Ofsted inspection criteria. Moreover, awareness and implementation of Prevent in schools across the sector generally was low, and it was not uncommon for schools to consider the promotion of cohesion, or 'British values', as fulfilling any responsibilities for countering extremism.

It is noteworthy that all the schools involved had 90–100% ethnic minority (in many cases Pakistani and Bangladeshi heritage) pupils and they were all located in areas of Muslim residence in the south-east and to the north-west of the city.[128] In this respect, they became subject to the spatial security logics that have governed the development and application of Prevent since 2007 – nationally, and locally in Birmingham. The Prevent agenda that was developed in 2007

---

[127] Not all conservative Muslim groups are associated with violent extremism. Indeed, some Salafi organisations have been active in combatting violent extremism – such as STREET (Strategy to Reach, Empower, and Educate Teenagers) in South London. In 2009, a tip-off from a Salafi mosque in Bristol to Avon and Somerset police led to the interception, arrest and conviction of Isa Ibrahim who had been plotting to bomb the Broadmead shopping centre in Bristol.

[128] In Annex 4, page 115, the Clarke Report provides a map of the locations of the 21 schools which shows their clustering in the south-east (from Washwood Heath to Sparkbrook) and north-west (in Lozells) inner ring of the city.

identified areas with 5% or more Muslims as Prevent priority areas. According to Paul Thomas, this was later revised to areas with 4000 or more Muslims.[129] In so doing, it cast a Muslim presence itself as a security risk, stigmatising sites of Muslim residence. Birmingham was identified as a priority area under this logic – as a consequence of the proportions and numbers of Muslims living in the city.

Birmingham is a site of significant Muslim residence – it is the fourth largest area of settlement after London boroughs. According to the 2011 census, 234,411 (21.8%) of Birmingham's population are Muslims – which is significantly higher than the England and Wales figure of 4.8%. Muslims in Birmingham are predominantly of Pakistani heritage, but the city is home to ethnically diverse Muslim groups, including Bangladeshis, Indians, and increasingly Somalis, Kurds, Turks and Iranians.[130] Muslims are also highly spatially concentrated in the city: 69% of Birmingham's Muslims live in nine of Birmingham's 40 wards: Washwood Heath, Hodge Hill, Nechells, Bordesley Green, Sparkbrook, South Yardley and Springfield to the east and south-east inner ring of the city, and Aston and Lozells and East Handsworth to the north-west. In three of those wards, Muslims make up over 70% of the population: in Washwood Heath (77.3%), Bordesley Green (73.9%) and Sparkbrook (70.2%).[131]

The spatial logic that guided the Prevent strategy in 2007 was further refined in Birmingham by the local crime safety delivery body, the Safer Birmingham Partnership (SBP), which in 2009 identified 11 Priority Neighbourhoods in Birmingham for targeted Prevent activity.[132] A strategic assessment by the SBP proposed that:

[129] Thomas, (2010) 'Failed and friendless', page 443.
[130] Department for Communities and Local Government (2009) *Summary Report: Understanding Muslim Ethnic Communities*, London: DCLG.
[131] Census 2011.
[132] The 11 priority neighbourhoods were: Aston Pride; Lozells; Handsworth; Soho Finger & Gib Heath; Ward End & Pelham; Washwood Heath & Saltley; Bordesley Green; Bordesley Green & Small Heath; Farm Park & Sparkbrook North; Sparkhill North & Central; Balsall Heath. Safer Birmingham Partnership (2009) *Building Resilience to Violent Extremism: Delivering the Prevent Strategy in Birmingham*, Birmingham: SBP, page 8.

arguably terrorism affects all the communities across Birmingham, but it is the Muslim communities who will be engaged with regards to the PVE agenda. This is because Muslim communities are most vulnerable to radicalisation, and the agenda seeks to provide support to the people and groups who are making a positive contribution to this agenda. The focus for the delivery of PVE work is specifically directed to support Muslim communities of the four key constituencies of Perry Barr, Ladywood, Hodge Hill and Hall Green.[133]

Significantly, in deciding that 'the majority of the projects will be centred on those areas as it is recognised that this is where most vulnerability lies', it drew on demographic data on Muslim presence – echoing the belief that the latter, rather than primarily intelligence, provided the key evidence base for identifying and locating security risks.

The spatial logics of security policy in Birmingham are further revealed in the operation of Project Champion some four years earlier. Project Champion was a police scheme that targeted two areas of Muslim residence in the city for enhanced surveillance. It was led by West Midlands Police (WMP) and entailed the installation in 2010 of 216 closed circuit television (CCTV) and Automated Number Plate Recognition (ANPR) cameras in Sparkbrook and Washwood Heath (with seven other adjacent wards affected), with the aim of creating a 'surveillance ring' around these areas. Initially, it was presented to local communities as a crime safety initiative aimed at tackling car theft and drug crime. The scheme was launched with flawed community consultation, and its counterterrorism purpose deliberately concealed. A campaign group of local residents, civil liberties campaigners and Muslim activists, in alliance with local councillors and journalists, revealed that Project Champion was in fact a counterterrorism initiative, and prompted the admission that it had been approved by ACPO(TAM) (Association of Chief Police Officers – Terrorism

---

[133] Ibid, page 8.

and Allied Matters), which had drawn down £3 million of Home
Office funding for the scheme.[134] This led to a public outcry and to
the Assistant Chief Constable of WMP issuing a public apology to
a meeting of community groups on 4 July 2010.[135] The nature and
covert purpose of the scheme and the poor consultation with local
communities were condemned in two public reports by Birmingham
City Council[136] and Thames Valley Police.[137] Ultimately the cameras
were hooded and finally dismantled in 2011.

The use of overt and covert surveillance that was attempted by
Project Champion was based on longstanding narratives of these
areas as risky, and this was consonant with the spatial logics that
governed the identification of Prevent Priority Neighbourhoods. This
characterisation of areas of Muslim settlement as a security risk was
similarly manifest in responses to the allegations of a Trojan Horse plot
that emerged in 2014, in which assessments of the threat to the schools
focused on sites of Muslim presence (in relation to neighbourhoods,
school populations and school governing bodies) and where the issues
were framed from the outset through the lens of extremism.

This was evident in the ways in which the investigations into Trojan
Horse were quickly securitised, with the then Secretary of State for
Education, Michael Gove, appointing a former Counter-Terrorism

[134] See West Midlands Counter Terrorism Unit (2008) 'Memorandum: Report to Chief Constable and Chief Executive of Police Authority seeking delegated authority concerning element of Project Champion', 3 September 2008. Available at: www.whatdotheyknow.com/request/36652/response/107429/attach/6/Champion%20Delegated%20Auth%20for%20Main%20Contract%20Award%206%20Oct%202009.pdf. The review confirmed that ACPO (TAM) approved the scheme and allocated £3 million in January 2008, and that this had been the outcome of an almost two-year process of negotiation with ACPO (TAM).

[135] See 'Police apologise for Project Champion Birmingham spy camera scheme', *Birmingham Mail*, 5 July 2010. Available at: www.birminghammail.co.uk/news/local-news/police-apologise-for-birmingham-spy-camera-127653.

[136] Birmingham City Council (2010) 'Project Champion: scrutiny review into ANPR and CCTV cameras: a report from Overview & Scrutiny', 2 November 2010. Available at: www.birmingham.gov.uk/downloads/file/460/project_champion_scrutiny_review_into_anpr_and_cctv_cameras_november_2010.

[137] Thames Valley Police (2010) *Project Champion Review*, London: TVP. Available at: www.statewatch.org/news/2010/oct/uk-project-champion-police-report.pdf.

Police Officer, Peter Clarke, to lead the DfE investigation – rather than an educationalist – an appointment that framed the issue from the outset as one with potential security/terrorism implications. The elision of Trojan Horse with counterterrorism was also evident in Ofsted's focus on the schools' failure to implement Prevent and its criticisms of schools' lack of awareness of how to identify 'risk of potential radicalisation and extremism'. As we discuss in more detail in Chapter Three, in fact, the requirement for and guidance on the implementation of Prevent in schools were not fully developed in 2014. Thus, the schools were punitively assessed according to criteria that were underdeveloped and inconsistently applied across the sector. In the process, the Clarke Report and Ofsted inspection regime implicitly identified schools with majority Muslim pupils as particularly prone – or, in the lexicon of Prevent, *vulnerable* – to extremism. In so doing, they performed the function of symbolically producing Muslims as synonymous with extremism.

Yet, as the various reports on the Trojan Horse affair conceded, and notwithstanding their criticisms of various governing and teaching practices, there was no evidence of radicalisation taking place in the schools implicated in the affair. The Kershaw Report concluded: 'There is no evidence of a conspiracy to promote an anti-British agenda, violent extremism or radicalisation in schools in East Birmingham',[138] whilst the Clarke Report found there was no evidence of 'terrorism, radicalisation or violent extremism' in the schools – rather religious conservatism or a 'hardline strand of Sunni Islam'. A contemporaneous report by the Trojan Horse Review Group for Birmingham City Council was highly critical of Ofsted's narrow vision of British values and its conflation of faith-based ideology with radicalisation.[139] Furthermore, the presenting officer in the NCTL hearings brought by the DfE to disbar a number of the teachers from the four schools that came to be seen as being at the centre of the

---

[138] Kershaw Report, page 4.
[139] Trojan Horse Review Group, Report to Leader of Birmingham City Council, 18 July 2014. Available at: www.birmingham.gov.uk/info/20179/news_and_media/984/trojan_horse_review, page 11.

affair argued that these cases are 'not about an evil plot to indoctrinate young children in extremist ideology or anything like it'; rather, they are 'about the failure to respect diversity'.[140] We will challenge even this judgement, but, for the present, it is sufficient to note the lack of clarity in the definition of precisely what was at issue and the slippage between accusations of 'extremism' and 'conservatism'.

Conclusion

The Trojan Horse affair in Birmingham was rapidly followed by investigations into schools in other areas of Muslim settlement, including Bradford, Luton and Tower Hamlets. Subsequently, the construction of the nature of the Trojan Horse threat in Birmingham provided a key legitimating rationale for the government's elaboration of an expansive counter-extremism policy that is applicable to public institutions generally, and takes the presumed facts of the Trojan Horse plot as evidence of the need for such an approach. Thus, the narrative of extremist entryism based on the claims surrounding the Trojan Horse episode are used to underpin the further expansion of counter-extremism policies in the UK more broadly and potentially to other sectors and institutions. For these reasons, the claims about extremism in the Birmingham schools, and their significance for the teaching of Muslim children and the teaching of British values, should be subject to careful scrutiny.

Before we do so, in the following chapter we examine how Prevent became entangled with community cohesion in school policies and the implications of this for how the Birmingham schools were evaluated. As we shall see, the lack of clarity about what schools were required to do under Prevent, and the highly punitive approach that Ofsted took in its evaluation of the schools, are further complicated by the confusion that arose as a consequence of regulatory requirements placed on schools in relation to promoting community cohesion.

---

[140] NCTL Opening Note *NCTL v Monzoor Hussain, Arshad Hussain, Raswan Faraz, Hardeep Saini and Lindsey Clark*, paragraph 9.

THREE

Community cohesion, schooling and Prevent

The previous two chapters have set out the debate on 'British values' and the security agenda associated with Prevent. In this chapter, we will look at how these have been translated into policies for schools and how those policies have been implemented. The latter includes the role of Ofsted inspections, but we will save that discussion until after we have presented the obligations on schools for teaching religious education and daily collective worship in Chapter Four. The reason for this is that the promotion of 'British values', any duties under Prevent, and requirements concerning religious education are all governed by a single legislative framework, that of section 78 of the Education Act 2002, which informs Ofsted inspections.

This Act states that:

the curriculum for a maintained school or maintained nursery school satisfies the requirements of this section if it is a balanced and broadly based curriculum which – (a) promotes the spiritual, moral, cultural, mental and physical development of pupils at the school and of society, and (b) prepares pupils at the school for the opportunities, responsibilities and experiences of later life.[141]

Ofsted inspections, as we shall see, are directed toward section 28, within which they make their judgements about community cohesion, religious education and Prevent. The guidance provided to schools on these matters, then, is of crucial importance.

One of the immediate consequences of the publicity surrounding the Trojan Horse affair was that the DfE reinforced the requirement on publicly funded schools in England to actively promote 'shared values', now called 'fundamental British values'.[142] The new guidance states that 'schools should promote the fundamental British values of democracy, the rule of law, individual liberty, and mutual respect and tolerance of those with different faiths and beliefs'. It states further that schools should, 'enable students to acquire a broad general knowledge of and respect for public institutions and services in England'.

Schooling community cohesion

The timing of this new initiative implied that the Trojan Horse affair was evidence of a failure to promote shared 'British values', or engagement with and respect for democracy, tolerance or respect for the rule of law, and that the failure derived, in part, from insufficient guidance to schools. This is not the case. Successive governments have seen schools as being crucial to foster community cohesion, which has included these values, especially in the context of perceived ethnic and religious differences.

---

[141] Education Act 2002. Available at: www.legislation.gov.uk/ukpga/2002/32/section/78.

[142] Department for Education (2014) 'Promoting fundamental British values as part of SMSC in schools. Departmental advice for maintained schools', London: Department for Education, November. Available at: www.gov.uk/government/uploads/system/uploads/attachment_data/file/380595/SMSC_Guidance_Maintained_Schools.pdf.

We have shown in Chapter One how public discourse on community cohesion increasingly placed 'values' at the forefront of concerns. This is a major part of the Guidance on the Duty to Promote Community Cohesion issued to schools by the Department for Children, Schools and the Family (now the DfE) in 2007 in which there was an emphasis on 'shared values'.[143] However, the implementation in schools also stressed the material correlates of values, namely the need to address inequalities (something missing from the later 2014 guidance). This followed the 2007 report of the Commission on Integration and Cohesion, *Our Shared Future*, which placed an emphasis on a new model of rights and responsibilities and a commitment to equality involving a need to 'deliver visible social justice, to prioritise transparency and fairness, and build trust in the institutions that arbitrate between groups'.[144]

In its response, the Labour government of the day accepted the recommendations of the Commission and incorporated them into the Education and Inspections Act 2006 (with effect from 1 September 2007), with Ofsted to begin reporting on them from September 2008. The 2007 guidance to schools is important with regard to the Trojan Horse affair because it sets out what schools were required to address within the curriculum and other practices and the terms by which they were to be evaluated in the inspections by Ofsted. In effect, these standards are those that applied to Park View and the PVET and against which they should have been judged. As we shall see, when we come to discuss them directly, neither the Kershaw Report nor the Clarke Report make any reference to this guidance (or, indeed, any other guidance offered to schools), as a benchmark against which to judge their curricula and practices.

[143] Department for Schools, Children and the Family (2007) 'Guidance on the duty to promote community cohesion', London. Available at: http://webarchive.nationalarchives.gov.uk/20130401151715/http://www.education.gov.uk/publications/standard/publicationDetail/Page1/DCSF-00598-2007.
[144] Commission on Integration and Cohesion (2007) *Our Shared Future: Final Report of the Commission*, Wetherby: Crown Office, page 8. Available here: http://resources.cohesioninstitute.org.uk/Publications/Documents/Document/Default.aspx?recordId=18.

The guidance defines the meaning of community cohesion for schools:

> By community cohesion, we mean working towards a society in which there is a common vision and sense of belonging by all communities; a society in which the diversity of people's backgrounds and circumstances is appreciated and valued; a society in which similar life opportunities are available to all; and a society in which strong and positive relationships exist and continue to be developed in the workplace, in schools and in the wider community.[145]

It also goes on to state that:

> The Commission's report also underlines the importance of equality – both the importance of tackling inequality gaps, but also the importance of making this social change visible to all communities, communicating fair treatment at all times. Schools' role here is crucial: by creating opportunities for pupils' achievement and enabling every child and young person to achieve their potential, schools make a significant contribution to long term community cohesion.[146]

In effect, then, the guidance places opportunities at the forefront and goes on to link these to 'shared values':

> As a starting point, schools build community cohesion by promoting equality of opportunity and inclusion for different groups of pupils within a school. But alongside this focus on inequalities and a strong respect for diversity, they also have a role in promoting shared values and encouraging their pupils

[145] Department for Schools, Children and the Family (2007) Guidance, page 3.
[146] Ibid, page 4.

to actively engage with others to understand what they all hold in common.[147]

This guidance remained in effect until 2014, when new guidance was issued (after the Trojan Horse affair and implying that it represented a failure to promote shared values),[148] which seemed to break the link between shared values and their material correlates – that is, equal opportunities (or at least makes no mention of the latter). As we will see in Chapter Five, the categories against which inspection reports were to be written were also changed (in January 2012) prior to the 2014 inspections of the schools, to remove a direct link to the criteria set out in the guidance. However, the government affirmed that those criteria still remained as the basis of inspections even if they were not mirrored exactly in the descriptors of each section in which reports were to be presented and against which performance was to be evaluated.[149]

The application of community cohesion policies to schools was one of the areas where the Commission on Integration and Cohesion's recommendations were most fully implemented. Moreover, the recommendations had resonance with the everyday understandings of members of diverse communities. Jayaweera and Choudhury, for example, found that their interviewees regarded schools as an important means not only for improving opportunities, but also for facilitating social interaction among different groups. However:

in interviews with policy-makers and practitioners, teachers from a high-achieving inner-city school with a predominantly South Asian student population complained that the national discourse on minority ethnic underachievement in education creates the impression that schools with large minority ethnic

---

[147] Ibid, page 6.

[148] Department for Education (2014) 'Promoting fundamental British values'.

[149] Department for Education (2011) 'Freedom of Information Release', 28 February. Available at: www.gov.uk/government/publications/community-cohesion/community-cohesion.

populations are bad and underperforming, and this in turn undermines attempts to attract white children to such schools.[150]

In other words, segregation (not, it should be noted, self-segregation) limited the extent to which the Commission's aims of increasing the interactions among minority ethnic and white children could be realised, but this was itself associated with negative perceptions of pupil performance at schools with majority ethnic minority pupils.

The means by which schools meet their broad obligations under section 78 of the 2002 Education Act are twofold – organisational arrangements (for example, assemblies and other arrangements for providing pupils with a voice; systems of discipline, for example with regard to bullying and the like) and in the curriculum. For maintained schools under local authority control, the latter means compliance with the National Curriculum. For academy schools, the curriculum is determined according to their funding agreement with the Education Funding Agency (an agency of the DfE).[151] As we have already said, Park View became an academy in 2012, and thus was able to modify its curriculum away from that otherwise mandated – although it should be noted that the ability to do so does not mean that it did. The accusation of Andrew Gilligan is that it did do so – or more specifically, something happened to change the school after 2012, the date of its stellar Ofsted report and its move to academy status – but this is not consistent with his arguments of laxity on the part of Birmingham council officials, since they were not responsible for the school after its transition to academy status.[152] Nor is it consistent with the accusations of the Clarke and Kershaw Reports, or the proceedings at the NCTL hearings, which condemn its practices prior to 2012, as we shall see.

---

[150] Jayaweera and Choudhury (2008) 'Immigration, faith and cohesion', page 118.
[151] It should be noted that the 'national curriculum' is a framework for different subjects that has most salience prior to formal examination. All schools must address the curricula set out by the relevant examining bodies for GCSEs and A/S levels, which are, in their turn, agreed with the Department for Education.
[152] Gilligan, 'Trojan Horse'.

Personal relationships and sex education

The National Curriculum also includes provision for citizenship education, religious education, and personal, social, health and economic education (PSHE), as part of section 78 of the 2002 Education Act. The Guidance on Community Cohesion had particular applicability to the curriculum on citizenship education, but it was also expected to apply to, and be embedded in, the other special areas (religious education and PSHE) as well as in some specific subjects, for example history and English, just as guidance on PSHE might be applied in the teaching of biology, for example. Indeed, in addressing the areas covered by the guidance, they are generally viewed to be something in which attention is paid to the 'whole curriculum' and not just to its component subject parts.

Schools properly, and necessarily, face in two directions: towards government and the requirements and obligations it places on schools, and towards the communities that they serve. We have seen that the latter are frequently diverse in their religious beliefs and traditions, or may have beliefs and traditions different from those of other communities. These different beliefs and traditions can be directly reflected in schools which are designated as 'faith schools', but schools which are designated as non-faith, community schools are also expected to take account of the concerns specific to the communities they serve. This is made explicit, for example, in the Guidance on Sex and Relationship Education.

This guidance is designed to apply to special lessons devoted to the topics, or in specific subjects (such as biology), or, for LEA schools operating the National Curriculum, in the syllabus for citizenship education. The guidance recognises that there are cultural and religious sensitivities in teaching about sex and relationships. It recommends that the curriculum be developed to accommodate these sensitivities, and that there should be consultation among governors, teachers and parents about such issues. For example, it states that 'the teaching of some aspects of sex and relationship education might be of concern to teachers and parents. Sensitive issues should be covered by the school's policy and in consultation with parents. Schools of a particular religious ethos may choose to reflect that in their sex and relationship education policy'.[153] It should be noted that the guidance refers to schools of a particular 'religious ethos'. This is not an ambiguity in the document, where it really means to refer to 'faith schools'. As we have already stated, England does not have 'secular schools', even if many parents and their children are secular. We will discuss the requirements on schools with regard to religious education and daily acts of collective worship in the next chapter, but here we want to note that reference to 'schools of a particular religious ethos' is careful phrasing to indicate that there will be maintained community schools – 'non-faith' schools – with a 'religious ethos' that reflects the communities in which they are located. In this respect, the guidance itself incorporates and provides for the core value of 'tolerance for religious diversity'.

The guidance goes on to propose that 'schools should ensure that pupils are protected from teaching and materials which are inappropriate, having regard to the age and cultural background of the pupils concerned. Governors and head teachers should discuss with parents and take on board concerns raised, both on materials which are offered to schools and on sensitive material to be used in the classroom'.[154] Finally, it is also recognised that these sensitivities include teaching about such matters in mixed classes. Thus, 'teachers will need to plan a variety of activities which will help to engage boys as well as girls, matching their different learning styles. Single sex groups may be particularly important for pupils who come from cultures where it is only acceptable to speak about the body in single gender groups'.[155] The guidance reinforces the point, stating that:

---

[153] Department for Education and Employment (2000) 'Sex and Relationship Education Guidance', London: Department for Education and Employment. Available at: www.gov.uk/government/uploads/system/uploads/attachment_data/file/283599/sex_and_relationship_education_guidance.pdf, paragraph 1.7.

[154] Ibid, paragraph 1.9.

[155] Ibid, paragraph 1.23.

it is therefore important for policies to be both culturally appropriate and inclusive of all children. Primary and secondary schools should consult parents and pupils both on what is included, and on how it is delivered. For example, for some children it is not culturally appropriate to address particular issues in a mixed group. Consulting pupils and their families will help to establish what is appropriate and acceptable for them.[156]

Some readers may be uneasy at this point that the guidance makes too many concessions to 'difference'. Although we disagree – and have set out in the chapter on 'British' values why a commitment to multiculturalism is likely to serve general values of democracy, the rule of law and religious tolerance, rather than conflict with them – this is not the matter at hand. The point here is that of the standards to which schools are asked to adhere. Schools are asked to engage with the communities from which their pupils come. In the case of Birmingham schools, this will involve engaging with communities with different faith traditions and beliefs, including Islam. These, then, are the standards that should apply in any judgement of Park View and its educational trust, PVET and the other schools that were being appraised.

Schools and the implementation of Prevent

As noted in Chapter Two, at the time of the Trojan Horse allegations and Ofsted inspections, Prevent was not yet a statutory requirement in schools – this was not introduced until 2015. In 2008, the then Department for Children, Schools and Families (DCSF) developed a 'toolkit to help schools contribute to the prevention of violent extremism', which was 'intended as guidance' and explicitly did 'not impose any new requirements on schools'.[157] This guidance focused

---

[156] Ibid, paragraph 1.25.

[157] Department for Schools and Families (2008) 'Learning together to be safe together: a toolkit to help schools contribute to the prevention of violent extremism', Nottingham: DCSF. Available at: http://dera.ioe.ac.uk/8396/1/DCSF-Learning%20Together_bkmk.pdf, page 6.

largely on schools' role in upholding democratic values and fostering community cohesion, with some specific advice on monitoring children's vulnerability to violent extremism or terrorism. It situated these responsibilities within already existing legal and contractual provision. The Prevent agenda was directly linked with community cohesion in this period, as we have seen, but there was no requirement placed on schools with regard to Prevent independently of the Guidance for Promoting Community Cohesion until 2015. Indeed, the responsibility to promote community cohesion has generally been seen by schools as their primary responsibility and inclusive of their obligations under Prevent.

The implementation of Prevent in schools was discussed in the government's 2011 Prevent strategy, but comprehensive guidance to schools on implementing the revised approach to Prevent was not in fact issued by the Department for Education until July 2015 – after it had become a statutory duty. The 2011 Prevent strategy, and subsequent policy documents, enfolded the implementation of Prevent within schools' existing safeguarding duties. As the 2011 Prevent strategy document stated:

> Schools can help to protect children from extremist and violent views in the same ways that they help to safeguard children from drugs, gang violence or alcohol. Schools' work on Prevent needs to be seen in this context. The purpose must be to protect children from harm and to ensure that they are taught in a way that is consistent with the law and our values. Awareness of Prevent and the risks it is intended to address are both vital. Staff can help to identify, and to refer to the relevant agencies, children whose behaviour suggests that they are being drawn into terrorism or extremism.[158]

The guidance to schools on Prevent that was issued in 2015 (after the Trojan Horse inquiries) similarly asserted that: 'Protecting children

---

[158] Home Office (2011) *Prevent Strategy*, page 69, para. 10.45.

from the risk of radicalisation should be seen as part of schools' and childcare providers' wider safeguarding duties, and is similar in nature to protecting children from other harms (e.g. drugs, gangs, neglect, sexual exploitation), whether these come from within their family or are the product of outside influences.'[159]

The characterisation of Prevent as simply an extension of schools' existing safeguarding duties has been challenged by teaching professionals. The National Union of Teachers (NUT) passed a motion at its annual conference in 2016 calling for the reform of Prevent, arguing that the implementation of Prevent in schools was *not* compatible with the understanding of safeguarding among teaching professionals, which emphasises the need to create safe spaces for children to express views or discuss difficult issues.[160]

A report by the Open Society Justice Initiative on the implementation of Prevent in education and health was similarly concerned with the way in which the safeguarding duty in schools is in tension with the requirements of the Prevent duty:

> Although the government describes Prevent as a form of 'safeguarding' (a statutory term which denotes promotion of welfare and protection from harm), the two sets of obligations have materially different aims, particularly with respect to children. In contrast to the Prevent strategy, for which the primary objective is preventing terrorism, the primary objective of the duty to safeguard children under domestic legislation is the welfare of the child. This reflects the obligation under article 3(1) of the Convention on the Rights of the Child to make the best interests of the child a primary consideration in all actions relating to children. Accordingly, while compliance with

[159] Department for Education (2015) *Prevent Duty*, page 5.
[160] Thus, the conference noted that 'The statutory duty placed on schools, colleges and local authorities sits alongside a responsibility to ensure a safe space for children and young people to explore their relationship with the world around them'. NUT Prevent motion 2016: http://schoolsweek.co.uk/nut-prevent-strategy-motion-what-it-actually-says/.

safeguarding obligations would only permit referral to Channel while prioritising the best interests of the child, the Channel duty guidance does not specify that as a mandatory or even a relevant consideration. All of the case studies in this report relating to children – including one in which a four-year-old child was targeted – appear to be instances in which the best interests of the child were not a primary consideration.[161]

The shift in the Prevent strategy to countering extremism (rather than preventing violent extremism) is based on the definition of extremism that was set out in the revised 2011 strategy as: 'vocal or active opposition to fundamental British values, including democracy, the rule of law, individual liberty and mutual respect and tolerance of different faiths and beliefs'.[162] For schools, promoting fundamental British values has become a key element of the implementation of Prevent. This was initially introduced in 2012 by the DfE as part of Teachers' standards and framed as a requirement of teachers 'not [to] undermine fundamental British values'. By 2014, this was enhanced to a requirement on teachers to 'actively promote' fundamental British values. The Counter-Terrorism and Security Act 2015 went further, requiring teachers to promote them inside and outside of school and identify young people at risk of radicalisation.[163]

In 2014, at the time of the Trojan Horse affair, the role of schools in implementing Prevent was non-statutory and outlined in an array of documents. Indeed, schools' responsibilities under Prevent and how they linked to other statutory obligations were at the time subject to considerable regulatory confusion. Furthermore, the extent to which

---

[161] Open Society Justice Initiative (2016) *Eroding Trust: The UK's Prevent Counter-Extremism Strategy in Health and Education*, New York: Open Society Foundations. Available at: www.opensocietyfoundations.org/reports/eroding-trust-uk-s-prevent-counter-extremism-strategy-health-and-education, pages 17–18.

[162] Home Office (2011) *Prevent Strategy* , Glossary, page 107.

[163] See HM Government (2015) *Revised Prevent Duty Guidance: for England and Wales*, version 2, revised 16 July 2015. Available at: www.gov.uk/government/uploads/system/uploads/attachment_data/file/445977/3799_Revised_Prevent_Duty_Guidance__England_Wales_V2-Interactive.pdf.

the monitoring of schools' compliance with Prevent was a routine aspect of Ofsted's inspection regime in 2014 is also unclear.

There is no publicly available detailed explanation of the rationale for the selection of the 21 Birmingham schools that were subjected to Ofsted inspections. According to Ofsted, 15 schools were inspected at the request of the Secretary of State for Education, whilst six were inspected due to 'Ofsted's concerns about the effectiveness of safeguarding and leadership and management in these schools'.[164] At the time of the Trojan Horse school inspections, the Ofsted school inspection handbook that had been issued in January 2014 and the handbook that had been updated in April 2014 carried few references to extremism, and this was mostly in relation to pupil behaviour and safety, stipulating that 'When judging behaviour and safety inspectors should consider … the extent to which pupils are able to understand, respond to and calculate risk effectively, for example risks associated with extremism'. There was a brief reference to preventing extremist behaviour as an example of ways leadership might demonstrate capacity to bring about further improvement.[165] This was later amended, so that by 2016 the handbook included specific references to awareness of and keeping pupils safe from radicalisation and extremism within the criteria for evaluating leadership and management.[166] But it was not an explicit element of the inspection criteria for leadership and management in 2014. It was *after* Trojan Horse that this requirement became an explicit element of the Ofsted regime. Thus the 2015 Counter-extremism strategy stated: 'Ofsted inspections now routinely assess schools on how well they promote fundamental British values and safeguard pupils from the risk of extremism. All Ofsted inspectors

[164] Michael Wilshaw letter to Michael Gove, 9 June 2014, 'Advice note provided on academies and maintained schools in Birmingham to the Secretary of State for Education, Rt Hon Michael Gove MP, as commissioned by letter dated 27 March 2014'. Available at: www.gov.uk/government/publications/advice-note-on-academies-and-maintained-schools-in-birmingham.

[165] Ofsted (2014) *School Inspection Handbook*, April 2014, page 42.

[166] Ofsted (2016) *School Inspection Handbook*, August 2016, pages 38, 42 and 43.

are trained so that they understand the link between extremism and the general safety and wellbeing of children and young people.'[167]

In 2014, then, the requirement to implement Prevent in schools, guidance to schools on how to implement Prevent and the monitoring or enforcement of implementation in schools were all relatively vague.

In fact, as part of its preparation for the government's revised Prevent strategy in 2011, the DfE commissioned research from Ipsos Mori to see how schools understood their obligations under Prevent.[168] Once again, we draw attention to the fact that this report set out what schools across the country were doing, yet it was not itself referred to by either the Clarke Report or the Kershaw Report in reaching judgements about Park View or other schools. Nor was it a reference point for the round of Ofsted reports in 2014 that found Park View and other schools in Birmingham to be wanting in their implementation of the Prevent agenda. In fact, when we come to a detailed treatment of those reports, we will see that there are grounds for believing that Park View was doing *more*, not *less*, than other schools.

The report for DfE distinguishes between practices associated with community cohesion and those associated with the Prevent agenda. It finds, but is not surprised by the finding, that:

> schools' awareness of Prevent is lower than their awareness of the statutory duty to promote community cohesion, perhaps reflecting the fact there is no statutory duty to engage in Prevent-related work and the relatively recent publication of Department guidance. Half of schools (50%) say they know a fair amount or more about the policy compared with 95% claiming at least a fair amount of knowledge about the statutory duty.[169]

---

[167] Home Office (2015) *Counter-Extremism Strategy*, page 26.

[168] Chris Phillips, Daniel Tse and Fiona Johnson (2010) *Community Cohesion and PREVENT*, Research Report 0085 for the Department for Education. Available at: www.gov.uk/government/uploads/system/uploads/attachment_data/file/182300/DFE-RR085.pdf.

[169] Ibid, page 11.

Knowledge of the Prevent agenda is greater among secondary schools (64%) than primary schools (47%). Only 48% of schools were confident (fairly confident, or better) in their knowledge of the Prevent agenda, compared with 93% expressing confidence in their knowledge of their duty to promote community cohesion. However, according to the report, 'secondary school knowledge of and confidence about Prevent is higher in more deprived areas and urban centres, particularly London. Schools with an ethnically diverse school roll or a large proportion of BME pupils are likely to know more and feel more confident'.[170]

Whereas half (49%) of schools use the curriculum to build resistance to violent extremism, 94% use it to promote community cohesion. However, while the knowledge of obligations to community cohesion was high, there was variation in terms of understanding issues of religious diversity and ethnic minority disadvantage. The report comments that:

> to some extent, more ethnically diverse schools are more active on community cohesion but the picture is complex. For example, secondary schools' perceived knowledge of ethnic origins and cultures appears greatest in both the most ethnically diverse schools (where presumably it is seen as a particularly pressing issue) and in the least ethnically diverse schools (perhaps reflecting a view that in a homogenous school there is little complexity to understand). Schools with 'middling' levels of ethnic diversity tend to claim the least knowledge.[171]

It is important to recall from our discussion of Prevent in Chapter Two, that it was organised spatially. Areas with 5% or more Muslims were designated as Prevent priority areas. On this criterion, Birmingham was one of the areas identified as a priority area. This spatial logic was further developed by Birmingham City Council itself, which

---

[170] Ibid, page 11.
[171] Ibid, page 14.

identified 11 priority neighbourhoods for its targeted Prevent activities, including the neighbourhoods of the 21 schools investigated under the Trojan Horse affair. From the perspective of many of those within these communities this was perceived both to suggest that Muslim presence itself was a security risk, and to stigmatise the places where Muslims lived.

Notwithstanding their unease at being singled out, it had the paradoxical consequence that as the DfE's commissioned report pointed out, 'schools with an ethnically diverse school roll or a large proportion of BME pupils are likely to know more about Prevent and feel more confident about Prevent'.[172] The government denies that the Prevent agenda put an undue focus on Muslim communities, but this is somewhat belied by the Trojan Horse affair and the media reporting of concerns over schooling in Birmingham. It is precisely schools of the kind caught up in Trojan Horse affair that the government's own research showed were more likely to be doing most to address issues of violent extremism. The various inquiries into the Trojan Horse affair failed to consider the pattern across the sector, while holding Park View and other schools to have deviated significantly from what it expected (and, by implication, considered to be the norm).[173]

Among the topics addressed by the DfE-commissioned study was the extent to which staff in schools had received training in Prevent. It showed that most schools in England did not conduct training, with a majority of schools responding that no member of teaching or support staff or senior leadership team or governors had received Prevent-related training (Table 3.1).

---

[172] Ibid, page 14.

[173] Similar issues apply to the NCTL misconduct hearings – the report also shows that knowledge of duties, etc was greater among senior teachers than ordinary teachers, yet the latter were charged with the same putative failings as their senior colleagues.

Table 3.1: Recipients of prevent-related training[174]

In the last year, which of the following, if any, have received continuing professional development/training on your school's contribution to preventing violent extremism?	Primary Schools	Secondary Schools
Base: All respondents	(321) %	(348) %
Respondent personally	23	25
Respondent's senior leadership team	14	22
Respondent's school's governors	7	6
Respondent's school's teaching staff	6	10
Respondent's school's support staff	6	6
None of these	66	58

Yet the Ofsted inspections of the 21 Birmingham schools nonetheless evaluated them on their awareness and implementation of Prevent, and several were (in some cases significantly) downgraded for their failures in this regard. In four of the five schools subjected to full inspections, among Ofsted's measures for improvement were recommendations that schools 'undertake extensive training in how to identify risk to pupils from extreme or radical views' or that they extend 'the use of "Prevent" strategies to raise students' awareness about the risks of extremism'. Similarly, among the further 16 schools that underwent Section 8 monitoring inspections, six were cited as requiring improvement, and, in line with the criticisms of the five schools subject to full inspections, this was typically in relation to issues relating to 'leadership and management' – with several of these schools instructed to put in place measures to tackle extremism or to implement Prevent. For example, Ofsted recommended that Graceland Nursery should 'train all staff in recognising risk of potential radicalisation and extremism', whilst it recommended that Adderley Primary should 'engage fully with the local authority in relation to the "Prevent" programme'.

In other words, the downgrading of Birmingham schools on the basis of their failings in this regard was for failings that were common

---

[174] The table is compiled from data provided by Phillips et al, op cit, page 94.

across the sector (while Ofsted gradings are intended to provide comparative judgements). Indeed, Park View, the school at the centre of the Trojan Horse concerns, was criticised for its failings in this regard, even though it *was* taking measures to implement the Prevent agenda: thus, the Ofsted report criticised the fact that the school's 'use in liaison with the police, of the government's "Prevent" strategy to identify and avoid extremism has only taken place for students in years 7 and 8'.[175] This describes *more* than was being done at other schools.

This was in part because, across the sector, schools tended to envelop responsibilities to implement Prevent within their activities to promote community cohesion – as did many other agencies. Indeed, the Prevent agenda overlapped across a range of areas of delivery, with the DCLG, police, local authority, education and other actors, merging it with the promotion of community cohesion. This was regarded by the 2011 review of Prevent as precisely the source of confusion about the 'securitisation' of integration and cohesion.[176]

Consequently, the 2011 Prevent strategy stated that, although 'Prevent will depend on a successful integration programme':

> as a general rule, Prevent and cohesion programmes must remain distinct, though coordinated with one another. Counter-terrorism Prevent funding must not be used extensively for community interventions which have much wider social objectives. The Government has already decided that responsibility for Prevent will lie with the Home Office (in the OSCT) and responsibility for integration with DCLG.[177]

In fact, this line of argument did little to clarify the situation with regard to schooling. The responsibility for integration, or community cohesion, was passed to the DCLG, but nothing was said specifically

---

[175] Phillips et al (2010) *Community Cohesion and PREVENT*, page 6.

[176] See Therese O'Toole, Daniel Nilsson DeHanas and Tariq Modood (2012) 'Balancing tolerance, security and Muslim engagement in the United Kingdom: the impact of the "Prevent" agenda', *Critical Studies on Terrorism*, 5: 373–389.

[177] Home Office (2011) *Prevent Strategy*, page 30.

about the responsibilities of the DfE, notwithstanding that the latter was responsible for the Guidance for Promoting Community Cohesion that was statutorily binding on schools.

Section 10 of the 2011 Prevent strategy addressed institutions and sectors where there was a risk of radicalisation, and included a short section on education. It proposed that, 'radicalisation tends to occur in places where terrorist ideologies, and those that promote them, go uncontested and are not exposed to free, open and balanced debate and challenge'. In this context, it also argued that 'schools are important not because there is significant evidence to suggest children are being radicalised – there is not – but because they can play a vital role in preparing young people to challenge extremism and the ideology of terrorism and effectively rebut those who are apologists for it'. The strategy further set out the existing obligations on schools, including 'the obligation to promote community cohesion deriving from the Education and Inspections Act 2006', as being designed to address these issues.[178] Insofar as the 2011 Prevent strategy identified any areas of concern, these were directed toward madrassahs and a variety of educational arrangements that were offered at hours per week below those that would have brought them under regulatory frameworks. The latter were frequently designed as supplements for home-schooled children.[179]

In fact, the most telling comments are about issues of regulatory confusion at the DfE. These did not involve the nature of underlying regulatory standards and guidance, but the complexity of the system with regard to different types of schools and different frameworks applied to each. However, the concerns are not directed toward publicly funded schools, but rather the independent sector. It is worth quoting at length:

[178] Ibid, paragraphs 10.1, 10.10, 10.15.
[179] One of the consequences of the Trojan Horse affair has been an increased proportion of pupils in Birmingham who are home schooled.

concerns have been raised about the robustness of the regulatory system for independent schools and in particular about the clarity of the Independent School Standards (the regulations against which independent schools are inspected). In 2009 Ofsted conducted a survey which concluded that, overall, the regulations are fit for purpose, but that there is a lack of clarity in the language of the regulations. If the regulations are not clear, or are not clearly understood, there are clear risks that schools might not fully understand their obligations and that extremist or intolerant messages may go undetected by inspectors. This is of particular concern, given that open-source reporting has suggested that extremism may be more of a problem within some of these institutions than in publicly-funded schools.[180]

This might appear to be prescient, in that the events at Park View and the earlier very positive Ofsted report might suggest that those inspectors had missed precisely what inspectors noticed in 2014. However, when we look at those reports in detail, we will see that the situation is the opposite. The earlier inspectors did understand the obligations on the schools and reported on them very directly. It is the later inspectors who introduced new 'obligations' under the Prevent agenda, despite there being no relevant regulations pertaining to them, other than the ones reported on by the earlier inspectors, against which the schools were judged to be outstanding.

Finally, we should conclude on what might be involved in challenging extremism within a school. Increased anxiety after the Trojan Horse affair, and in the light of the 2014 Guidance on the Promotion of British Values, has led to reports that schools have shied away from addressing contentious issues and that Muslim pupils have feared to express their views on, say, Palestine, or the war in Syria. Earlier guidance had stressed that the curriculum must be balanced and not promote particular political views (in recognition of children and young people as vulnerable to persuasion). However, this was not

---

[180] Home Office (2011) *Prevent Strategy*, paragraph 10.20.

intended to preclude the presentation of partisan views. Nor does it mean that balance has to be provided in each lesson, with contested views presented side by side, for example. Balance was to be achieved across the curriculum, and other practices of the school, not within each lesson considered individually. Indeed, the very thrust of the 2007 Guidance on the Duty to Promote Community Cohesion was to regard the objectives of community cohesion as a matter for the whole curriculum, notwithstanding that there will be specific parts of the curriculum that have a more prominent role.

Conclusion

We have already mentioned Foucault's idea of 'governance through failure', but we begin to see a different issue emerging. This is one where policies are promoted and implemented, but the scaffolding that supports those policies is dismantled. At the same time, intermediary bodies lose their role in ensuring those standards. For example, it is not simply that guidance provides schools with a clear idea of what they should be doing, but their relationships with other schools provide a means of debating best practice. In addition, local authorities have provided support and further means of assurance. However, the shift away from local authority responsibility as part of the academies programme has brought many schools under the direct authority of the DfE. At one and the same time, schools are placed in smaller networks (of academy trusts, at best, or as single academies, at worst), and under the broad oversight of a DfE with little capacity to replace the functions of local authorities, while being subject to 'efficiency savings' as part of financial austerity imposed by the Treasury.

Of course, this does not mean that there were failures of governance and implementation with regard to published standards, simply that government itself became vulnerable to the charge of 'failure', especially if such a claim is taken up within the media. This is particularly significant in areas of media anxiety where an expectation has been raised about problems of 'community integration'. The removal of the supporting scaffolding means that different bodies which might expect to have some responsibility are operating with reduced day-to-day knowledge. In this context, the charge of 'failure' becomes a means of governing, regardless of whether that failure is evident in practice. In the next chapter, we will see how this is connected with requirements on the teaching of religious education and daily acts of collective worship.

FOUR

Religious education, collective worship and publicly funded education

The Trojan Horse affair is largely about the claim that some schools in Birmingham – and Park View school in particular – allowed an undue religious influence over the curriculum and other practices in the schools. The further implication has been that this has undermined an appreciation of diversity and religious tolerance on the part of the children, and, therefore, has been in conflict with 'British values'. There has also been the claim that segregation of boys and girls has taken place and that this, too, is detrimental to equalities of opportunity, although, as we saw in the last chapter, the guidance to schools is explicit that the separation of girls and boys is good practice for some activities where there are cultural sensitivities about the suitability of mixing.

One of the key themes in reporting on the case is that practices which were alleged to have taken place at Park View school might have been unobjectionable had it been a 'faith school', but they were a problem because it was not. The implication of many reports (including, most egregiously, the Clarke Report) is that schools that are not 'faith schools' are, therefore, intended to be 'secular'.[181] As we shall see, this is not the case – all schools, whatever their designation – faith, non-faith, or whether they are LEA maintained, academy or 'free' – are required to hold daily acts of collective worship and teach religious education. The main difference between faith and non-faith schools concerns the recruitment of teachers and other staff – for example, whether a particular faith-background can be required – and pupil selection – for example, whether this can be from a particular faith background (though even the latter is regulated).[182] In schools with a religious foundation, religious education and collective worship will reflect the Trust deeds of the school, whereas those schools without a religious foundation will either follow the locally agreed syllabus or, in the case of academies and free schools, a religious education syllabus of their choosing in line with their contract with the EFA.

Before we address the allegations against PVET directly, we want to set out more fully the nature of the obligations concerning religion in schools in England (there are some differences with regard to other devolved jurisdictions in the UK, especially Northern Ireland and Scotland). We will begin by setting out the general context of religious practice and belief in England and the apparent paradox of declining religiosity alongside the continued existence – even growth – of faith schools. We will then discuss the specific requirements of religious education and collective worship in non-faith schools and the nature of the agreed syllabus for religious education in Birmingham.

---

[181] As the Clarke Report put it, there was 'a deliberate attempt to convert secular state schools into exclusive faith schools in all but name', page 48.

[182] New faith academies have since 2007 been required to select no more than 50% of pupils on the basis of faith. However, the government has proposed that this cap be removed. See *Schools that Work for Everyone*, September 2016. Available at: https://consult.education.gov.uk/school-frameworks/schools-that-work-for-everyone/.

Religion and post-secular society

Around a third of all state-funded schools in England are faith schools, or 'schools of a religious character' as they are more properly termed. This reflects the history of educational provision, where the Church of England initially developed schools to provide basic education alongside schooling in the Christian faith from the 19th century onwards (of course, the so-called 'public schools' for the wealthy were also primarily religious foundations and were established much earlier). The 1870 Education Act was the first to make provision for public education, but it did so as a supplement to existing Church of England (and other) schools. The suppression of Roman Catholicism after the Reformation meant that Roman Catholic schools did not reappear until the 1850s with the re-establishment of Roman Catholic dioceses, when education was taken up as a central part of rebuilding the church's presence in England. Similar developments are associated with some of the non-conformist denominations – especially Methodism – which also established schools with the general lifting of laws against non-established religions in the middle of the 19th century.

The current significance of faith schools in the provision of schooling in England is seemingly in contrast with the declining significance of religious belief. The British Social Attitudes Survey shows a rise in the proportion of people who say they have no religion from just under a third in 1983 to nearly a half in 2014. There is a particularly sharp decline in those describing themselves as Anglicans from 40% to 17% across the same period. In contrast, there is a rise from around 1% of the population to just under 10% for those practising non-Christian religions. Almost half of those surveyed by YouGov in 2012 said that they would not describe their beliefs and values as spiritual or religious, while less than 10% described their values and beliefs as religious.[183]

---

[183] Figures cited from the Report of the Commission on Religion and Belief in British Public Life (2015) *Living with Difference: Community, Diversity and the Common Good*, Cambridge: Woolf Institute. Available at: www.woolf.cam.ac.uk/uploads/Living%20with%20Difference.pdf.

These figures are provided in a report by the Commission on Religion and Belief in British Public Life published in 2015. The report goes on to suggest that the decline in practising Christianity tends to make the rise of other religions more visible. This is further reinforced by the fact that the age structure of minority religious communities is different from that of the rest of the population. It is much younger and so those practising minority religions are likely to increase as their communities have proportionately more children, while those practising Christianity are likely to continue to decline (with Catholics and non-conformist Christians becoming proportionally more significant). According to Andrew Brown and Linda Woodhead, half of all practising Anglicans are over 60 and only one in 10 teenagers are practising Anglicans.[184]

This situation is exemplified in Birmingham. It has long been a city of religious and ethnic diversity, having been a centre of Roman Catholic revival in the mid-19th century (with the building in 1841 of the first Catholic cathedral since the Reformation), and subsequent migration from Ireland, especially in the 19th and early 20th centuries, but continuing into the 1950s and 1960s associated with manual labour on the new road networks that were being built. New Commonwealth migration to Birmingham has also been longstanding, but increased significantly in the 1960s. It included migrants (in fact, citizens of the British Commonwealth) from Christian religious backgrounds from the Caribbean and Africa and also Muslims from Africa, India, Bangladesh and Pakistan, as well as Hindus and Sikhs from India.

The general situation, then, is one of a decline in religion in the population as a whole, alongside an increase in religion reflecting the rise in specific ethnic minority groups, something that is especially significant in Birmingham. The latter are, in turn, an increasing proportion of those with school-age children, or likely to have them in the future. This explains the paradox that although, in aggregate terms, there is a decline in religion, there is an increased demand for faith

---

[184] Andrew Brown and Linda Woodhead (2016) *That Was the Church That Was: How the Church of England Lost the English People*, London: Bloomsbury.

schools, and demands for an extension of provision to serve minority religions. Indeed, the two are intertwined. The perception that non-faith schools were 'secular' initially gave rise to a preference for faith schools among parents from minority religions, even where the faith expressed in the school was not their own.[185] However, an increasing number of minority communities began to organise with an interest in establishing their own faith schools, and, at the same time, evangelical Christians concerned about increasing 'secularism' within schools also sought to establish faith schools organised around evangelical Christianity.[186] Geoffrey Walford, for example, writes that, 'during most of the post-war period, growing secularism and multiculturalism had led to a de-emphasis on Christian religious teaching and to a large-scale abandonment of the theoretically compulsory daily act of worship in all schools'.[187] This was so, notwithstanding legal requirements.

The rise of faith schools was also facilitated by other legislative changes. The first was the *Education Reform Act*, introduced by the Conservative government in 1988. This was a precursor to the idea of academy schools, in so far as it allowed schools to opt out of LEA control to become grant-maintained schools under central government responsibility. It also permitted a new independent school to be established as a grant-maintained school. However, there was little progress on increasing religious diversity among faith schools under these arrangements, although additional Church of England and Catholic schools and one Jewish school were established.[188] Renewed impetus came from the New Labour government's White Paper on *Excellence in Schools* in 1997 and the subsequent *School Standards and Framework Act* of 1998. This abolished grant-maintained schools and paved the way for the academies programme, with a new type of school

---

[185] For example, around half of the pupils at King David Primary School in Birmingham, a small Jewish faith school, are Muslim.

[186] G. Walford (2000) *Policy and Politics in Education. Sponsored Grant-Maintained Schools and Religious Diversity*, Aldershot: Ashgate.

[187] G. Walford (2008) 'Faith-based schools in England after ten years of Tony Blair', *Oxford Review of Education*, 34(6): 690.

[188] Ibid.

called City Technology Colleges. Under this framework, new faith schools were actively encouraged, including those of a non-Christian character. It was in 1998 that the first maintained Muslim faith school was established.[189] By January 2017 this number had increased to 27 in England, but still amounts to only 0.1% of maintained faith schools in England,[190] whilst Muslims make up 4.8% of the population of England and Wales according to the 2011 Census.

This provides a different context for the government's exhortations about 'British values' of religious tolerance. The implication of government discourse is that it is religious minorities that are potentially intolerant. However, it is also ethnic minority communities that are most likely to express religious values and the wider public to have concerns about that religious expression. Indeed, as secularism has increased among the wider public, there has been growing criticism of the very existence of faith schools, especially among groups representing humanists – and, by extension, about requirements for religious education and collective worship in non-faith schools.

Legislating religious education

A requirement that all publicly funded schools should teach religious education and have a daily act of collective worship was set out in the 1944 Education Act and has been reaffirmed since, especially in the 1988 Education Act, under Conservative Secretary of State for Education, Kenneth Baker. Exemptions were allowed on an individual basis, both for teachers and for pupils, but there was no obligation to provide an alternative for pupils exercising that right not to

[189] This was the Islamia Primary School in Brent. This was shortly followed by the Al-Furqan School in Birmingham, a school which comes to figure significantly in the Trojan Horse affair, albeit somewhat obliquely.

[190] See House of Commons Briefing Paper (2017) *Faith Schools in England; FAQs.* Briefing Paper Number 06972, 13 March 2017. Authors Robert Long and Paul Bolton.

participate.[191] The 1988 Act introduced the National Curriculum, but, although made mandatory, religious education was not incorporated into it as it was perceived that this would reduce flexibility and diminish the responsibility of local bodies to determine a curriculum suitable for local needs. However, the Act's provisions for religious education and collective worship were designed to reinforce religious education after a period in which it was perceived that it had become diluted, and collective worship abandoned in many schools. Both religious education and worship were to be Christian-based. They should 'reflect the fact that the religious traditions in Great Britain are in the main Christian whilst taking account of the teaching and practices of the other principal religions represented in Great Britain', and that a daily act of collective worship should be 'wholly or mainly of a broadly Christian character'.[192]

Most commentators – for example, speakers in Parliament during the passage of the 1988 Act – thought that there should be teaching of other religions, but that the teaching of Christianity was of fundamental importance as a matter of British heritage and values. As Kenneth Baker put it, 'A fundamental part of any religious education should be the Christian faith. That faith was brought to these islands by St Augustine and it has woven its way through our history'.[193] Indeed, to some extent, the revival of interest in religious education was not simply a response to a perceived rise of secularism, but was part of a response to growing numbers of ethnic minorities from other than Christian traditions and the idea that religious education could serve integration with 'British values'. This idea was given new expression by David Cameron in his King James Bible speech in 2011, when

[191] For detailed treatments of the Acts and the associated parliamentary debates, see W.K. Kay and L.J. Francis (eds) (1998) *Religion in Education*, Leominister: Gracewing.

[192] 1988 Education Act. Part 1. Chapter 1. Section 8(3) and 7(1). Available at: www.legislation.gov.uk/ukpga/1988/40/contents.

[193] Hansard, House of Commons Debate, 23 March 1988, vol 130, cc398–426. Available at: http://hansard.millbanksystems.com/commons/1988/mar/23/the-national-curriculum.

he declared that 'We are a Christian country. And we should not be afraid to say so' – signalling a shift from a multi-faith paradigm that characterised New Labour's approach to a more Christian heritage focus under the coalition government.[194]

The significance of the 1988 Act is also that it formally established the framework within which religious education and collective worship should be reviewed and implemented. It had been a matter of a syllabus agreed at the local level since the 1944 Education Act, through a conference made up of four committees. The later Act established that this format, now described as an Agreed Syllabus Conference (ASC), was something all local authorities were required to set up. It continues to be the body responsible for local authority maintained schools, although, as we shall see, academies and faith schools (in so far as they have become academies) lie outside its jurisdiction. It is formally separate from the Standing Advisory Council on Religious Education (SACRE), but, like the latter, is made up of four committees, which vote separately as committees, with unanimity required across all of them.[195] The committees are defined 'functionally' on the basis of different interests in religious education. Thus, there is a committee representing the local authority, one representing the teaching profession, one representing the Church of England (as the established church) and one initially representing other Christian denominations, later extended to other faiths. The syllabus has to be reviewed every five years, but it is not required that major revisions should take place each time.

The 1988 Act runs together religious education and collective worship, but it is clear that religious education provides the context within which collective worship should take place. A school assembly at the beginning of the day should include collective worship of a mainly (or wholly) Christian character albeit not specific to any

---

[194] Prime Minister's King James Bible Speech, 16 December 2011. For discussion, see O'Toole et al (2013) *Taking Part*.

[195] Unanimity is required for determining the syllabus, although a SACRE can advise local authorities on the basis of a majority view.

particular denomination.[196] The idea was that such an assembly would provide the moral and spiritual framing for the school day. However, the Act also recognised that the opportunity of individual withdrawal from participation on the grounds of religious conscience would be a problem if exercised widely by those from minority religious backgrounds. In consequence, it was allowed that there could be separate 'determinations' to vary the framework of collective worship to reflect the needs of the school and its particular intake of pupils. These determinations would be authorised by the local SACRE and reviewed on a five-yearly basis.

It should be noted that any determination granted by a SACRE would take place in a wider context of the religious education curriculum for the school which was also approved by the local SACRE. In this situation, the issue is one of balance (achieved within a curriculum that contextualises collective worship), not whether or not a school is 'overly religious'. Publicly funded schools are free to express a distinctive religious ethos, and that ethos can be Christian or, subject to determination, any other faith. They can also operate without a religious ethos, but they are required, nonetheless, to provide collective worship (usually, in this situation, it will be of a mainly Christian character).

In this context, it is not only schools that operate with a set of established expectations, but also Ofsted inspectors, who could assume an agreed context for religious education and collective worship in the schools they inspected. The implementation of the religious education curriculum and school assemblies are part of Ofsted inspections and are incorporated under section 78 of the Education Act 2002, which requires schools to have a curriculum that 'promotes the spiritual, moral, cultural, mental and physical development of pupils at the school and of society, and prepares pupils at the school for the opportunities, responsibilities and experiences of later life'.[197]

---

[196] The 1988 Act changed the requirement for collective worship at the end of the school day and also allowed it to be among groups of pupils rather than a whole school event.

[197] 1988 Education Act.

The SACREs represent a unique form of deliberative process and exercise of local judgement. While there will be those who object to the religious requirements on schools and who believe that schools *should be secular*, their religious character is nonetheless determined by Parliament and sanctioned by law.[198] However, the content of the curriculum proceeds through a very specific form of consensus building across different interests and different religious traditions. It is significant that the next major piece of schools legislation disrupted this form of decision making. The 2010 Academies Act was designed to speed up the process by which schools left the responsibility of the LEA and became the direct responsibility of the DfE. The Act determined they would not be bound by the National Curriculum as part of their greater freedoms and exercise of autonomy.

As we have seen, religious education and collective worship was mandated in the 1988 Act without being part of the National Curriculum since they were to be overseen by the SACREs. Religious education continued to be outside the National Curriculum for schools remaining under local authority responsibility, and it continued to be a requirement on academies and free schools. However, the Secretary of State for Education, Michael Gove, argued that SACREs should have no responsibility for that requirement. Academies and free schools, whether faith schools or not, would agree their religious education curriculum as part of their contracts with the EFA. At the same time, determinations for other than collective Christian worship were also to be administered by the DfE. We have already suggested that the latter department was likely to be under considerable administrative pressure in the context both of the increasing number of academy schools and of the efficiency savings demanded by the Treasury. Indeed, a Freedom of Information request revealed that no determinations were issued by the DfE between 2010 and 2015, suggesting that no procedures

---

[198] The British Humanist Association and the Secular Society have each proposed that religious education should include humanism and also that there should be no requirement of daily acts of collective worship. The Commission on Religion and Belief in British Public Life, in its turn, has recently recommended both proposals, perhaps influenced by publicity over the Trojan Horse affair.

for making and renewing them were put in place, in contrast to the situation with schools under LEA responsibility.[199]

With the government's intention to accelerate the number of academies, SACREs were concerned about the undermining of their role. In effect, their concern was that what was happening was a dramatic revision of the 1944 Act by stealth, albeit one that did not involve a changed commitment to religious education, for which secularists had been arguing. The requirements for religious education and collective worship remained, but no longer subject to the local processes of consensus building and moderation that the SACREs represented. Equally, a significant amount of work to develop an agreed syllabus was diminished as the government encouraged, through financial inducement and by mandate for failing schools, a dramatic increase in the number of academies (especially at secondary level). For example, by 2016 82% of maintained primaries were under local authority responsibility, with 17% academies (mostly in multi-academy trusts) and 1% free schools and other, while just 35% of secondary schools were under local authority responsibility, 59% were academies (of which 30% were in multi-academy trusts) and 5% free schools and other.[200] Academies could choose to adopt the agreed syllabus, but they were not obliged to do so, and, in any case, their responsibility was to the funding agreement signed with the EFA. The scaffolding supporting religious education that had been carefully built since 1944 was being dismantled, and intermediaries between schools and the DfE were being diminished. Academies were granted greater freedoms, but those freedoms were to be exercised under the central control of the DfE.

[199] Cited in the Expert Witness statement of Marius Felderhof (2015) *NCTL v Hussain, Saini, Clarke, Farwaz & Hussain*.

[200] 'Academies and maintained schools: what do we know?', *Full Fact*, April 2016. Available at: https://fullfact.org/education/academies-and-maintained-schools-what-do-we-know/.

The Birmingham agreed syllabus, 2007

Notwithstanding the complaints of secularists about the very idea of religious requirements on publicly funded schools – and both authors are themselves secular in orientation – the Birmingham SACRE-agreed syllabus is a very significant achievement. It indicates the value of the deliberative processes of its constituent committees and conferences.

As we have already indicated, SACREs are required to provide five-yearly reviews of any agreed curriculum, but there is no obligation to undertake major changes. In the two years prior to the 2007 review Birmingham SACRE decided to embark on a major reorganisation of the curriculum. This had been preceded by several decades of engagement with issues of multi-faith education deriving from the specific circumstances of Birmingham described above. As long ago as 1975, Birmingham had established a leading position for its multi-faith curriculum in which the study of six faith traditions was recommended – Christianity, Buddhism, Hinduism, Islam, Judaism and Sikhism. Indeed, the Birmingham SACRE had invited representatives from Hinduism, Islam, Judaism and Sikhism onto the 'non-denominational committee'. It had also appointed an *ex officio* consultant associated with the British Humanist Association, who was active in publicising the revision of the curriculum within the city.[201]

In fact, the 1975 curriculum included humanism and communism as part of the syllabus, as examples of secular values, albeit they were not specified as required aspects. This gave rise to considerable controversy, both within the City Council Chamber and in Parliament, as well as in local and national media. Conservatives were particularly hostile to the teaching of communism, but there was also hostility to multi-faith religious education, which re-emerged in the formulation of the 1988 Education Act that reinforced the requirement for religious education and collective worship to be 'mainly Christian'.

---

[201] See S.G. Parker and R.J.K. Freathy (2011) 'Context, complexity and contestation: Birmingham's Agreed Syllabuses for Religious Education since the 1970s', *Journal of Beliefs and Values*, 32(2): 247–263; Parker and Freathy (2012) 'Ethnic diversity, Christian hegemony'.

The 1995 Birmingham syllabus reduced the number of religions that should be studied, in the light of a debate over whether knowledge *about* religions was the crucial issue or knowledge of the personal qualities that religions sought to develop. This became the topic of the 1992–95 Agreed Syllabus Conference, which argued for a more values-led syllabus, where the concern would be to learn *from* religion, rather than to learn *about* religion. It was proposed that this emphasis, rather than the number of religions studied, would better realise the aims of the spiritual, moral and cognitive *development* of children that was the purpose of religious (and other) education and was enshrined in section 78 of the 2008 Education Act.

Between 2005 and 2007, the Birmingham SACRE undertook the reconstruction of this values-based curriculum. This was done under the guidance of Dr Marius Felderhof from the Department of Theology and Religion at the University of Birmingham, on secondment to Birmingham City Council and acting as Drafting Secretary. The approach to a values-based curriculum was child-centred in so far as it was organised in terms of the idea of 'dispositions'. A 'disposition' is understood by Felderhof to be 'a prevailing quality of character marked by an inclination, or will, to act in a particular way or by a tendency to a certain kind of action'.[202] The idea, then, would be to enumerate dispositions and consider how they are exemplified within different religious traditions: that is, how they are interpreted and the narratives that are told, as well as specific practices that are associated with them.

The Agreed Syllabus Conference was tasked with reaching agreement on the relevant dispositions – for example, 'being temperate', 'being joyful', 'being attentive to suffering', 'being fair and just', 'being accountable and living with integrity', 'cultivating inclusion, identity and belonging'. Given that this involved agreement among representatives of all faiths, the dispositions had to be agreed as common across all of them. In this way, the dispositions are

---

[202] 'The 2 dispositions', Faith Makes a Difference. RE in Birmingham (n.d.). Available at: www.faithmakesadifference.co.uk/dispositions.

'universalisable' and, therefore, avoid a potential criticism made by some critics of multi-faith education that it encourages a form of relativism.

In the end, 24 dispositions were identified and organised into six clusters. Each asks the child to reflect on the meaning of dispositions and the kinds of actions that they might enjoin. The clusters and their accompanying dispositions are described in Table 4.1.

Table 4.1: The 2007 Birmingham agreed religious syllabus[203]

Cluster	Dispositions
Developing Creativity *How should we imagine and express what matters?*	Being Imaginative and Explorative Appreciating Beauty Expressing Joy Being Thankful
Developing Compassion *How and why should we care?*	Caring for Others, Animals and the Environment Sharing and Being Generous Being Regardful of Suffering Being Merciful and Forgiving
Developing Choice *What should we stand for?*	Being Fair and Just Living by Rules Being Accountable and Living with Integrity Being Temperate, Exercising Self-Discipline and Cultivating Serene Contentment
Developing Community *How and where should we contribute and relate to others?*	Being Modest and Listening to Others Cultivating Inclusion, Identity and Belonging Creating Unity and Harmony Participating and Being Willing to Lead
Developing Commitment *What ventures should we undertake?*	Remembering Roots Being Loyal and Steadfast Being Hopeful and Visionary Being Courageous and Confident
Developing Contemplation *How do we come to understand what matters?*	Being Curious and Valuing Knowledge Being Open, Honest and Truthful Being Reflective and Self-Critical Being Silent and Attentive to, and Cultivating a Sense for, the Sacred and Transcendence

[203] The chart is constructed from information provided by the curriculum website, Faith Makes a Difference RE in Birmingham. https://www.faithmakesadifference.co.uk/dispositions/clusters.

While the syllabus is aligned with the obligations under section 78 of the 2008 Education Act, it is not claimed that the spiritual, moral and cognitive development of children, or promoting community cohesion, is the sole preserve of religious education. The purpose is to show the contribution that different religious traditions can make. The guidance to teachers is explicit:

> whilst they must communicate the Christian tradition they will select other material on the basis of certain principles to reflect the family background of the children, their ages, aptitudes and interests, and use whatever will deepen and broaden their horizons, or whatever will contribute to social solidarity and cohesion in a religiously plural community, i.e. there is no tick list approach to religious traditions.[204]

As with the 1975 curriculum, humanists in Birmingham also lobbied strongly that, with increased secularism (albeit less marked in Birmingham, and particularly among its minority ethnic populations), humanism should also be included. This was rejected on the basis that the statutory requirement was for a *religious* education curriculum and this did not include *alternatives to* religion. Reference to humanism as a possible subject in the curriculum had been included in proposed Non-Statutory Guidance on Religious Education, but this was removed after what the British Humanist Association argued was concerted lobbying from the Birmingham SACRE.[205] However, the city had taken legal advice in 1975 which said that humanism and Marxism could not be included in the religious education curriculum 'in their own right',

---

[204] The Basic Curriculum in Birmingham Summary of the 2007 Birmingham Religious Education Syllabus, page 3. Available at: www.faithmakesadifference. co.uk/sites/faithmakesadifference.co.uk/files/Summary_2007_Birmingham_RE_ Syllabus_2_0.pdf.

[205] 'Birmingham taxpayers' money used to urge systematic discrimination against non-religious in RE', British Humanist Association, 12 June 2014. Available at: https://humanism.org.uk/2014/06/12/birmingham-taxpayers-money-used-council-urge-systematic-discrimination-non-religious-re/.

but only as critiques of religion. The 1975 legal advice was passed on to the DfE at the time of the consultation on the Non-Statutory Guidance (2009). This advice was accepted by the DfE, who had privately indicated that they had received similar advice from their legal advisers.[206] The draft Non-Statutory Guidance on Religious Education was subsequently revised to reflect the legal advice.

Notwithstanding that the syllabus was developed through a process of building agreement, it did not mean that there were no other dissenting views, in particular, that it was too much of a multi-faith curriculum. However, the point to emphasise is that it was the *locally agreed syllabus* taught in Birmingham schools, as required by the 1988 Act and reiterated in the 2008 Education Act.

What should also be evident is that the clusters and the dispositions are not, in themselves, directly hostile to a secular world view (except, perhaps, the disposition of 'Being silent and attentive to, and cultivating a sense for, the sacred and transcendence'). What would be absent would be secular exemplifications of the dispositions, and this is what the British Humanist Association took exception to. However, these are part of the school curriculum otherwise in relation to the teaching of 'shared (or British) values' of democracy, the rule of law, etc, or in citizenship education within the National Curriculum. While the Secretary of State for Education, Michael Gove, responded to the Trojan Horse affair by stating that all schools would be required to 'promote British values',[207] and this was taken up by the British Humanist Association to argue for modification of the guidance on

---

[206] Private communication from Dr Marius Felderhof. The situation changed again in a High Court ruling in November 2015 that the Department for Education had acted unlawfully in failing to give pupils the opportunity to learn about non-religious worldviews (such as humanism) at GCSE. See *R (Fox) v Secretary of State for Education* [2015]. Available at: www.judiciary.gov.uk/wp-content/uploads/2015/11/r-fox-v-ssfe.pdf.

[207] As reported in 'Ofsted finds "culture of fear and intimidation" in some schools', *The Guardian*, 9 June 2014. Available at: www.theguardian.com/politics/blog/2014/jun/09/ofsted-publishing-trojan-horse-plot-reports-and-michael-goves-statement-politics-live-blog#block-5395e28ce4b0a6aad6394ac8.

religious education,[208] it should be clear by now that all schools were under an obligation to teach religious education and have daily acts of collective worship *and* to promote shared values as part of the duty to promote community cohesion. As the Birmingham agreed syllabus put it, religious education should 'contribute to social solidarity and cohesion in a religiously plural community'.[209]

As already mentioned, the 2010 Academies Act changed the situation. Not only were schools encouraged to leave local authority control by becoming academies, this also meant that they would be outside the oversight of the local SACRE (although religious education and daily worship remained mandatory). Birmingham SACRE made a strong representation to the Secretary of State for Education, Michael Gove, arguing that the problem of the proposed arrangements was that they removed moderating influences on governors and teachers who could develop a curriculum without even the engagement of their local faith organisations, let alone the collective experience of the various committees represented within the local SACRE. Michael Gove's response was typically robust and dismissive. He saw no merit in the argument, reaffirming his commitment to religious education, but stating, in effect, that it would be better to treat a locally agreed syllabus as like a product in the marketplace: it would be chosen if it met pupils' needs as determined by the governing body and head teacher of a school.

It is worth quoting from his letter in full:

> members of Standing Advisory Councils on Religious Education (SACRES) and Agreed Syllabus Conferences (ASCs), including Church of England representatives, have the right to put forward their views when developing an agreed syllabus. The most productive approach must be for ASCs to offer challenging and rigorous syllabuses that academies will want to adopt as they see

---

[208] See, for example, 'Birmingham schools findings reflect need for wider review of place of religion in schools', British Humanist Association, 9 June 2014. Available at: https://humanism.org.uk/2014/06/09/34029/.

[209] The Basic Curriculum in Birmingham Summary (2007), page 3.

they can meet their pupils' needs. I acknowledge the validity of the argument Mr Hordern makes about the law as it applies to academies. All academies must continue to provide religious education, as set out in their funding agreements. All academies must adhere to their funding agreements and we have no plans to change this requirement. Nevertheless, beyond these basic requirements, I am committed to academy and free schools' freedoms to choose whether they opt into local arrangements, and I see no reason why these freedoms should impact adversely on community cohesion or inter-religious cooperation.[210]

Conclusion

Have we found the 'smoking gun'? After all, the worries of SACRE about the risks associated with the freedoms assigned to academies seem to have been borne out in the Birmingham Trojan Horse affair. Park View became an academy and was subsequently accused of 'Islamification' of its curriculum and collective worship. This would be too easy an interpretation. Our argument is that there was no such 'Islamification' at PVET schools. However, the dismissal of the risks by Mr Gove and his lack of concern that SACREs were a safeguard against them may explain his peremptory response to the Trojan Horse affair when it blew up, even if it doesn't explain the situation at the school. As we shall show, Park View did adopt the Birmingham agreed syllabus when it became an academy, even though it was not obliged to do so. More properly, it carried on with the syllabus it was already teaching. It had an incentive to do so, not least because its chair of governors, Tahir Alam, was himself a prominent member of the Birmingham SACRE and had been actively involved in developing it.

---

[210] Cited in Expert Witness statement of Marius Felderhof (2015) *NCTL v Hussain, Saini, Clarke, Farwaz & Hussain.*

FIVE

Governance, school reform and change management

We have set out the wider context for understanding the Trojan Horse affair – specifically, the public discourse over British values, social integration, cohesion and the Prevent agenda. We have also set out how these were translated (or not) into guidelines for schools and the extent to which they were established as statutory requirements. Such requirements also include the provision of religious education and a daily act of collective worship. Schools are subject to inspection with regard to these requirements and other aspects of their performance; for example, the academic achievements of their pupils and their management and governance. The nature of this governance regime, in its broadest sense, is the topic of this chapter.

As we have indicated, there has been a programme of radical changes to the organisation of schools associated especially with the academies programme and other initiatives to improve school performance which were announced by the then Secretary of State in the Labour government in March 2000.[211] The academies programme had further

---

[211] The Learning and Skills Act 2000 provided for the creation of city academies, subsequently renamed academies under the Education Act 2002 and permitted in all areas rather than just cities.

impetus under the coalition government following the 2010 Education Act. The academies programme removes schools from LEA control and places them under the central authority of the DfE. Schools enter into contracts with a new body of the DfE, the Education Funding Agency (EFA), through which the funding for academies is monitored and disbursed. This process has disrupted existing networks of relationships and means of communicating 'best practice' within LEAs, and has replaced them with new networks facilitated by the DfE, or self-organised among academies themselves, for example, through the formation of multi-academy trusts and consultancies. In addition, in the last chapter we saw how the SACREs have been displaced from their role in developing and monitoring religious education and collective worship in schools, with no clear alternative provision within the arrangements for academies and free schools.

The origins of the academies programme lie in policies to address educational disadvantage and 'failing' schools. However, it has been a declared intention of both the New Labour government that developed the programme and of the subsequent coalition and Conservative governments that all schools in England should become academies.[212] With the exception of 'failing' schools, which have been required to become 'sponsored' academies under the guidance of another successful school, the process is supposedly consensual, with a variety of incentives – from financial benefits and freedoms over staffing, and, since 2010, freedom from the constraints of the National Curriculum – offered to encourage schools to make the transition as 'converter' academies. Notwithstanding the higher political consensus across different governments, it has often been a highly conflictual process, as we shall see, with teachers' unions and local communities frequently

---

[212] Opposition brought about a 'U-turn' following an announcement that such a programme was to be pushed through under Secretary of State Nicky Morgan in 2016, but the intention remained. See the report by Rachael Pells, 'Full academisation of schools still a reality, despite government U-turn, think tank confirms', *Independent*, 10 May 2016. Available at: www.independent.co.uk/news/education/education-news/full-academisation-of-schools-still-reality-despite-government-u-turn-nicky-morgan-think-tank-a7023156.html.

opposed to the changes, especially where the process has been seen to reduce local involvement in schools (notwithstanding claims to the contrary).[213]

This has exposed a paradox. The academic performance of schools is more tightly inspected and any weaknesses that are exposed are seen as indications of problems of management and governance. At the same time, the external governance of schools has become less ordered and coherent. This disjunction has created the conditions for a second narrative about the 'Trojan Horse affair'. The dominant media narrative and the position put forward by the government has been one of 'extremist ideology' on the part of school governors and teachers, leading to changes in the curriculum and other negative practices that make for a socially conservative and intolerant ethos in the schools in question. The second narrative – and it is one favoured by the liberal press and many academics – is that the problem did not lie with a plot to impose an 'extremist ideology', but represented a failure of external governance.[214] In other words, the problems in the schools were a consequence of failings at the DfE and the new system of external governance that the academies programme represented. Schools were able to detach themselves from moderating influences (both of SACREs and of LEAs, more generally) and the closer scrutiny that LEAs would represent.

It is important to stress, once again, that our argument is different, even if we share the view that external governance arrangements are confused. This second narrative, no less than the first, presupposes that there were indeed problematic practices – that is, practices that were in conflict with statutory requirements and guidelines – taking place at the schools. The fact that there are weaknesses in the new forms of school governance put in place by the DfE does not mean that any particular school is, itself, mismanaged or poorly governed. The achievements of Park View school are such that, prima facie, they are

---

[213] See, for example, Francis Becket, 'Too much power', *The Guardian*, 13 May 2008. Available at: www.theguardian.com/education/2008/may/13/schools.newschools.

[214] See, for example, Baxter (2016) *School Governance*.

evidence of good governance. After all, as we shall see, the idea that school failure is to be laid at the door of ineffective school governors and senior teachers has been at the very heart of the inspection regime and the new governance arrangements for academies.

Moreover, as we will also see, the DfE was engaged with the school on precisely the basis of it being a highly successful school that should become a 'converter' academy and 'sponsor' other less successful schools. For example, it was in contact with Park View in 2012 to encourage it to become a multi-academy trust and to take over two other schools which were failing, or had failings of leadership, Nansen Primary and Golden Hillock secondary. We will also see in a later chapter that the DfE asked PVET to take over a third school, Al-Furqan primary school. This was also an underperforming school, but it was a faith school. The DfE apparently saw no contradiction in requesting that a non-faith Trust should sponsor a faith school. This was because it understood there to be a 'faith ethos' at PVET, an ethos that was later to prove to be at issue in the accusations laid against it. The Trust decided that this was incompatible with its own status and withdrew from the process, but not before it had gone some way towards implementation of the planned incorporation. This was in full view of the DfE, precisely because of the delicacy of the proposed arrangements. No concerns about PVET were raised by staff at the DfE. However, as we shall see, this episode is not part of the EFA's review of events, which ended its funding agreement, and nor do the Kershaw and Clarke Reports mention it, though it transpired that the Clarke team was aware of it. Indeed, the Clarke Report was advised by officials from the DfE, including one who had been involved in the EFA Review of PVET following the airing of the allegations in the Trojan Horse letter and who should have known about the DfE's support for, and oversight of, PVET's proposed takeover of Al-Furqan school.[215] It forms no part of the EFA Review or the Clarke Report.

---

[215] Education Funding Agency, *Review of PVET*.

School governance, from 'system' to 'network'

As we saw in the previous chapter, the 1870 Education Act was the first to make provision for public education, but it did so as a supplement to existing Church of England (and other) schools. The 1944 Education Act was the first properly to regularise education through a system of primary and secondary schools, publicly funded under local authority control. The Act allowed three types of secondary school – grammar, technical and secondary modern – although their different types of provision could also be combined in a single, 'comprehensive' school. In addition, a category of independent school with direct grant funding was also maintained and, as we have seen, schools with a religious character – what are now generally called faith schools – were brought within the system of local authority funding, though some also continued as 'direct grant' schools.

The 1944 Act achieved a high degree of consensus across political parties, although divisions were already becoming apparent around academic selection and the move toward comprehensive schools in 1965 (when some local authorities retained grammar schools).[216] Nonetheless, the responsibility for educational provision in a local area rested with the local authority and its education department. The latter are responsible for the distribution of funding, the allocation of pupils, and the recruitment and employment of teachers. They also own the schools' premises and land (although some schools with a religious character are owned by their respective religious organisations).

Since the Children's Act of 2004, the provision of educational services has been combined with other children's services under a Director of Children's Services, with responsibilities for looked after

[216] This has become a live issue, once again, with the announcement that the government wishes to allow new selective grammar schools (and also allow faith schools to select on the basis of religion). See the report by Heather Stewart and Peter Walker, 'Theresa May to end ban on new grammar schools', *The Guardian*, 9 September 2016. Available at: www.theguardian.com/education/2016/sep/09/theresa-may-to-end-ban-on-new-grammar-schools. The policy was put on hold after the 2017 election delivered a minority conservative government.

children and social work with children and families. This is significant in the Birmingham context since the children's social care services in Birmingham had been subject to intervention from the Department of Health between 2002 and 2005, following a zero-star performance rating. Continued concerns with different aspects of social work practice culminated in a special report to the Secretary of State for Education and the Minister for Children and Families in February 2014. The report referred to 'an historically isolated department developing a dysfunctional management and practice culture, one that was largely immune from outside challenge and hence resistant to both internal and external pressures for improvement'.[217] This coincided with the Trojan Horse affair and contributed to the idea of problems of governance at the local authority which included the Director with responsibility for schooling since that was also included within children services, albeit not directly implicated by the report.

Individual schools in England that are publicly funded through local authorities are subject to direct oversight from their LEA. However, increasing numbers of schools are now outside local authority jurisdiction, as academies or free schools. They are able to recruit and appoint teachers without reference to the local authority and also to make their own admissions, albeit under a National Admissions Code and in line with their contract with the EFA.[218]

This development followed a new approach to education and its governance by the then Labour government between 1998 and 2010. The main concern was to develop a holistic approach – as reflected in the Children's Act of 2004 – and to encourage innovations that would drive up school performance. LEAs were perceived to be bureaucratic

---

[217] *Report to the Secretary of State for Education and the Minister for Children and Families on ways forward for Children's Social Care Services in Birmingham,* February 2014. See paragraph 9.1. Available at: /www.birmingham.gov.uk/downloads/download/873/report_to_the_secretary_of_state_for_education_and_the_minister_for_children_and_families_on_ways_forward_for_childrens_social_care_services_in_birmingham.

[218] See the details on Academy admissions on the government's website: www.gov.uk/guidance/academy-admissions#admissions-arrangements.

in organisation and unable to bring about necessary change in practices. In effect, the charge was that they had become captured by various professional interests – whether those of the bureaucracy itself, or of teachers and other educational experts – and this was detrimental to the interests of children, especially those in disadvantaged circumstances. Whereas entrenched social inequalities had previously been argued to determine outcomes, the focus was shifted to *aspirations* (on the part of parents and their communities) and *expectations* (of teachers), in order to drive up standards regardless of circumstances. This is something that was initially promoted by Chris Woodhead when he was Chief Inspector and head of the Office for Standards in Education (Ofsted) from 1994 to 2000 and would also be adopted by Sir Michael Wilshaw when he became Chief Inspector of Schools in 2012. The approach was taken up enthusiastically by Michael Gove when he became Secretary of State for Education in 2010. He famously referred to civil servants, teachers' unions and professionals working within education, including academic researchers, as 'the Blob', something that needed to be fought as vigorously as Steve McQueen fought the alien jelly threatening Pennsylvania in the film of that name.[219]

The approach was to emphasise 'outcomes rather than structures'. Innovations that addressed outcomes were to be supported wherever they came from. Thus, the development of new schools – initially called city academies – outside local authority control were encouraged, with sponsorship investment (of £2m) from private companies or charities (including private schools and universities). This emphasis on 'outcomes' also introduced a greater focus on targets and performance tables to rank schools, as we shall see when we come to consider the role of Ofsted (the agency of the DfE tasked with inspecting all schools). If the number of academy schools was not initially large as a proportion of all schools, the academies programme gathered pace and accelerated after the Conservative–Liberal Democrat coalition

---

[219] See Dennis Sewell, 'Michael Gove vs the Blob', *The Spectator,* January 2010. Available at: www.spectator.co.uk/2010/01/michael-gove-vs-the-blob/.

came to power in 2010 with the express intent that all schools should become independent of local authorities.

As we saw in the last chapter, by 2016 82% of maintained primaries were under local authority responsibility, with 17% academies (mostly in multi-academy trusts) and 1% free schools and other, while just 35% of secondary schools were under local authority responsibility, 59% were academies (of which 30% were in multi-academy trusts) and 5% free schools and other.[220] A similar pattern is found in Birmingham, where out of a total of 299 primary schools 98 (33%) are academies or free schools, and out of 82 secondary schools 53 (65%) are academies or free schools (there are 5 'all through' schools, of which 3 are academies or free schools).[221]

A 2005 White Paper, *Higher Standards, Better Schools for All*, set the tone for this development by proposing another type of school – a trust school – which was to have some of the freedoms of an academy, but would remain under local authority jurisdiction. Schools were encouraged to become federation trusts in order to share best practice with a successful trust school leading the federation of other schools under its tutelage. A new position of National Schools Commissioner was set up to coordinate advice to schools, subsequently with regional commissioners and associated Head Teacher Boards.[222] A National College of School Leadership had been set up in 2000, which became part of the National College for Teaching and Leadership in 2013, when it took over the regulation of teacher standards following the abolition of the General Teaching Council for England (as part of the government's drive to reduce the number of 'quangos'). These DfE agencies commission 'teaching schools' and 'national leaders in education' to provide support for underperforming schools.

These developments may be regarded as incremental changes that have had wide-ranging consequences. On the one hand, the old structures remained in place, albeit diminished in scope, to which were

---

[220] 'Academies and maintained schools: what do we know?', *Full Fact*, April 2016.

[221] Information provided by Education Services Birmingham.

[222] Significantly, the Headteacher Board for the West Midlands has no ethnic minority member.

added new bodies and new processes. However, these additions were outside the older hierarchical structure of local authority control and so the new system has been described as closer to a network mode of governance.[223] Some commentators have referred to the changes as constituting a form of 'marketisation of services', as indicated by the rhetoric of entrepreneurship and competition that accompanied them. However, while for-profit private companies are involved in sponsorship and the provision of services, this does not capture the fact that many other providers are charities, or directly responsible to the local authority. The 2005 White Paper referred to local authorities as shifting from 'provider to commissioner',[224] but while this may have been the intended direction of travel, it was travel that was incomplete in a number of important respects. Some publicly funded schools were entirely outside local authority jurisdiction and, for them, a local authority had no commissioning role. On the other hand, other schools remained entirely under local authority control, where it remained a provider of services, rather than a commissioner.

Stephen Ball describes the new arrangements as a 'heterarchy', which 'replace[s] some bureaucratic and administrative structures and relationships with a system of organization replete with overlap, multiplicity, mixed ascendancy and/or divergent-but-coexistent patterns of relation'.[225] For Ball, this also allows the proliferation of new policy actors – consultants and self-organised groups representing new entities, as well as new state agencies – which blur the distinction between public and private sector. The developments make the settings in which schools operate more complex and difficult to report by journalists. This complexity can also sustain a narrative that, rather

---

[223] See Stephen Ball (2011) 'Academies, policy networks, and governance', in Helen M. Gunter (ed) *The State and Education Policy: the Academies Programme*, London: Continuum.

[224] Department for Education and Skills (2005) *Higher Standards, Better Schools for All: More Choice for Parents and Pupils*, October 2005, page 11. Available at: www.educationengland.org.uk/documents/pdfs/2005-white-paper-higher-standards.pdf.

[225] Ball (2011) 'Academies, policy networks, and governance', page 148.

than a multiplicity of overlapping responsibilities, there are potential gaps where 'deviant' practices can arise unnoticed.

The changing role of governors

Since these changes were initiated under a Labour government, subsequent governments have continued with the emphasis on driving improvements in school performance and increasing parental choice and community involvement in schools. Once again, local authority governance is understood to be vulnerable to capture by professional interests of teachers, or the general inertia attributed to bureaucracy. This has had paradoxical consequences in that one of the instruments that has been used to bring about the desired changes has been to strengthen the role of governing bodies of schools, recommending that they should be more businesslike and act more like corporate boards. This culminated in a White Paper in 2016 in which the Secretary of State, Nicky Morgan, announced that not only would all schools in England be transferred out of local authority control by 2022, but the requirement to have parent governors would end.[226] This policy proposal was quickly withdrawn, but it was a clear indication of government priorities and a deep ambiguity over the meaning of community involvement in schools.

At present, schools are required to have a Board of Governors which meets on a regular basis to consider the activities of their school. Governors are volunteers – about 300,000 are needed across schools in England (with estimated vacancies currently at 30,000)[227] – whose purpose is to ensure clarity of mission, ethos and strategic direction of the school, to ensure its academic performance and compliance with

[226] In a White Paper published in March 2016, *Educational Excellence Everywhere*. Available at: www.gov.uk/government/uploads/system/uploads/attachment_data/file/508550/Educational_excellence_everywhere__print_ready_.pdf.

[227] See the report by Peter Stanford, '30,000 volunteers wanted – but who'd be a school governor?', *The Telegraph*, 6 January 2014. Available at: www.telegraph.co.uk/education/educationopinion/10553621/30000-volunteers-wanted-but-whod-be-a-school-governor.html.

the various statutory requirements on schools (for example, as set out in earlier chapters) and oversee the management of the budget. However, governors should not engage in the day-to-day activities of schools – operational matters – which are the responsibility of the management team within the school under the head teacher. Clearly, while some of these responsibilities are common across all schools, how they are to be discharged varies according to the type of school.[228] The Board of Governors in academy schools, for example, has responsibility for the appointment of teaching staff, while for a local authority school it does not.

Appointment to a Board of Governors for schools under local authority responsibility is determined on 'functional' grounds, in much the same way as the composition of a SACRE. However, how those with a 'stakeholder' interest in schools are identified has changed along with the changes to types of schools and the movement away from local authority control. Thus, for local authority schools, there are governors selected from among parents, governors selected from school staff (with the head teacher usually being a member of the Board), governors appointed by the local authority, and co-opted governors representing the community, who are appointed by the governing body. Lastly, following the development of the academies programme, there are governors representing foundation, sponsorship and partnership bodies, if this is applicable. The chair of governors is appointed by the Board of Governors, but cannot be a member of staff at the school.

Various studies have attested to the fact that governors tend not to be representative of the communities in which schools are located,

---

[228] *Governors' Handbook: for Governors in Maintained Schools, Academies and Free Schools*, published in January 2014, comprises 111 pages and has a matrix chart on page 6 of five core functions and whether or not they arise for governors according to the six different types of publicly funded schools. Available at: www.gov.uk/government/uploads/system/uploads/attachment_data/file/270398/ Governors-Handbook-January-2014.pdf.

with many living outside the area.[229] At the same time, the role of parent and community governors is becoming increasingly attenuated. This has had paradoxical consequences in that one of the instruments that has been used to bring about the desired changes has been to strengthen the role of governing bodies of schools, recommending, as we have seen, that they should be more businesslike and act more like corporate boards.[230] The expectation of academy schools is that their Boards would be smaller with a higher preponderance of nominees from sponsors and foundation bodies. For example, guidance by the then Department for Education and Skills states:

> to determine the ethos and leadership of the academy, and ensure responsibility and accountability, the private sector or charitable sponsor always appoints the majority of governors. This is the case even when a local authority is acting as co-sponsor for wider purposes. The number of governors on an Academy governing body is not prescribed, but the expectation is for the body to be relatively small.[231]

As Stewart Ranson and Colin Crouch write in a report on governance for the Centre for British Teachers Education Trust (CfBT), a consultancy that has subsequently been re-named as the Education Development Trust, 'a system which since 1944 has placed the governance of schools in the hands of a council of locally elected people, supported by an experienced professional bureaucracy, the local education authority, with its committee of elected councillors, is

---

[229] See for example, R. Deem, K. Brehony and S. Heath (1995) *Active Citizenship and the Governing of Schools*, Buckingham: Open University Press; C. Dean, A. Dyson, F. Gallannaugh, A. Howes and C. Raffo (2007) *Schools, Governors and Disadvantage*, York: Joseph Rowntree Foundation.

[230] See, for example, the BBC report by Patrick Howse, 'School governors "should be more business-like"', 13 January 2014. Available at: www.bbc.com/news/education-25713820.

[231] Department for Education and Skills (2004) *What are Academies?* Available at: https://tinyurl.com/ybb754m3.

being replaced by self-governing trusts led by corporate sponsors'.[232] For them, this represents a move toward an idea of schools governed by an executive board together with a charismatic head teacher to bring about change, against possible resistance. In other words, it is not simply that school governance is ad hoc and incoherent, but that it is composed of different elements founded on contradictory principles, those of democratic and professional accountability, on the one hand, and of corporate autonomy, on the other. During the period in which the Trojan Horse affair unfolded, expectations on governing bodies were divided between these principles. Under each set of principles, governing bodies are expected to challenge the direction of the school, but in moving from a local authority school to an academy school, the composition of a governing body would be expected to change, with the 'sponsor' taking over a dominant role in the appointment of governors and the head teacher having increased autonomy.

A number of the charges made against PVET involve the role of governors and the 'inappropriate' demands made by them. Once again, it is necessary to caution against the idea that these were examples of a lack of 'professionalism' that was being warned about by government ministers, and others, and were beginning to be widely reported in the media.[233] After all, Park View Academy was a highly successful school and was criticised for practices that were associated with that success and were being introduced into underperforming schools it was sponsoring under its Trust.

The inspection regime

The drive to professionalise boards of governors and to make them more businesslike, as Jacqueline Baxter argues, is directed at school

---

[232] S. Ranson and C. Crouch (2009) 'Towards a new governance of schools in the re-making of civil society', Research Paper, Institute of Education, University of Warwick, page 48. Available at: www.educationdevelopmenttrust.com/~/media/EDT/Reports/Research/2009/r-school-governors-and-the-partnership-arrangement-report-2009.pdf.

[233] Baxter (2016) *School Governance*, op cit.

performance as represented through academic results and Ofsted inspection reports.[234] Indeed, the performance of school governors was itself made a criterion for Ofsted inspection in 2012, and the Secretary of State, Michael Gove, endorsed this in a speech comparing boards of governors to '19th century parish councils',[235] and, therefore, in need of a good shake-up.

Schools have been subject to a regime of inspection since the inception of public funding for schools. Inspections under the auspices of His/Her Majesty's Inspector of Schools were largely designed to improve practices and to be supportive, and were not public. This changed in 1992 with the creation of Ofsted. This was part of John Major's Conservative government's 'Citizen's Charter', or contract with the public, for the delivery of public services and a commitment to transparency and information. In the realm of education, this involved a commitment to clear criteria for inspection and the publication of the reports. The development of the National Curriculum in the 1988 Education Act meant that schools could be assessed against common standards of achievement. All subsequent educational initiatives have had implications for school inspections and have involved incorporation into the criteria. As we have seen in earlier chapters, one set of criteria has been associated with section 78 of the Education Act 2002.

The inspections form part of what Michael Power has called an 'audit culture', where performance is judged according to measured outcomes, which are constructed into indices and rank orders, frequently also associated with 'value for money'.[236] Governments no

---

[234] Ibid, see especially chapter 4.

[235] Michael Gove, Speech at Freedom and Autonomy for Schools National Association conference, 5 July 2012. Available at: www.gov.uk/government/speeches/michael-gove-on-fasnas-first-twenty-years.

[236] Michael Power (1997) *The Audit Society*, Oxford: Oxford University Press. This has been associated with the Audit Commission set up by the Local Government Finance Act of 1992, with powers extended to audit of Local Education Authorities in 1997 (powers shared with Ofsted). In line with the shift in the public sector from 'provider' to 'commissioner', the Audit Commission was replaced after 2010 with local control over audit services purchased within the market.

longer issue directives or seek to govern directly, but set targets which different bodies and agencies must strive to achieve. By means of such accounting devices, performance can be made transparent to different parties and can be judged relative to others, thereby constituting a competitive environment where best practice must be sought out. Thus parents can judge the standing of the schools available to their children, school governors have criteria by which to judge the performance of head teachers, and funding bodies can identify underperforming schools as well as successful ones. In this way, audit and its associated performance measures become part of 'heterarchical' governance.

Not all information about schools can be generated by performance data – such as that relating to examinations results, data on attendance and exclusions and the like, available on an annual basis and part of internal monitoring by schools. Some information is associated with the judgements of inspectors about what they find on their visits to the schools, derived over several days from their attendance at classes, school assemblies and meetings and interviews with pupils and staff, and scrutiny of school documents such as reports to governors and lesson plans. Generally, while the character of reports has changed over time, they have enabled the identification of underperforming and outstanding schools in the context of the modification of the criteria (deriving from statutory guidance). Currently, the grades are: outstanding, good, requires improvement and inadequate.

As we have seen, criteria associated with the Guidance on the Duty to Promote Community Cohesion became part of Ofsted inspections in 2008. This was guidance associated with promoting 'shared values' *and* addressing inequalities. Notwithstanding its own emphasis on the importance of 'British values', as outlined in David Cameron's Munich speech, the coalition government appeared to retreat from this. The Education Act 2011, for example, removed the requirement for Ofsted to inspect and report directly on a school's performance in relation to community cohesion that had been introduced in 2008. However, the duty on schools to promote it remained. The DfE explained in a Freedom of Information release that, 'it is intended that inspections will be focused around four core areas, pupils' achievement, the quality of teaching, leadership and management, and pupils' behaviour and safety'. It adds further that, 'The government believes that there remains an unacceptable gap in achievement for different groups of children, including those from certain minority ethnic backgrounds, economically disadvantaged pupils and other vulnerable groups. Tackling this is a priority within the Government's education reform programme, including the planned changes to school inspection.'[237]

Conclusion

We have described changing governance of English schools. The process was contested and especially at local level, where parents, teachers and local politicians sought to defend local authority schools.[238] In this context, the fact that the identification of failing schools through Ofsted inspections would also trigger the conversion of a school into an academy meant that the Ofsted inspections themselves became politicised. This was reinforced by the fact that, as the overall balance of types of school changed, so inspectors were recruited from sponsors of academy schools and private consultancies with what some regarded as vested interests in the promotion of academies over local authority schools.[239]

This politicisation was viewed with some relish by the Chief Inspector of Schools, Sir Michael Wilshaw, who made well-publicised attacks on failures of governance and stressed the need to challenge teachers to improve performance. He had himself been a successful and high-profile teacher at a failing school in a disadvantaged area and did not regard social and economic inequality as an excuse for poor achievement among pupils. In this respect, his approach was to

---

[237] Department for Education (2011) 'Freedom of Information Release', 28 February.
[238] See for example, case studies presented in the edited collection by Helen M. Gunter (2011) *The State and Education Policy: The Academies Programme*, London: Continuum; see also Richard Hatcher (2009) 'Setting up academies, campaigning against them: an analysis of a contested policy process', *Management in Education*, 23(3): 108–12.
[239] For discussion, see Baxter (2016) *School Governance*.

encourage schools to 'disrupt' low aspirations on the part of parents and low expectations on the part of teachers.

In a lecture given at the Ark Schools Trust (an educational charity responsible for 35 schools) in November 2011, on the occasion of being appointed as Chief Inspector, Sir Michael reflected on his career as a head teacher in London, where he had successfully transformed two schools. He referred to the industrial action by teachers and the vested interests and complacency of local authorities that accepted low academic achievement, especially in schools in disadvantaged areas. He argued that good leadership by a head teacher supported by strong governors could produce dramatic improvement. In the past, he commented, 'it took a very brave head, or a foolhardy one, to focus on school improvement and the issue of staff competence … [however] the performance agenda in schools and the demands for greater accountability, mean that there is now a greater expectation that heads tackle the issue of capacity more quickly when children are being manifestly and consistently failed'.[240]

Indeed, he cited improvement as evidence of effective leadership and quoted his predecessor to establish the continuity of view at Ofsted. David Bell, in 2003, had written:

> it is important to stress that although schools in these areas find it difficult to improve, there are some that can cope and are doing well. Indeed, some schools are doing extremely well compared to schools nationally. Inspections show that the higher-attaining disadvantaged urban schools are better led and managed. What makes the difference is the clarity, intensity and persistence of the school's work and the rigour with which it is scrutinised. At best, all the energy of the school serves the same end, raising standards. Good leaders in these schools have vision and can apply it in practical ways. They are flexible, spot opportunities

[240] Sir Michael Wilshaw, 'Good schools for all – an impossible dream?', 28 November 2011. Available at: http://arkreboot.bitmachine.co.uk/sites/default/files/111129_mw_speech_4pm_with_logo_final_0_0.pdf, pages 3–4.

and deal imaginatively with problems. They 'grow their own' solutions.[241]

Sir Michael went on to criticise the four inspection grades and the then descriptor 'satisfactory' for grade 3 and also commented that achievement also needed to consider 'context', such that some schools that seemed to be performing well would be revealed as 'coasting'. Thus, he stated that, 'Ofsted should be critical of those schools which may be achieving to national averages and beyond, but whose uncontextualised value-added is below or just above the mean. So called "coasting schools" should take note'.[242]

Unsurprisingly, the changes continued to be conflictual both within local communities, between local communities and their schools, and within schools between some teachers and senior leaders. In Birmingham, this situation was compounded by the fact that some communities – especially, ethnic minority communities – had longstanding concerns about schools failing their children and the response of the local authority. If Birmingham City Council comes to be charged with failing to respond to notifications of a Trojan Horse 'plot', a charge that is also associated with perceptions of a wider failure of leadership within its child services, it is necessary to note that a larger long-term failure had been that of the underachievement of ethnic minority pupils.[243] However, that failure was being turned around and Park View, and PVET more generally, was part of that process.

As we shall see, not only was Park View school an outstanding school with academic achievements above the national average, it was far from 'coasting' – its pupils were drawn from one of the most disadvantaged wards in the country. Yet it became charged with inadequate leadership and management.

---

[241] Ibid, page 8. David Bell's speech to the Fabian Society, 'Access and achievement in urban education', *The Guardian*, 20 November 2003 is available at: www.theguardian.com/education/2003/nov/20/schools.uk3.

[242] Wilshaw, 'Good schools for all', page 9.

[243] Birmingham was one of the first local educational authorities to address such issues by gathering data on performance by ethnic minority pupils.

★★★

Conclusion to Part One

In Part Two, we focus on the specific charges and allegations that were made against the teachers and schools involved in the Trojan Horse affair. We conclude Part One of our discussion of the policy context to the Trojan Horse affair with some summary observations.

Firstly, we noted that there was a suspicion that the schools involved were failing to prepare children for life in modern Britain and were thus in breach of their responsibilities to promote 'fundamental British values'. As we discussed in Chapter One, fundamental British values are contested on a variety of grounds – not least in relation to their 'Britishness'. In recent times, however, they have also been set in opposition to the accommodation of religious or cultural diversity. We argue, however, that far from undermining shared 'British values', accommodating diversity can in fact serve to enhance them – and that is what we suggest the schools were doing.

Secondly, we addressed the issue that the schools were failing properly to discharge their responsibilities under the government's Prevent policy. We showed that, at the time of the Trojan Horse affair, there was no statutory duty on schools to implement Prevent, and little guidance provided to them by the DfE to do so. Although, as we go on to discuss in detail in the following chapters, no evidence of extremism was found in the schools, the 'facts' of the Trojan Horse affair have been used to justify the expansion of the government's counter-extremism agenda – with significant implications for Muslim communities and civil liberties in Britain – not least if the government presses ahead with drawing more forms of 'extremism' into its remit.

Thirdly, we discussed the obligations that schools do have to promote community cohesion. We noted that, for many, their compliance with this obligation was seen as fulfilling their responsibilities to promote shared 'fundamental British values' and counter extremism. We also showed that, in any case, awareness and understanding of Prevent was very uneven across the sector, whilst the holding of schools to account for their failure in this regard was unevenly applied to some schools – those in areas of Muslim settlement and with high proportions of Muslim pupils and teachers – and not others. This was because, at the time of the affair, the Ofsted inspection regime actually carried few formal requirements in this regard. Nonetheless, many of the schools – including those associated with the PVET – were significantly downgraded on this aspect, despite their continued high performance in relation to pupil achievements.

Fourthly, we set out the requirements of *all* schools to provide for religious education and worship. The characterisation of the schools involved in the Trojan Horse affair as 'secular' – as they were described in the Clarke Report – is simply incorrect. As we showed, these requirements by default require an emphasis on Christian worship and values, but there are provisions for the setting of a locally agreed religious education syllabus, and dispensations to schools for non-Christian acts of worship, in order to reflect the religious identities of pupils in the schools. These provisions were in place in Birmingham and were seen as essential to responding to its diverse population and to raising the educational performances of particularly its minority ethnic children – who had endured decades of educational disadvantage.

Finally, our discussion of the policy context pointed to the 'heterarchic' nature of school governance in Birmingham, and elsewhere, as a consequence of the emergence of new arrangements for school management and governance associated with the government's academies programme, which occurred alongside the continuation of existing arrangements for the structure and management of schools. These combined to create substantial regulatory confusion over the proper role of the LEA, the DfE, school governors and school leadership. It was in these unclear circumstances that the role of Park View in taking over the leadership of other schools, or the expression of Islam in the schools, were presented as evidence of a sinister process of Islamification. As we go on to show in Part Two, these allegations are simply unfounded.

PART 2

The case

SIX

Introducing the case

This has been a rather lengthy build-up to the direct discussion of the school(s) at the centre of the Trojan Horse affair, in particular Park View Academy and its Educational Trust (PVET). It has been necessary for two reasons. First, to set out the wider debates around 'British values' and the role of religion in schools, and second to set out the complexity of governance arrangements and the regulation of schools, including the major changes which have taken a significant proportion of schools out of LEA control. Of course, another part of the wider context has been concerns about violent extremism, concerns that have been focused on Muslim communities in particular. This has been especially significant in Birmingham, where the misconceived 'Project Champion', as we have seen, was directed at the very places where the schools were located.

Achieving integration

Notwithstanding the public anxieties that were fuelled by media reports and government claims about failures to integrate, we have also seen that the social scientific evidence is that British Muslims have a high degree of commitment to values of democracy, the rule of law and religious tolerance. They also have a greater commitment to religious values than the wider population, which is much more secular in its orientation. But the two are not mutually exclusive precisely because religious tolerance purports to protect expressions of religious faith, including in schools. The presence of a specific religious ethos in a school does not, on its own, indicate a hostility to people of other religious faiths or no faith. The significant role of faith schools within the English school system, of course, testifies to that truth and, as we have seen, legislation requires all schools to provide religious education and collective worship. While this might have little significance in schools where the parents of pupils are predominantly secular in their orientation, we should not expect a similar indifference to the legal requirement where parents do have significant religious commitments. Nor should we expect those parents to be required to meet their needs only within a designated faith school. Indeed, all schools are legally required to provide religious education and collective worship. Moreover, specific guidance on how to meet the religious needs of children in non-faith schools is provided by many bodies, from government, to local authorities, SACREs and organisations representing faith groups.

Greater religiosity on the part of Muslims, then, is not an indication of potential intolerance to other religions, even where it may be correlated with a more conservative view on specific social issues, such as, for example, same-sex relationships or pre-marital sex. Nor are such conservative views specific to Muslims. After all, Clause 28 of the 1988 Local Government Act made it an offence 'to promote the teaching in any maintained school of the acceptability of homosexuality as a pretended family relationship'.[244] It was not repealed until 2003, when David Cameron, among other Conservative MPs, voted against repeal. The recently elected Conservative government has entered into a 'supply and confidence' agreement with the Democratic Unionist Party of Northern Ireland, which has socially illiberal policies toward abortion and same-sex marriages, for example.

---

[244] See Local Government Act, 1988. The specific clauses of section 28 are available at: www.legislation.gov.uk/ukpga/1988/9/section/28.

Moreover, we have also seen that schools are recommended to take the sensitivities of parents, and the local communities within which schools are located, into account when considering how they teach about personal relationships. This may include some teaching not taking place in mixed classes. This is important because criticism of PVET has involved the separation of girls and boys for some teaching and for physical education, despite this being part of the guidance offered to schools about best practice. Such guidance is found across many local authorities with a significant pupil intake from Muslim religious backgrounds providing advice on the likely sensitivities of parents. Moreover, 'homophily' – pupil preference for same sex socialising during meals and breaks, as well as when sitting in classes – is well documented and is independent of religious orientation.[245]

We will see that guidance co-authored by Tahir Alam and published by the Muslim Council of Britain – *Towards Greater Understanding: Meeting the needs of Muslim pupils in state schools* – is considered by the Clarke Report to be part of the 'ideological agenda in Birmingham'.[246] Yet that publication provides guidance on the common practices of Muslims with religious commitments, including dietary requirements, modesty of dress, obligations for prayer, as well as information about festivals, fasting during Ramadan and collective worship. What is recommended is not different to practices of other local educational authorities with a high proportion of Muslim pupils. For example, Wandsworth Borough Council issued guidance to its primary schools in 2015, 12 months after the Trojan Horse affair, and covered the same topics with similar advice.[247] The importance of creating

---

[245] For a discussion, see Eleonor E. Maccoby (2002) 'Gender and group process: a developmental perspective', *Current Directions in Psychological Science*, 11(2): 54–58.

[246] The document is summarised in annex 6 of the Clarke Report and published in full as an annex to the Kershaw Report. For the discussion in the Clarke Report, see Chapter Five.

[247] The document thanks the schools' service, headteachers and Muslim representatives on Ealing SACRE for sharing their 2007 guidance. See Wandsworth Borough Council, May 2015, *Guidance for Primary Schools with Muslim Pupils*.

school environments that support religious expression is evident in recommendations from other bodies. For example, the Open Society Institute project on 'Muslims in the UK – Policies for Engaged Citizens' (part of its EU Monitoring and Advocacy Programme), reported on the low educational attainment of Muslim pupils in a context where 'education is crucial to integration and social cohesion in a diverse multicultural and multi-faith society'.[248]

The conclusion was that more needed to be done to create an encouraging environment, through more examples from Islamic culture and history, more role models for pupils within the teaching staff of schools and through giving Arabic and other community languages full status as modern languages within the curriculum. More specifically, it concluded that there should be:

> national guidelines on ways to meet the distinctive needs of Muslim pupils, incorporating best practice at the level of the Local Education Authorities. These should include issues of clothing; school meals; school attendance during, and acknowledgement of, Islamic festivals; Muslim needs during Ramadan; meeting Muslim hygiene and cleanliness requirements; providing prayer facilities for Muslim students for the midday prayer; and permission for attendance of a mosque for the Friday midday prayer.[249]

Many reports on the Trojan Horse affair accused the schools of being 'overly religious' and that this was illegitimate for community schools that were not designated as faith schools.[250] However, we have seen that all schools are legally required to teach religious education and to have a daily act of collective worship. From a secular perspective, perhaps, the issue is to teach pupils *about* different religions and their

---

[248] Open Society Institute (2005) *British Muslims and Education*, page 104. Available at: www.fairuk.org/docs/OSI2004%207_Education.pdf.

[249] Ibid, page 174.

[250] We will see in a later chapter that this argument is found in both the Clarke and Kershaw reports and is, therefore, promoted in the wider media.

beliefs, but, from the perspective of those with religious commitments, their commitments are something to be *expressed* in daily life and exist as deep guides to conduct. Many schools honour the requirement of collective worship in the breach because of the secular orientations of the parents of children at their schools, *but it is, nonetheless, a legal requirement.* Moreover, while the statutory requirement is that collective worship should be 'wholly or mainly of a broadly Christian character' (albeit not of a specific denomination), it is possible for schools to apply for a 'determination' to vary this requirement and to hold assemblies where the collective worship reflects another faith. As we shall see, Park View had such a 'determination' for Islamic worship since 1997, although constraints of space (brought about by building works) – problems faced by other schools – meant that the school had to rotate assemblies, with pupils only having one assembly per week. The determination lapsed in 2012, shortly after it became an academy, but its practices did not change and, as we have seen, the DfE issued no determinations, indicating its failure to institute a process after it had relieved SACREs of that function for academy schools.

We have also shown that, despite recurrent calls to promote 'British values' in schools as if discovering a new 'failure', this has been part of guidance for schools and a statutory requirement since 2007, something which Ofsted has addressed in its inspection reports. The 'shared values' stressed in the guidance to schools on promoting community cohesion – democracy, the rule of law, individual liberty and tolerance of those with different religious faiths and beliefs – are the same as those put forward in guidance subsequent to the Trojan Horse affair. As we have seen, the situation has been more ambiguous with regard to the Prevent agenda. As we set out in Chapters Two and Three, addressing it was not a statutory requirement until *after* the Trojan Horse affair. As the 2011 report for the DfE indicated, schools were fully aware of their obligations toward community cohesion, but most schools conflated this with Prevent – not least because, until 2011, there was substantial operational and conceptual overlap between Prevent and community cohesion.[251] In practice, this meant that specific

---

[251] Phillips et al (2010) 'Community cohesion and Prevent'.

awareness of Prevent was relatively underdeveloped across the sector. The exceptions were secondary schools and especially those with a high proportion of ethnic minority pupils – like Park View and other schools in East Birmingham. Nonetheless, the Ofsted inspections in 2014 did argue that the Birmingham schools at the centre of the affair should have done more to address Prevent, most likely reflecting the view of the DfE's Due Diligence and Counter Extremism Division, whose members made up half of the team for the EFA Review of the PVET, which recommended ending its contract. No evidence was provided of any hostility to Prevent and, indeed, the school did make provision, as we shall see in the next chapter. In the view of the inspectors it was 'insufficient' – against no specified expectation of what would be sufficient – and, it was proposed, this placed pupils at a 'safeguarding' risk.

A similar situation applies to changing governance. The general process of change, of pushing through the academies programme, and the very public discourse of underachieving schools – poor teaching and insufficiently challenging leadership from head teacher and governors, and complacent local authorities – also contributed to public anxieties about the equal opportunities afforded to children in publicly funded schools. This was a particularly acute issue for ethnic minority communities which had longstanding concerns about their children being poorly served. The consequence of the emphasis on performance targets was that they were presented with data about the failure of the schools attended by their children and were exhorted to engage with their improvement. Indeed, a particular failure was associated with the performance of children (especially boys) from Pakistani and Bangladeshi backgrounds.

For example, Sir Tim Brighouse, Chief Education Officer in Birmingham from 1993 to 2002, regarded underachievement by ethnic minority pupils as among the most important issues of his tenure. It was something that he reported was pressed upon him by parents. He writes that:

among the groups I met was the Saltley Parents Association, a group of Pakistani heritage parents who were concerned about a range of schooling issues – in particular what they perceived, I discovered rightly, as low standards and expectations within some of the schools which their children were attending in east Birmingham. I also met headteachers from the area, a few of whom saw some of the actions of a small minority of male parents and governors from the local community as challenging, perhaps even threatening, and as exemplifying an 'agenda' of increasing the influence of their particular culture on the school.[252]

Saltley School was identified by the Clarke Report as one of the schools where undue pressure was put on the head teacher, but Sir Tim Brighouse regarded these pressures as legitimate and ones that were also placed upon him in his leadership of Birmingham schools.

Sir Tim Brighouse accepted that the issue of improvement was paramount and improvement across Birmingham schools was significant under his watch. An Ofsted report on the performance of the LEA in 2002 rated its achievements as outstanding. It commented that:

the LEA has done much, with its schools, to overcome the educational effects of this high degree of disadvantage. Since 1997, the attainment of pupils has risen at almost all levels at a rate faster than the national average. In 1998, OFSTED reported that Birmingham was a very well run LEA. It is now clear that it is much more than that. It is one of a very small number of LEAs which stand as an example to all others of what can be done, even in the most demanding urban environments.[253]

---

[252] 'Witness statement of Tim Brighouse, before the Professional Conduct Panel Case No. 12139. In the matter of: The National College for Teaching and Leadership and Monzoor Hussain (and others)', paragraph 3.

[253] Ofsted/Audit Commission Inspection of Birmingham Local Education Authority, April 2002. Available at: https://reports.ofsted.gov.uk/sites/default/files/documents/local_authority_reports/birmingham/012_Local%20Authority%20Inspection%20as%20pdf.pdf, paragraph 5.

The report also noted: 'Birmingham's proportion of minority ethnic pupils (43 per cent) is four times the national average. Pupils are from many and diverse ethnic groups, with almost 50 first languages spoken in their homes. Given this context, there is a corporate lead to see such pupils not as a minority but as part of a single equal opportunities society in the city.'[254]

Sir Tim Brighouse observed that his appointment coincided with the Macpherson Inquiry in 1999 into the murder of Stephen Lawrence, with its identification of problems of 'institutional racism', as well as the Runnymede Trust's 1997 report identifying issues of 'Islamophobia'.[255] As a result, Birmingham LEA had introduced policies to address racism within the provision of education, something that was also highly commended in the Ofsted report.[256] Birmingham was unusual among LEAs, as Ofsted acknowledged, in collecting data relating to the differing performance of pupils from their different heritages, socioeconomic groups and gender and the Ofsted report commented that this was effective in monitoring performance and directing support. Park View School and its success is part of this drive to improvement. However, collecting data, monitoring and measuring against targets do not in themselves explain how success is achieved. There are strong reasons to believe that providing a school culture that is sensitive to and respects that of its pupils is part of the answer.

For example, studies of African Americans and Latinos in the USA suggest that their success in schools derives from building self-

---

[254] Ibid, paragraph 69.

[255] Brighouse, Witness statement, paragraphs 18 and 9 respectively. See also Report of an Inquiry by Sir William Macpherson, February 1999. *Report of the Stephen Lawrence Inquiry*. Available at: www.gov.uk/government/publications/the-stephen-lawrence-inquiry; Runnymede Trust (1997) *Islamophobia: A Challenge for us All*. Available at: www.runnymedetrust.org/publications/17/74.html.

[256] Ofsted / Audit Commission Inspection, April 2002, paragraphs 148–9. For example, 'the local authority convened its own commission after the publication of the report of the inquiry into the death of Stephen Lawrence. While the commission's report was critical of aspects of the local authority's work, the local authority has taken on board the commission's recommendations, and individual departments are taking forward relevant recommendations', paragraph 148.

confidence among pupils. This, in turn, derives from positive cultural identification both with the dominant culture and that of their own ethnic (or religious) group. This is what Edward Telles and Vilma Ortiz describe as 'bi-cultural identification'.[257] They find that a decline in positive identification with their own ethnic group amongst pupils leads to a decline in academic performance (as does a singular identification with that ethnicity), as pupils internalise the dominant culture's low valuation and expectations of them. Similarly, Miwa Yasui and her colleagues show that positive ethnic identification is associated with psychological adjustment, while Carol Wong and colleagues show that if pupils perceive themselves to be discriminated against, then this is associated with declining grades and less psychological resilience, which are mitigated by stronger ethnic identification.[258] This was a view that was shared by the Swann Report of 1985, *Education for All*, which recommended that schools and curricula should reflect and provide for the cultural identities of children, as well as tackle direct and indirect discrimination, in order to raise the educational performance of minority ethnic children.[259]

Birmingham LEA's policies against discrimination and their reinforcement in schools (for example, through logs of racist incidents)

---

[257] Edward E. Telles and Vilma Ortiz (2008) 'Finding America: creating educational opportunity for our newest citizens', in Brian D. Smedley and Alan Jenkins (eds) *All Things Being Equal: Instigating Opportunity in an Inequitable Time*, New York: The New Press.

[258] Miwa Yasui, Carole La Rue Dorhan and Thomas J. Fishion (2004). 'Ethnic identity and psychological adjustment: a validity analysis for European American and African American adolescents', *Journal of Adolescent Research*, 19: 807–825; C. Wong, J. Eccles and A. Sameroff (2003) 'The influence of ethnic discrimination and ethnic identification on African American adolescents' school and socioemotional adjustment', *Journal of Personality*, 71: 1197–1232.

[259] Swann Report (1985) *Education For All. Report of the Committee of Enquiry into the Education of Children from Ethnic Minority Groups.* The report also noted: 'Far more can and should be done by schools to respond to the 'pastoral' needs of Muslim pupils, to ensure that there is a real respect and understanding by both teachers and parents of each other's concerns and that the demands of the school place no child in fundamental conflict with the requirements of his [sic] faith', pages 773–774, paragraph 6.10. Available at: www.educationengland. org.uk/documents/swann/swann1985.html.

serves one of the purposes of integration. However, for pupils from a Muslim faith background that means treating religious expression and practices as not being in conflict with the values of achievement and equal opportunities that a school is also pursuing. While secularists might find the association counter-intuitive, the positive consequences of religious expression within non-faith schools for pupils from backgrounds where there are strong religious commitments is attested to in much of the guidance provided by different bodies.

For example, Guidance on Offering Space for Prayer and Reflection in School, from Harrow SACRE, talks of the stresses of living a life where the parts of a self are divided, and that the provision of space for prayer, 'may allow pupils to bring their "whole self" to school, that is, to feel that they wholly belong to their school community'.[260] We have seen how the Birmingham agreed religious syllabus – taught by Park View – had a strong emphasis on values and dispositions and how these are exemplified in different religious traditions. A similar emphasis informs Harrow SACRE in the idea of 'exemplification' as one means of securing the spiritual and moral development of the child, as required by section 78 of the Education Act 2002. The school as a community involves children and adults learning from each other:

> within the curriculum there are subjects and aspects which explore how belonging to a religious community influences the moral and ethical decisions of individuals and which requires self-discipline in lifestyles. When there are pupils, and perhaps staff, modelling those choices regularly and independently, this allows both adults and children to learn about and from religions as observers, whose integrity and own backgrounds and beliefs are protected and respected … It also demonstrates that for many within religious communities, observance of religious obligations is about more than what people eat and wear and is about daily disciplines not just festival celebrations!

---

[260] Harrow SACRE Guidance on Offering a Space for Prayer and Reflection in School, page 3. Available at: www.harrow.gov.uk/www2/documents/s108380/sacre.

The testimony provided by pupils is moving: "'When I pray in the morning, I feel refreshed. Now I feel refreshed at lunchtime!'"; "Being quiet helps me not to feel distracted. It helps me not to be distracted in the afternoon"; "It helps me to reflect on what I've done and what I could change to be better"; "Praying helps me to forget bad things that have happened and make a fresh start".[261]

In other words, an 'Islamic ethos' in a school with a very high proportion of Muslim pupils is not a sign of a 'monoculture', as the Clarke and Kershaw Reports suggest. At least, were there to have been a 'monoculture' at Park View, it would be difficult to understand its success in achieving outcomes that are above the national average, despite having a pupil intake that typically has attainment levels below that average. Success is evidence of an effective and integrated school culture entailing a recognition by the school leaders that an Islamic ethos and academic achievement and equal opportunities are, in the context of their school, complementary and mutually necessary.

Moreover, involving parents and local communities in the governance of schools has been identified as key to addressing educational underachievement among particular ethnic minority pupils. Thus, in its 'Asian Heritage Achievement action plan', updated in 2003, Birmingham's Education Service set out the 'important role' of the LEA in encouraging the participation of parents and communities in school governance to support children's learning.[262]

A moral panic?

Jacqueline Baxter has shown that, with the intensification of the academies programme, the media was also amplifying concerns with stories of failures of governance at schools, as well as pointing to the complexity of the new arrangements and the difficulties of the DfE in managing them.[263] The new arrangements also disrupted the capacities

---

[261] Ibid, page 4.

[262] Birmingham City Council Education Service (2003) 'Asian heritage achievement action plan', 19 December 2003 revision. January 2004. Birmingham, page 6.

[263] Baxter (2016) *School Governance*, see especially chapter 3.

of LEAs, although, as we have seen, Birmingham LEA was not an example of an LEA that was failing to bring about improvements in its schools, notwithstanding the criticisms of other aspects of its children's services (those involving social care and looked after children).

Once again, even if the overall system of governance emanating from the DfE lacked coherence, such that 'deviant practices' *might emerge unnoticed*, it does not follow that this is what happened in the Trojan Horse affair. In fact, we shall show in the next chapter that everything that was subsequently claimed to be problematic about Park View school (and PVET) in the reports subsequent to the identification of an alleged plot to Islamicise schools had been subject to close attention in earlier reports and was commended as contributing to its success.

What we have described in the previous chapters are fertile conditions for what the sociologist Stan Cohen termed a 'moral panic'.[264] He developed the concept to understand how youth subcultures in the 1970s came to be the focus of intense public debate and anxieties about declining moral standards, giving rise to a coercive judicial response that outweighed the nature of any underlying problem. The general mechanism, according to Cohen, was the creation of a 'folk devil' – a stereotype of a dangerous figure, such as the teenage 'mods and rockers', or the 'mugger', or, now, the 'extremist Muslim'[265] – which is then amplified in media reporting as an explanation of unfamiliar practices presented as a threat to social order or decency. For a variety of reasons – partly to do with their liminal status between dependency and socially productive independence – young people, and anything associated with them, are a potent source of moral concern. Indeed, section 78 of the 2008 Education Act is itself framed in terms of precisely such concerns about the moral development of children and social integration.

'Moral panic' describes a process of 'amplification' and an 'excessive response' in relation to specific practices. In this case, the 'Muslim

---

[264] Stanley Cohen (1972) *Folk Devils and Moral Panics*, London: MacGibbon and Kee Ltd.

[265] See, for example, Farzana Shain (2011) *The New Folk Devils: Muslim Boys and Education in England*, Stoke-on-Trent: Trentham Books.

terrorist' has been amplified to call into question other Muslim practices. Our argument is that there are no egregious practices in the Trojan Horse affair, although there is amplification and an excessive response. The appearance of 'deviant practices' is something that has been constructed through the various interventions by government agencies and media reporting with no underlying reality, other than a suspicion of Muslims. This is why we referred at the beginning of the book to the Hillsborough affair as the closest analogy. In the Hillsborough affair, false claims were made about the behaviour of fans – drunkenness, the pilfering from dying victims, attacks on police – that deflected attention from serious police failings in crowd management and their cover-up.[266] The 'yobbism' of 'hooligan football supporters' creating a crush among supporters became the established narrative. It took a long campaign and new hearings to establish that what had been understood and condemned as an issue of 'public order' was, in fact, a matter of failures on the part of the police.

The puzzle in the Trojan Horse affair is to understand how a *successful* school could become the centre of a moral panic, and it is to this that we turn. Events unfolded quickly from the first media report in the *Times* on 2 March 2014, followed by Ofsted inspections of 21 schools ordered by the Secretary of State for Education, Michael Gove, beginning with Park View Academy on 5 March as a 'section 8' review, followed by a full (section 5) inspection on 17 March 2014,[267] in a context of a first wave of media publicity. Of the 21 schools, five were subjected to full (section 5) inspections and 16 to section 8 monitoring inspections. Eight of the 21 schools were academies, four of which were subject to full inspections, with the other school subject to a full inspection due to become an academy (this was Saltley School, scheduled to become an academy in March 2015). Of the 21 schools that were inspected by Ofsted, only 14 had had any allegations made against them according to the Clarke Report.

---

[266] See Phil Scraton (1999) *Hillsborough: The Truth*, Edinburgh: Mainstream Publishing.

[267] The terminology refers to the Education Act 2005. Section 8 inspections are short inspections carried out at the behest of the Secretary of State.

Of the five schools subjected to full inspection, three had previously been recently inspected, with two being rated 'outstanding' (Park View and Oldknow) and one as 'good' (Saltley School), not least because they had achieved significant increases in pupil attainments. After the March–April 2014 inspections, they were downgraded and all five of these schools were assessed as 4 – 'inadequate' – on the basis of 'safeguarding' issues and 'leadership and management' problems. In the five schools at the heart of the affair, 96%+ of pupils are ethnic minority, of largely Pakistani and Bangladeshi heritage. The other 16 schools had similar ethnic profiles (i.e. 90%+ ethnic minority pupils).

The inspections were concluded for those schools and reported on by Sir Michael Wilshaw in early May, with the EFA also concluding its review of PVET in May 2014. On the basis of interim Ofsted reports, Peter Clarke was appointed by the Secretary of State in mid-April to provide a wider report. This appointment was controversial insofar as it placed matters directly in a context of violent extremism, since Peter Clarke was formerly in charge of Counter Terrorism Command within the Metropolitan Police in London. At around the same time, Peter Kershaw was appointed by Birmingham City Council to report on implications for the local authority. The Kershaw Report was delivered on 14 July 2014 and the Clarke Report on 22 July 2014.

In the next chapter, we will address the first phase, associated with the Ofsted inspections and reports, and culminating with the EFA Review of PVET. In the following chapter, we will address the Clarke and Kershaw Reports before going on to discuss the National College for Teaching and Leadership professional misconduct hearings to which the Clarke Report gave rise.

The first media report on a Trojan Horse 'plot' appeared in the *Sunday Times* on 2 March 2014. Written by Richard Kerbaj and Sian Griffiths, it outlined an 'Islamist plot to take over schools'. It described a 'strategy document' sent in the previous November to Birmingham City Council. The document purported to come from disaffected Muslims involved in a plot to take over 'failing schools'. The article described this as a 'setback' for the government's academies programme since the alleged plot was using the 'freedoms' associated with the programme to facilitate the takeover. The first step, in a five-step strategy described in the document, Kerbaj and Griffiths report, 'is to identify poor performing schools in Muslim areas; then Salafist parents in each school are encouraged to complain that "teachers are corrupting children with sex education, teaching about homosexuals, making their children say Christian prayers and mixed swimming and sports"'.[268] The report also referred to an article the previous Sunday stating that Park View school was being investigated by the DfE for, 'allegedly side-lining non-Muslim staff and trying to teach Islamic studies, despite not being a faith-based state school'.

As should be evident, such a 'plot' would need to have a *successful* school at its centre in order for it to be facilitated by the academies programme, since that was a condition for a failing school to have 'sponsored' academy status. However, in its turn, this presupposes that a successful school could have the characteristics attributed to it by these (and other) reporters. As we saw in Chapter Five on governance and inspections, a successful school is understood by the DfE to be a consequence of effective teaching, leadership and governance at a school and it is something confirmed by Ofsted inspections. It is precisely the successful nature of Park View that is elided in discussions of the Trojan Horse affair, despite the fact that success is necessarily associated with a high degree of official scrutiny, especially where that success involves the DfE recommending that a school sponsors others to become academy schools under its patronage.

[268] Kerbaj and Griffiths, 'Islamist plot to take over schools', *Sunday Times,* 2 March 2014.

SEVEN

Enter Ofsted

As we said at the start of the book, there is an equivocation in secondary accounts of the Trojan Horse affair. Does it show evidence of 'extremism', or is it simply a case of poor practices on the part of religious conservatives that run counter to 'British values' and social cohesion and which were allowed to happen because of the poor governance of the schools? We quoted Tim Boyes, CEO of Birmingham Education Partnership (appointed by Birmingham City Council to oversee schools after the Trojan Horse affair), who wrote that, 'the problem that sits behind Trojan Horse is not about Islamic extremism, it's about schools unhelpfully locked into the closest parameters of their neighbourhoods'.[269] The 'parameters' of those neighbourhoods are understood to be those of conservative values, self-segregation and deprivation.

That characterisation of the problems of the schools does not however account for why the schools at the heart of these problems were otherwise succeeding. For instance, by January 2012 Park View Academy was in the top 14% of schools nationally in terms of its examination results. According to data presented in the Clarke Report, as we have seen, Park View Academy had a pupil intake that

---

[269] See 'Trojan Horse one year on', *Birmingham Mail*, 23 April 2015.

was 98.8% Muslim, with 72.7% on free school meals (an indicator of social deprivation) and just 7.5% of pupils had English as a first language. There are no separate data on the proportion of Muslim pupils in Birmingham schools, but the BME school population in Birmingham is 66.6%, compared to 28.9% nationally, while the proportion with English as a first language in Birmingham is 64.2% and 82.7% nationally, while the figure for free school meals is 28.9% in Birmingham and 15.2% nationally. Moreover, its 'feeder' primary, Nansen, was judged to be a failing school such that the pupils that arrived at Park View had attainments well below the national average. The achievement of its pupils would seem to indicate a school that had transcended the parameters of its neighbourhood, and, in fact, had encouraged its local community to embrace the value of education and the opportunities it afforded their children. Indeed, that was presumably why Sir Michael Wilshaw, newly appointed as Her Majesty's Chief Inspector of Schools and head of Ofsted, stated on a visit to the school in 2012 that 'all schools should be like it'.[270]

Just two years later, Sir Michael gave an Ofsted perspective on the Trojan Horse affair in a note to the Secretary of State for Education, Michael Gove, on 9 June 2014. This perspective was derived from the 21 Ofsted inspections – including of Park View – and meetings with lead inspectors, head teachers, professional associations and representatives from Birmingham City Council. His comments were emphatic, including that 'a culture of fear and intimidation has developed in some of the schools since their previous inspection', and, further, 'that there has been an organised campaign to target certain schools in Birmingham in order to alter their character and ethos'. Finally, he wrote that, 'in several of the schools inspected, children are being badly prepared for life in modern Britain'.[271]

The claims were disingenuous in their elaboration. For example, that 'some headteachers, including those with a proud record of

---

[270] See Vasagar, 'An Inspector calls', *The Guardian*, 27 March 2012.
[271] Wilshaw, 9 June 2014. 'Advice note'. All quotes are taken from the 'statement of findings', pages 2–8.

raising standards, said that they have been marginalised or forced out of their jobs. As a result, some schools previously judged to be good or outstanding have experienced high levels of staff turbulence, low staff morale and a rapid decline in their overall effectiveness'.

Park View school was at the centre of the affair, and, as we shall see, its head teacher had the proudest record in Birmingham of raising standards, yet it was she who was accused of participation in the 'Islamification' of the school. A significant decline in effectiveness and pupil performance came in the wake of the disruption of the school following from unremittingly hostile negative publicity – any decline came after the furore and the intervention by the DfE and in consequence of how it was handled.

Sir Michael elaborated further: 'some of the academies inspected, for example, did not meet the requirement to provide a broad and balanced curriculum or to provide the appropriate balance in religious education. In several of these academies, the general requirement to promote community cohesion was not being met'. He added footnotes to explain the different arrangements applying to academies – that they need not, for example, follow a locally agreed curriculum in religious education as sanctioned by the SACRE. However, as we have already commented, while academies need not follow the locally agreed curriculum for religious education, they may do so, and Park View Academy was following the curriculum, not least because Tahir Alam, head of the Board of Governors at the school (and also the wider Trust) was a member of Birmingham SACRE. Although he was not a member of the 2005–7 Agreed Syllabus Conference, as a member of SACRE he had a stake in the agreed syllabus and he gave advice to the local authority on its implementation.

In fact, in the 2014 Ofsted reports and in the Clarke and Kershaw Reports, little is said about the curriculum and most is inferred from Islamic collective worship and the ethos of the schools. In what follows, we will show how the very features that come to be associated with 'Islamification', and not simply the examination results, were commended by inspectors in a series of Ofsted reports that preceded the March 2014 intervention by Ofsted.

From failing to outstanding, the trajectory of Park View school

Park View school was, throughout the period, a small mixed-gender, community comprehensive school for pupils aged 11–16. It became an academy in April 2012. The school had a history of poor or weak performance. It was in special measures in 1996 and continued to have low standards of pupil attainment by the time of a second, comprehensive Ofsted report in 2001 (the report was undertaken by 15 inspectors over four days, and reviewed performance since an earlier interim report in March 1999, as required of schools in 'special measures'). However, while attainment was below the national average, there was significant improvement (especially when performance was measured against prior attainment and against the expectations associated with social disadvantage as measured by the proportion in receipt of free school meals). The school was judged to be satisfactory in most aspects. The proportion of pupils attaining A–C grades at GCSE was 7.2% in 1996, but had risen to 31% by 2001.

Monzoor Hussain, one of the senior teachers charged with professional misconduct by the NCTL following the Clarke Report, was the first Muslim teacher appointed to the school in 1996, by the then acting head teacher, Mike Nicholls. The latter had retired just before the 2001 Ofsted report. However, since then, the school has had continuity of leadership. Tahir Alam was chair of the governing body at the time of the 2001 report (he later became chair of the Board of Governors of PVET in 2012, while remaining a governor at Park View Academy). Lindsey Clark was appointed head teacher just after the 2001 report and remained through to the March 2014 report. Following the incorporation of two other schools into PVET in 2012, she became executive head of PVET. A feature of all the Ofsted reports from 2001 through to the 2012 report, which was the last report before the Trojan Horse affair hit the headlines, was the commendation of leadership at the school. Thus, in 2001 it was commented that 'morale in the school is good and the school has the will and capacity to improve further. Although without a permanent headteacher at the time of the inspection, the school is well-led and effectively supported by the governing body'.[272]

The Ofsted reports also describe effective engagement with parents and the local community. Initially, the school had attendance lower than the national average, especially at the time of pilgrimage in the Islamic calendar. However, across the reports, attendance is described as improving, and the school is commended for its engagement with parents and securing their involvement in the school. This also includes comments on the effectiveness of governors. In the 2001 report, it is stated that: 'governors contribute to the shared culture of improvement by providing effective support and appropriate challenge to the school'.[273] The 2007 report commented that 'the headteacher's clear commitment to the quality of the students' education has resulted in a rigorous focus on managing student attendance and eradicating unacceptable behaviour. Attendance is now excellent and behaviour, around the school and in lessons, is good. Good care, guidance and support ensure that all students are given every chance of succeeding in life'. It also commends the governors, who 'contribute well to the life of the school and are effective in planning its strategic direction. They are well-informed about development plans and provide high levels of support and challenge in relation to new initiatives. The school gives good value for money. Financial management is prudent'.[274]

The school was not inspected again until January 2012, as a consequence of passing an 'interim assessment'. The latter was based on data concerning pupil academic performance and attendance, but an inspection would have occurred had there been any complaints brought to the attention of Ofsted. The theme of good governance

---

[272] Only reports for 2014 onwards for schools at the centre of the Trojan Horse affair are available on the Ofsted website, https://reports.ofsted.gov.uk/inspection-reports/find-inspection-report/. The 2001 Report is Ofsted Inspection Report, Park View School, Inspection number 187797, 26 February to 2 March 2001. The quote is from page 6.

[273] Ibid, page 4.

[274] Ofsted Inspection Report for Park View School, Inspection number 286688, 20–21 June 2007, page 4, 7.

is continued in the 2012 report, although now the school is judged as 'outstanding', rather than 'good'. The report states unequivocally that:

this is an outstanding school. The headteacher and her team have very high expectations and provide outstanding leadership and management. The school provides an exceptionally caring and supportive environment for students and their families and is an important part of the local community. 'We are very proud to go to Park View' is typical of comments students made during the inspection.[275]

It elaborates further that:

the headteacher is supported very ably by the deputy headteacher and the leadership team. All staff are focused relentlessly on further improvement and work together outstandingly well. Plans are evaluated rigorously and followed through. Morale is very high. Promotion of equality of opportunity is at the heart of the school's work, creating a very positive and harmonious atmosphere.

In addition, the report remarks on how well this is augmented by the governing body:

the headteacher's informative reports, together with other relevant information, enable the governing body to monitor progress towards targets within the school development plan. The governing body provides excellent strategic direction and challenge and is involved fully and systematically in evaluating the school. Financial management is exemplary and the school offers outstanding value for money.

---

[275] Ofsted Inspection Report, Park View Business and Enterprise School, Inspection number 376921, 11–12 January 2012. Quotes from pages 4, 7.

Similar comments are made about 'safeguarding'. The new criteria for inspection reports were introduced in January 2012, but in the 2007 report it is stated that 'Diversity is valued and celebrated ... Good care, guidance and support ensure that students are given every chance of succeeding in life ... Students' personal development and well-being are good. Almost all achieve well and develop as confident young people who are able to make informed choices about their lives.'[276] The 2012 report is more direct: 'safeguarding policies and procedures are outstanding. They are reviewed regularly, so that adults and students have an excellent understanding of safety issues. Risk assessments are exceptionally thorough. Very careful checks are made of the suitability of adults to work with children'. The report also comments that 'there is very close liaison with external agencies to meet the needs of students whose circumstances make them the most vulnerable and potentially disaffected'.[277] The latter is a reference to Prevent concerns.

The inspectors are also fully aware of the 'Islamic ethos' of the school. It had a determination for Islamic assemblies provided by SACRE since 1997. Practices that will later be judged as negative, and as not preparing children for life in modern Britain, are given a very different interpretation. The criteria associated with section 78 of the Education Act of 2002 – against which it fails in March 2014 – are commented on directly in both the 2007 and the 2012 reports. In the first, it is stated that:

> students' spiritual, moral, social and cultural development is good and fully reflects the school's aim for 'respect, opportunity, learning and achievement to the highest standards'. Students enjoy the many opportunities to celebrate diversity and reflect on their lives, through the school's provision of collective worship and well-organised programme of assemblies ... Students make positive contributions to the community and have raised significant funding for charitable causes, most notably Comic

---

[276] Ofsted Inspection Report for Park View School, 2007, page 4.
[277] Ofsted Inspection Report for Park View School, 2012, page 8, page 7.

Relief. Students are proud to take responsibility as prefects, mediators, members of the business and enterprise steering group and the school council. As a result, they have influenced many decisions about school life.[278]

This is further developed in the 2012 report:

Students make excellent progress in their spiritual, moral, social and cultural development. There is a wide range of opportunities for spiritual development, for example, through the well attended voluntary Friday prayers meeting. Assemblies and tutorials promote a very strong sense of pride in the school community. This contributes very well to students' keen understanding of their rights and responsibilities, and they are profoundly aware of how their actions can affect others. Students have developed excellent reflective skills through the outstanding opportunities provided by the curriculum.[279]

As we have seen, the school is in one of the most disadvantaged areas of Britain and the reports indicate some difficulties that arise because of shortages of staff, or difficulties in appointing teachers for some parts of the curriculum. However, the Ofsted reports indicate a powerful and consistent arc of improvement since the school was in special measures in 1996. This is especially marked in the academic achievements of pupils. The various reports indicate that the pupil attainment on entry is 'often well below average'.[280] The report in 2007 noted continued improvement over 2001 and classed the school as grade 2 (good) on all criteria, stating that, 'this is an overwhelmingly good and improving school', and commenting further that 'sustained improvement at Key Stage 4 led to the school being identified as the most improved school

---

[278] Ofsted Inspection Report for Park View School, 2007, page 5.

[279] Ofsted Inspection Report for Park View School, 2012, page 8.

[280] Ibid, page 5.

in Birmingham in 2006, and the joint 15th most improved secondary school in the country'.[281]

The Ofsted report of January 2012 assessed the school as grade 1 (outstanding) on all criteria, putting it into the top 14% of secondary schools in England at the time. The report comments that, 'students achieve exceptionally well and make outstanding progress', and states further that 'the school's overall GCSE performance has shown a strong upward trend over the last three years. The proportion of students gaining five or more GCSEs at grades A*–C including English and Mathematics has been significantly above average for two consecutive years, with the outstanding curriculum provision and excellent partnership arrangements making major contributions'. The report also noted that 'Boys have performed less well than girls in the past but the school has put in place strategies that narrowed the gender gap in GCSE examination results in 2010 and 2011'.[282]

We saw in our discussion of the emerging 'heterarchical' form of governance in Chapter Five that one of the ways in which the DfE has sought to improve schools independently of local authority initiatives has been through the creation of new practice networks and the identification of 'exemplary' schools from which others might learn.

Park View had National Healthy School status (in which one of the four criteria is effective teaching of PSHE education and another is securing emotional health and well-being). The Healthy Schools programme was introduced in 1999 by the Department for Health and the then Department for Children, Schools and Families, and a National Healthy Schools Standard (NHSS) is 'flagged' in the Guidance on Sex and Relationship Education published in July 2001. It is stated that 'sex and relationship education is one of a number of specific themes which make up the Standard. The NHSS has specific criteria which ensure that schools can confidently set the context and ethos for the effective delivery of sex and relationship education'.[283] Park

[281] Ofsted Inspection Report for Park View School, 2007, page 4.
[282] Ofsted Inspection Report for Park View School, 2012, page 5.
[283] Department for Education and Employment (2000) 'Sex and Relationship Education Guidance', paragraph 1.9.

View was also identified as a National Support School, meaning that it should share its expertise in raising student performance with other schools, and, as we have already noted, its conversion to academy status was the occasion for the DfE to recommend it to 'sponsor' Nansen and Golden Hillock within a new multi-academy trust.

The final sentence of the 2012 Ofsted report for Park View contains no inkling of what is to come: 'Outstanding leadership practice and an exemplary track record since its last inspection fully illustrate the school's excellent capacity to improve further.'[284] In March 2014, just over two years later, that powerful arc of improvement since 1996 was over. The school was deemed to be inadequate and was back in special measures, following which pupil performance declined dramatically.

From 'outstanding' to 'inadequate'

The next inspections of the school – it had 'converted' to become Park View School Academy of Mathematics and Science in April 2012 – were under the full glare of media concern about a Trojan Horse 'plot'. The Secretary of State for Education, Michael Gove, initiated a section 8 inspection, which took place on 5–6 March 2014. This was followed by a full section 5 inspection on 17–18 March. The overall judgement of the school was shifted from 'outstanding' to 'inadequate', with 'achievement of pupils' downgraded from 'outstanding' to 'good' and 'quality of teaching' from 'outstanding' to 'good', while 'behaviour and safety of pupils' was downgraded from 'outstanding' to 'inadequate' and 'leadership and management' also downgraded from 'outstanding' to 'inadequate'.[285]

The decline of governance was yet more rapid at another school, Oldknow Academy (now Ark Chamberlain primary school). It had been inspected more recently, in January 2013, when it was judged to be 'outstanding' in all categories, with the comment that:

---

[284] Ofsted Inspection Report for Park View School, 2012, page 8.

[285] Ofsted Inspection Report, Park View Academy of Mathematics and Science, 5–6 March, 17–18 March 2014. Available at: https://reports.ofsted.gov.uk/inspection-reports/find-inspection-report/provider/ELS/138059.

its contribution to pupils' spiritual, moral, social and cultural development is exceptionally good. The very wide range of different cultures is celebrated, opportunities are provided for prayer at appropriate times, and assemblies reflect the different faith groups in the academy. The way in which the academy respects different faiths and cultures, for example, by ensuring there are separate changing rooms and single-sex physical education lessons, is greatly appreciated by parents and the wider community. The academy is a friendly and racially harmonious place, where discrimination of any kind is not tolerated.[286]

By April 2014, the situation was reversed and the school judged to be 'inadequate' overall, failing on 'safeguarding' and 'leadership', while 'attainment' and 'teaching quality' remain outstanding. The inspectors (one of whom was part of the inspection team at Park View) write that 'the curriculum is inadequate because it does not foster an appreciation of, and respect for, pupils' own or other cultures. It does not promote tolerance and harmony between different cultural traditions'.[287]

How might the disparities be explained? We will go through the Park View 2014 inspection report in detail. On the face of it, the downgrading of pupil achievement and quality of teaching seems to reflect, at most, a possible flattening off of the previous trajectory of improvement. Yet there does not appear to be any decline in performance, given that 'the proportion achieving five or more GCSE A★ to C grades, including English and mathematics has been well above the national average'.[288] Perhaps the school was, in Sir Michael Wilshaw's terms, 'coasting'?[289] However, that term was supposed to

---

[286] Inspection Report, Oldknow Academy, January 2013, page 7. The reports for Oldknow are available at: https://reports.ofsted.gov.uk/inspection-reports/find-inspection-report/provider/ELS/138052.

[287] Inspection Report, Oldknow Academy, April 2014, page 6.

[288] Op cit, page 5.

[289] Speech by Sir Michael Wilshaw, 28 November 2011, delivered at Ark Education trust. 'Good schools for all – an impossible dream?', page 8. Available at: http://arkreboot.bitmachine.co.uk/sites/default/files/111129_mw_speech_4pm_with_logo_final_0_0.pdf.

apply to schools where the contextual data indicated high attainment on pupil entry. The 2014 report provides no such contextual data; it does not mention the lower than average attainment on entry (from its 'feeder' school, Nansen), or the significance of the context of a high proportion of pupils coming from disadvantaged backgrounds, as indicated by the receipt of free school meals, though pupil intake remains similar to that recorded at the time of the earlier reports.

Nonetheless, it does mention that progress at Key Stage 3 is less than at Key Stage 4, although, of course, the disparity between the two is consistent with the fact that pupils have attainment well below the national average on entry. It also indicates that performance in 2014 for English and mathematics is set to improve over 2013. Year 11 pupils in receipt of free school meals attained slightly higher standards than other pupils in 2012, but 'the academy has not been able to sustain this' and it has reversed.[290] This is a comment that is a little odd, given the school's overall achievements in relation to the circumstances of its children, and the fact that children in receipt of free school meals generally perform worse across the sector. The comments on quality of teaching follow this line. Neither set of comments would seem to warrant a downgrade.

More puzzling is the radical downgrading of the 'behaviour and safety of pupils' and 'leadership and management', since these were especially commended in January 2012. It is clear that the focus of attention of the report is 'safeguarding' and the failures of leadership and management with regard to the same.[291] The school is urgently recommended to 'improve systems for safeguarding students so that statutory requirements are met and statutory guidance is fully adhered to … [including] by extending the use of "Prevent" strategies to raise students' awareness about the risks of extremism'.[292]

As we saw in Chapter Two, there was no statutory obligation to address the Prevent agenda directly and most schools conflated it with

[290] Op cit, page 5.
[291] Ibid, page 2: 'This inspection was initiated under section 8 of the Education Act 2005 with an initial focus on safeguarding, and leadership and management.'
[292] Ibid, pages 3–4.

the Duty to Promote Community Cohesion. In that context, the fact that 'use, in liaison with the police, of the government's 'Prevent' strategy to identify and avoid extremism has only taken place for students in years 7 and 8', describes more than was done at other schools. The report also states that, '*most staff* [our emphasis] have not received training in the "Prevent" programme, although there are now plans for this to take place'.[293] The indication of future plans (a reference to a response from the school made between the two visits from which the Ofsted report drew its findings) should not distract from the fact that *some* staff had received training. This is in contrast to most schools in England, as we showed in Chapter Three.

The implication is that the high proportion of Muslim pupils made the Prevent agenda a special concern for the inspection team, notwithstanding that this would not be a major focus of inspections otherwise. As we noted in Chapter Three, Prevent was only a minor element of the inspection criteria in the Inspection Handbook of January and April 2014, and only in relation to pupil behaviour and safety, not in relation to the core criteria for leadership and management, where it received relatively minor emphasis. This interpretation is reinforced by media reports that an initial draft report after the section 8 inspection in early March had not recommended such drastic regrading, begging the question of whether there had been an intervention from higher officials at Ofsted or the DfE.[294]

The perception of concern with issues specific to pupils from a Muslim background is reinforced by comments made about the absence of training for a 'significant number of staff' in child protection, 'tailored to the particular safeguarding context of the students in this academy, such as awareness of forced marriage or the early signs of extremist behavior'.[295] Mention is also made of boys and girls being taught separately in religious education (something

---

[293] Ibid, page 6.
[294] See Richard Adams, 'Ofsted inspectors make U-turn on "Trojan Horse" school, leak shows', *The Guardian*, 30 May 2014. Available at: www.theguardian.com/education/2014/may/30/ofsted-u-turn-trojan-horse-park-view-school-leak.
[295] Op cit, page 7.

to which we will return when we discuss the NCTL hearings) and personal development, notwithstanding that the latter is consistent with guidelines provided to schools, as we saw in a previous chapter, and to which positive reference is made in earlier Ofsted reports. The report comments that, 'the academy has a programme of personal development, and spiritual, moral, social and cultural development, alongside opportunities to develop leadership skills. Students are invited to develop moral understanding through the weekly themed Islamic assemblies. However, no opportunities exist for non-Muslims to attend alternative assemblies'.[296] It provides no comment on the context for this apparent lapse – for example the school roll was 618 pupils, of which 98.9%, as we have seen, were from Muslim backgrounds. Moreover, while parents are able to withdraw their children from collective worship, there is no statutory obligation to provide an alternative.

The overall view is a narrow curriculum that does not provide pupils with sufficient balance or prepare them 'for life in modern Britain and multi-cultural society'.[297] Notwithstanding that the Chief Inspector had himself emphasised academic success as a very large part of such preparation, the very achievements of the school give the Ofsted inspectors no pause. As we have seen, the school is criticised for differential achievement between Key Stage 4 and Key Stage 3, as if attainment at the former was not more important (in terms of GCSE results) and improvement between the two stages, when pupils had entered with lower than national average attainment, a key indicator of successful teaching. Moreover, Sir Michael Wilshaw had previously made such success a mark of effective leadership and argued that it was precisely what *would* prepare children for life in the 21st century.[298]

For the moment, we will conclude this section with a final jarring note. When staff changes became an issue after the suspension of some staff at Park View, including many of its senior leadership team, the

---

[296] Ibid, page 8.
[297] Ibid, page 4.
[298] Wilshaw, 'Good schools for all – an impossible dream?'

achievement of pupils declined very significantly. Indeed, it has not yet returned to anything approaching the levels recorded in March 2014. In short, while the March 2014 report castigated leadership and management for alleged failings in safeguarding, it was unable to explain why such poor leadership had not had negative consequences for pupil achievement.

The successor school to Park View Academy, Rockwood Academy, remained in special measures until March 2016, when it received gradings of 'good' on all criteria. In an echo of earlier Ofsted reports on Park View, the principal is commended for having 'focused with ambition, drive and determination on raising standards at the school and his work has energised teachers and leaders'.[299] However, pupil attainment remains below the national average. We have sympathy for the new leadership team in grappling with the disruptions brought about by the interventions from the DfE which ended the PVET contract with the EFA. Nonetheless, pupil attainment is significantly worse than that achieved by Park View, even when its final year students were taking examinations in the immediate aftermath of the eruption of the Trojan Horse affair, as Table 7.1 shows (Ofsted has removed data pertaining to Park View Academy and Golden Hillock prior to 2014, including earlier Ofsted reports). GCSE results in 2014 at Park View are worse than in 2013 because the exams were sat in the midst of the Trojan Horse disruptions and they go into a steep decline thereafter.

---

[299] Ofsted School Inspection Report, Rockwood Academy, 16–17 March 2016, page 3. Available at: https://reports.ofsted.gov.uk/inspection-reports/find-inspection-report/provider/ELS/138059.

Table 7.1: Comparative school performance Park View Academy (subsequently Rockwood Academy) and Golden Hillock (subsequently Ark Boulton), 2014–2016.[300]

Grade C or better in 5 GCSEs including English & maths	2012	2013	2014	2015	2016
Park View/Rockwood Academy	76%	73%	66%	58%	49%
Golden Hillock/Ark Boulton	43%	50%	N/A	41%	52%
Birmingham	N/A	N/A	58.2%	56.2%	59.9%
England state-funded schools	58.8%	60.6%	58.9%	59.2%	63%

For its part, in 2016 Nansen Primary was in the bottom 10% of schools in the country for reading and maths and average (60% of schools) for writing in terms of progress between Key Stage 1 and Key Stage 2. Ark Chamberlain primary (formerly Oldknow Academy when it was judged outstanding) is currently in the bottom 10% for reading and writing and average for maths.

Change management in politically charged times

As we have seen, Park View Academy was a successful school in precisely the terms set out by Sir Michael, and it had received commendations from Ofsted inspectors right up to the point of the Trojan Horse affair. Moreover, its Islamic ethos was associated with that success – explicitly so, in remarks by the inspectors on the school's engagement with parents and development of pupil confidence. When it became an academy, it was encouraged – a small school of just 600 or so pupils – by the DfE to sponsor two other schools as 'converter' academies, Golden Hillock secondary school and Nansen Primary school. Both were judged to be underperforming schools and PVET was charged with bringing its proven leadership and management capacity to bear. This would mean developing forms of monitoring and reporting in the other schools, utilising those in place and judged to be very effective at Park View, and planning for the integration of the governing bodies through an overall board of the Trust and the secondment of staff to facilitate those processes.

[300] Data from: https://www.compare-school-performance.service.gov.uk/.

For the moment, let us suppose that the leadership capacity might have declined. The 2014 Ofsted report refers to 'considerable staff changes since the academy opened almost two years ago'.[301] However, this is a little misleading and is a consequence of the creation of the PVET. Some of those previously in leadership positions within Park View school moved to take up interim appointments in Nansen and Golden Hillock. The head teacher of Park View became executive head of PVET, the head of governors at Park View remained, but also took on the position of chair of the governing body at PVET. In other words, there is continuity of personnel, but movement between positions. The review of PVET by the EFA also complained of the lack of clarity in staffing structures and that there were a number of staff in acting positions, including each of the head teachers of the schools in the Trust.[302] Once again, this follows from the very process of the formation of the Trust.

Moreover, the process of change was very rapid and relatively incomplete by the time of the EFA Review. The PVET was incorporated on 14 February 2012, with Nansen Primary joining on 1 October 2012, and Golden Hillock on 1 October 2013, just eight months before the review.[303] There was also a process where another school was under consideration for inclusion in the Trust, with Michael Gove signing an Academy Order in July 2013 to fast-track Al-Furqan to academy status for 1 November 2013. In the event, this did not proceed, but negotiations were underway through the same period as for Golden Hillock.

The review notes a number of areas where financial procedures were not properly established or were breached. However, given widespread reporting of irregularities at other Trusts,[304] it should be noted that none of these involved any impropriety and should be placed in the context of the earlier positive reports on financial procedures at Park View. As we shall see, in Chapter Nine on the NCTL hearings,

[301] Op cit, page 3.
[302] Education Funding Agency, *Review of PVET*, page 3.
[303] Ibid, page 8.
[304] See Baxter (2016) *School Governance*, see especially chapter 3.

financial irregularities form no part of the case against the teachers. Problems concerning lack of clarity in the roles of governing body members at Golden Hillock are also reported. Finally, the chair of the Board of Governors of PVET, Tahir Alam, is declared to have 'an inappropriate role in the day to day running of Park View School', as a consequence of his admission that he had 'been in the school every day in the last four weeks dealing with "issues"'.[305] This criticism is more than a little disingenuous since Mr Alam was describing the very period of the Ofsted inspections that downgraded the school from 'outstanding' to 'inadequate', when his intense involvement might be expected and welcomed rather than condemned.

It is well-established in the sociological literature that new management arrangements are disruptive of previous patterns of informal and implicit rules and practices that exist alongside a formal structure of rules.[306] This is always a source of tension and an object of concern in strategies of change management, which, in turn, encounter resistance as well as support. Management of change also includes a potential for the confusion of responsibilities. However, it is not likely that the very systems that the 2012 report had reviewed and commended would have degraded so quickly. In addition, former position holders remained within the Trust and were available for consultation. It is significant, for example, that pupil achievement remained above the national average. This is in striking contrast to the situation after the school was returned to special measures – performance declined rapidly and has not recovered to previous levels, as we have seen (while performance at Nansen and Golden Hillock had improved in the short period during which they had been part of PVET).

However, the creation of the Trust also made available new opportunities for promotion and acting 'above role' (and, therefore, being open to performance review in that role), but also for anxiety

---

[305] Education Funding Agency, *Review of PVET*, page 5.

[306] See, for example, G. Salaman (2001) *Understanding Business Organisations*, London: Routledge; P. Banfield and R. Kay (2012) *Introduction to Human Resource Management*, Oxford: Oxford University Press.

and disappointment. In the context of the fact that the inspection was occasioned by media reports about a Trojan Horse plot and problems of leadership and safeguarding, this also created conditions for retrospective staff complaints. Once again, we will look at these more thoroughly in the context of the Kershaw and Clarke Reports. However, it is striking that a leadership team that was relatively unchanged in terms of personnel would, in the space of two years, shift from being praised for its promotion of equal opportunities, both for pupils and staff, to being condemned for failing to do so.

The one that got away

It is hard to avoid the conclusion that the main criticism of Park View was that it was overly 'Islamic' and that this, in turn, was associated with a 'plot' to 'Islamise' other schools. Yet, as we have seen, the 'takeover' of other schools was itself the normal process associated with the academies programme. In the narrative associated with the Trojan Horse affair, the involvement of the DfE is kept in the background, yet all sponsorships ('takeovers') are signed off by the Secretary for State for Education and have active involvement of officials associated with the academies programme. As we have seen, there was a fourth school associated with the PVET, namely Al-Furqan primary school. It had been deemed 'inadequate' at its last Ofsted inspection, and had had an interim Executive Board and interim head teacher appointed. However, the school features neither in the EFA's review of the PVET, nor in the Clarke Report. What makes it so significant is that it was an Islamic faith school.

We will not rehearse all the criticisms directed by the EFA Review at the 'Islamic ethos' of PVET, but they charge the Trust with restricting the social, moral, spiritual and cultural provision to 'a conservative Islamic perspective', practices of 'segregating girls and boys in some classes which could constitute less favourable treatment of girls', and evidence of an 'inappropriate external speaker being invited into Park View School to speak to children'. Concern about the 'Islamic ethos' of the schools was also expressed, noting that, at Park View, 'the school is not faith-designated, but has an Islamic focus', and that there were posters in Arabic in classrooms and in corridors, 'advertising the virtues of prayer and promoting Friday prayers'. It is also noted that around 80% of girls at Park View were wearing white hijabs, 'although there was no evidence to suggest a strict Islamic dress code was being enforced'.[307]

It is also noted that PVET schools offer Islamic collective worship, though none had an active determination (that of Park View having expired in April 2013). We shall take up this issue in the next chapter, but, for the moment, we can note that such determinations were previously provided by the local SACRE, but with academies that role passed to the DfE. It seems that the latter put in place no mechanisms for doing so (at least, this is what can be inferred from the fact that a Freedom of Information request by Birmingham SACRE elicited the information that no determinations had been made by the DfE). Worryingly, the Kershaw Report misrepresents this request by the SACRE. As we saw in Chapter Four, Birmingham SACRE was concerned about capacity at the DfE. Its request to the DfE was to ask how many determinations had been granted, to which it had the response that there were none. Kershaw inverts this and states:

> we are informed by Birmingham SACRE that a Freedom of Information request revealed that no free school or academy in Birmingham has submitted a request for a Notice of Determination or renewal of an expired Determination and that therefore 'all schools and academies in the city, which do not have a determination granted by SACRE before they became academies, should hold a Daily act of Collective Worship of a wholly or mainly or broadly Christian nature'.[308]

However, in the view of the SACRE it was improper to have this expectation of schools with very high proportions of Muslim pupils

---

[307] Education Funding Agency, *Review of PVET*, pages 3, 7, 8.
[308] Kershaw Report, page 35.

and their point was that, unlike the SACRE, the DfE had failed to follow up renewals, thereby leaving schools in an ambiguous position. They did not expect a school that had had a determination since 1997 to revert to Christian worship in 2013 because of poor procedures at the DfE.

We will address the issues of 'Islamic ethos' in the next chapter, noting for the moment only that there is little evidence of any change after 2012 when the ethos was commended. Our purpose here is to draw attention to the fact that the DfE was seemingly happy for a Trust *without* a faith designation to incorporate a school *with* a faith designation. The reason why the department thought that this was not a problem was precisely because it recognised the very 'Islamic ethos' of PVET about which the EFA Review and Kershaw and Clarke Reports subsequently express dismay. In both official and media reports, as we have seen, it is frequently expressed that Park View itself confused its status as a non-faith school with that of a faith school, yet here we see that the confusion attributed to it belongs with the DfE. Of course, the truth of the matter is that non-faith schools can have a faith ethos. However, it is somewhat unexpected that the DfE would recommend that a non-faith Trust should sponsor a faith school.[309]

One feature of a faith school is that it can recruit staff on the basis of their faith (although it doesn't have to) and can also insist upon certain modes of address of teachers (in this case, use of Ustad/Ustada as an honorific before a member of staff's surname). It can also insist upon prayer and other accommodations of religious requirements. The NCTL professional misconduct hearings against senior teachers at Park View disclosed minutes of discussions between members of the Al-Furqan governing body, that of PVET (its executive head

---

[309] The Secretary of State, Michael Gove, did commission a report by the Permanent Secretary at the department into 'possible warnings' to DfE of extremism in Birmingham schools. However, this does not address the role of the department in facilitating the sponsorship of schools by Park View. See Department for Education (2015) *Review into Possible Warnings to DfE Relating to Extremism in Birmingham Schools*, 16 January 2015. Available at: www.gov.uk/government/speeches/review-into-possible-warnings-on-extremism-in-birmingham-schools.

teacher), the Birmingham LEA and the DfE. The minutes are from July 2013, with other minutes provided for a meeting of the Interim Management Board Meeting of Al-Furqan in September 2013. There are also emails in September from lawyers representing the Al-Furqan governing body.

The documents are revealing. They show a difference of opinion over the relative importance of academic improvement over Islamic ethos (with the trustees responsible for Al-Furqan concerned that the former was being given greater weight), the worries of the (non-Muslim) interim head teacher that another (Muslim) head teacher might be appointed, and discussions of secondment of a deputy head teacher from Oldknow primary school (on the basis of the Islamic ethos of that school, as well as its outstanding academic achievements) to work with the interim head teacher. Oldknow school was not part of PVET, but Nansen Primary did not have the record of achievement to warrant secondment of its staff to Al-Furqan (teachers from Park View were seconded to Nansen). Other discussions involve the process of linking the governing body of Al-Furqan with that of PVET, specifically in the person of Tahir Alam, asking him to join the Interim Executive Board of Al-Furqan while its new governing body and its integration with the Board of Governors of the PVET was being negotiated.

In the event, the incorporation of Al-Furqan into PVET, which the Secretary of State had scheduled for November 2013, did not go ahead. The trustees of Al-Furqan did not believe that arrangements would sufficiently protect the Islamic ethos of their school and PVET could not endorse the practices of an Islamic faith school as their own. Notwithstanding, that it was deemed by the EFA to operate from a 'conservative Islamic perspective' and, by Sir Michael Wilshaw and others, to be at the centre of a concerted and hardline effort to Islamise schools, it was moderate in its understanding of what an 'Islamic ethos' meant in a non-faith school and was unwilling to breach that line.

We will be dealing with the Kershaw Report in the next chapter, but it should be noted that Al-Furqan is briefly mentioned there. Reference is made to bringing back the use of the honorific Ustad/

Ustada following its removal by the Interim Executive Board in 2013.
The report also states that:

> we were informed [redacted] that when a [redacted] woman was
> recommended as a [redacted] protested on the basis that a woman
> 'would not have strong enough character' and stated that what
> the school needed was a 'man with a beard.' We were told that
> [redacted] of Park View Academy agreed with this statement
> and stated that [redacted] Park View Academy and Trust [sic]
> wanted to appoint another candidate.[310]

The minutes demonstrate otherwise and also show that the
representative of PVET, Lindsey Clarke, was exerting no such pressure.
Kershaw appears to be unaware that the DfE was supporting the
incorporation of Al-Furqan into PVET. Indeed, a later comment in the
Kershaw Report refers to a 'petition' sent to the chair of the Interim
Education Board and copied to PVET and governors at Oldknow,
where Kershaw states, 'it is unclear why these individuals would have
been involved in issues concerning Al-Furqan School'.[311]

Significantly, the negotiations between Al-Furqan and PVET were
conducted in the presence of an official from the DfE. However, it
seems that no one came forward from the DfE to explain the situation
to the Kershaw team, although it subsequently emerged during the
NCTL hearings that an official had been interviewed for the Clarke
Report, an interview that would have been available to the Kershaw
Report. 'We were informed …' occupies a particular role in both the
Kershaw and Clarke Reports, but what is striking is the very matters
about which they were either *not* informed, or which they chose not
to reflect upon as part of their investigations. The Clarke Report, in
addition, had advisers from the DfE, one of whom had been directly
involved in the EFA Review of PVET. The fact that PVET had been
asked to sponsor Al-Furqan would have been part of the files at DfE.
It is the Clarke and Kershaw Reports to which we now turn.

[310] Kershaw Report, page 25.
[311] Ibid, page 47.

EIGHT

The Clarke and Kershaw Reports

We have seen how, in the light of media reports of a 'plot' to 'Islamicise' schools in Birmingham, Ofsted set in motion section 8 inspections of 21 schools in Birmingham in early March 2014, followed by 5 full section 5 inspections. The supposed 'plot' was revealed in a letter and supporting document sent to the Birmingham City Council leader in November 2013, but apparently not acted upon. Three of the five schools subjected to full inspections were part of PVET, with Oldknow Academy, another school previously judged to be outstanding, one of the others. Sir Michael Wilshaw delivered Ofsted's verdict on the affair on 14 June 2014. He declared that 'a culture of fear and intimidation has developed in some of the schools since their previous inspection', and, further, stated that 'there has been an organised campaign to target certain schools in Birmingham in order to alter their character and ethos'. He also stated that 'some headteachers, including those with a proud record of raising standards, said that they have been marginalised or forced out of their jobs. As a result, some schools previously judged to be good or outstanding have experienced high levels of staff turbulence, low staff morale and a rapid decline in their overall effectiveness'.[312]

---

[312] Wilshaw, 9 June 2014. 'Advice note'. All quotes are taken from the 'Statement of findings', pages 2–8.

However, as we have shown, this does not accord with what the previous Ofsted reports had described. Park View Academy was an effective and outstanding school, on the basis of which it had been asked to sponsor two other less successful schools, Nansen Primary and Golden Hillock secondary school. Indeed, it is precisely as a consequence of the Trojan Horse affair that a head teacher, Lindsey Clarke, with 'a proud record of raising standards' would be subjected to a professional misconduct hearing at the National College for Teaching and Learning (the body responsible for teacher standards), along with other members of her senior teaching team who were also involved in that success. The only cases brought by the NCTL involve teachers associated with PVET (and Oldknow).

As we saw in Chapter Five, the academies programme itself has generated 'staff turbulence' within schools, not least because it was associated with a concerted attempt to improve academic standards by calling head teachers and other teaching staff to account. Parents and members of ethnic minority communities had for some time been concerned that schools were failing their children. The academies programme encouraged governing bodies to challenge head teachers and the strategy of schools toward improving performance. This also had an impact upon LEAs, which were faced with schools either being required to become academies, because they were deemed inadequate (and, therefore, no longer responsible to them), or opting to 'convert' to academies.

Notwithstanding the public statements about failures in governance, including the bureaucratic and complacent nature of LEAs, made by government ministers and the Chief Inspector of Schools, it would be grossly unfair to suggest that LEAs were not also concerned to improve standards. As we saw in Chapter Six, Birmingham LEA, in particular, had outcomes above the national average.

We have also described the new governance arrangements as 'heterarchical' and 'networked', meaning that there was no longer a single, hierarchical system of governance with clear roles for LEAs. In addition, the nature of school governing bodies was also subject to change, but in ways which were not entirely consistent with the new arrangements that were emerging. The formula for academies was essentially that they 'may, but need not' adopt the requirements placed on schools under LEA control. For example, they could adopt the locally agreed syllabus from their SACRE, but need not do so. In a similar way, while schools under the direct control of the local authority would have LEA-nominated governors, academies might seek such nominations, but they need not.

Given that the putative Trojan Horse plot is widely understood to have been formulated within Muslim communities, the expectation might be that the supposed illegitimate pressure on head teachers came from parent governors, or community governors. In fact, it is LEA-appointed governors who are identified as being those who were most involved in such pressures, suggesting that they were participating in an official policy of challenging schools. For example, the Kershaw Report states, 'there is clear evidence that a significant number of those governors acting unreasonably have been local authority governors'.[313] The report does not pause to reflect on its significance in the light of Birmingham LEA's policies of school improvement (in fact, as we shall see, the report erroneously states that Birmingham LEA lacked such policies).

In April 2014, no doubt informed by early sight of the Ofsted reports, the Secretary for State for Education, Michael Gove, appointed Peter Clarke as an Education Commissioner to investigate allegations arising from the Trojan Horse letter, and, at more or less the same time, Birmingham City Council appointed Ian Kershaw to investigate the same, and its implications for their practices. The setting up of two reports on the same matter reflected the confusion in governance between hierarchical and heterarchical forms. The local authority retained responsibility for schools that were not academies, but the DfE could act on its own authority without need for consultation with the local authority since some of the schools were under its direct responsibility. Both chairs agreed to share evidence (except where it had been given in strict confidence) and both reports were published

---

[313] Kershaw Report, page 12.

at more or less the same time, Kershaw on 18 July and Clarke on 22 July. Their findings concurred with those of Ofsted (whose 2014 reports are cited by Kershaw, but not by Clarke). The Trojan Horse narrative would now become firmly established.

The Kershaw and Clarke Reports: (mis)identifying the problem

A number of commentators have suggested that Michael Gove was predisposed to believe in the existence of a Trojan Horse plot, pointing to a book he had written on the dangers of 'Islamism'.[314] The book identified a problem of extremist ideology within Islam. As we saw in Chapter Two, this was the kind of argument that became more dominant within the Prevent strategy after the election of the Conservative–Liberal Democrat coalition government in 2010, albeit that it did not give rise to statutory requirements on schools until 2015 after the Trojan Horse affair. His appointment of Peter Clarke, the former Metropolitan Police head of Counter-Terrorism, seemed to confirm this bias. Indeed, the West Midlands Chief Police Constable, Chris Sims, expressed his concern about the appointment and that people would draw 'unwarranted conclusions' from Clarke's previous role about what was under investigation in the schools.[315] In fact, West Midlands Police had also conducted an inquiry (not made public) and decided that there was no basis for them to act.

In response to these concerns, Peter Clarke stated that 'I made it clear to all interested parties that I saw my task as to establish the facts of what had happened'. He goes on to comment that 'the investigation has been extensive and has been able to reach clear conclusions based on firm evidence. With the assistance of my team, I have gathered nearly

---

[314] See Michael Gove (2006) *Celsius 7/7: How the West's Policy of Appeasement Has Provoked Yet More Fundamentalist Terror – And What Needs to be Done About it Now*, London: Phoenix.

[315] As reported by Helen Pidd and Vikram Dodd, 'Police chief condemns appointment of terror officer over "Islamic schools plot"', *The Guardian*, 15 May 2014' Available at: www.theguardian.com/uk-news/2014/apr/15/police-chief-counter-terror-officer-islamic-schools-plot-birmingham.

2,000 documents, generated over 2,000 pages of interview transcripts from some 50 witnesses, and drawn on a wide range of material from diverse sources'.[316] He does not reveal something that emerged at the NCTL hearing of professional misconduct against senior teachers at PVET, as we shall see, namely that half the inspection team involved in the EFA Review of PVET were from the DfE's Due Diligence and Counter Extremism Division, nor that three members from the EFA review were appointed as advisers to his investigation (with one, Ann Connor, acting as the main author of chapter 4 on the 'specific patterns of behaviour observed'). This, perhaps, explains the way in which the Clarke Report, in contrast to the Kershaw Report, focuses most of its attention on PVET.

The setting up of the two investigations is also bound up with changing governance arrangements. The Kershaw investigation was charged with looking at the role of Birmingham City Council and its education services. Under an earlier mode of governance – that is, the hierarchical system designed for the delivery of a public service – an investigation would have been led by a team from another local authority (much as investigations into police forces are led by other police forces) with a similar range of schools and issues of pupil achievement. However, under 'heterarchical' arrangements, the arbiter of good practice is less straightforward. In the event, the investigation was conducted by a management team from an academy trust, Northern Education, under its Managing Director Ian Kershaw, an educationalist.

Northern Education has a 'corporate' system of governance similar to that recommended for academy schools in government guidance.[317] It currently runs 20 schools, equally divided between primary and

[316] Clarke Report, pages 7, 8.
[317] Department for Education and Skills (2007) *What are Academies*? It states: 'to determine the ethos and leadership of the academy, and ensure responsibility and accountability, the private sector or charitable sponsor always appoints the majority of governors. This is the case even when a local authority is acting as co-sponsor for wider purposes. The number of governors on an Academy governing body is not prescribed, but the expectation is for the body to be relatively small'.

secondary schools. To put that in context, there were 437 schools in Birmingham at the time of the report.[318] It is based in the North East of England, an area with a below average (for England) proportion of ethnic minorities. For example, Birmingham has a population that is 63.26% White British and 19.6% Asian and Asian British and 6.57% Black and Black British, compared with, for the North East, 92.3% White British, 2.7% Asian and Asian British and 0.76% Black and Black British.[319] As we also saw in Chapter Four, the ethnic minority population is disproportionately younger and, therefore, more likely to have children in school than the population as a whole and so differences between the two regions in terms of the ethnic minority composition of its school pupils are likely to be even greater.

In this context, then, it might be expected that the Kershaw Report would comment on the ethnic minority makeup of the schools and also on the issues of underachievement on the part of ethnic minority pupils, especially those from a Muslim heritage. It does not. Nor does the Clarke Report, except in Annex 5, which provides short summary statements about his findings from each school (which includes brief descriptions of the pupil intake at each school, but without comment on their implications). More concerning, as we shall see, is that neither report disentangles an appropriate timeline in relation to the different schools, thereby conflating complaints associated with when schools were in 'special measures' with those when they were judged 'outstanding'. In addition, they criticise Birmingham City Council for failing to act with regard to complaints. Yet some of these complaints coincide with the council taking action – for example, in the case of Golden Hillock – by arranging academy sponsorship; that is, the council taking the issue of poor pupil achievement seriously forms the context of the 'complaints'. However, earlier complaints at Golden Hillock are treated on a par with those arising after academy sponsorship is put into place.

[318] Kershaw Report, page 3.
[319] Guardian Datablog (an 'experimental data' release from ONS providing local authority level data for 2009). Available at: www.theguardian.com/news/datablog/2011/may/18/ethnic-population-england-wales#data.

This confusion arises, in part, because of the pivotal role of PVET and the Clarke Report's failure to consider that such a role might derive from its qualities as an outstanding school, rather than from a 'plot' by its staff. Thus, reported complaints against the governing body at Golden Hillock (referring to criticisms of the school's poor performance prior to PVET's involvement) might reasonably be regarded as in the process of being resolved by the good offices of the Trust. After all, the information available to Birmingham City Council was that Park View school had been judged 'outstanding' and had the support of the DfE in sponsoring other schools as part of a multi-trust academy. Paradoxically, although Birmingham City Council was no longer responsible for Park View Academy, as a consequence of its academy status, it made itself vulnerable to criticism precisely because it was actively involved in the process of sponsorship as part of its own commitment to achieving higher school standards. It is not clear how 'sponsorship' could be regarded as occurring simply at the instigation of teachers and governors with an intent to 'Islamicise' a school. As we saw in Chapter Six, Sir Tim Brighouse, former Chief Education Officer in Birmingham between 1993 and 2002 viewed underperformance by ethnic minority pupils as a major challenge of his period of office and one that was associated with vigorous complaints from parents, complaints whose legitimacy he accepted.

The Kershaw Report gets into these difficulties because of the lack of knowledge of its team with regard to the special issues of schools in Birmingham and, in part, because of its acceptance of the narrative of the Trojan Horse letter itself. This is something that is shared with the Clarke Report. Neither thinks it necessary to test the veracity of the letter – it was widely believed to be a 'hoax' – and each argues that it is only concerned with the allegations and whether there is evidence to support them. In this way, the Trojan Horse plot narrative is built into the reports and alternative accounts of the same 'facts' are elided. Indeed, the mode of proceeding militates against testing those 'facts' and the problem of the initial letter (and its accompanying document) is compounded. The letter is a series of allegations and the reports gather witness statements that multiply those allegations, rather than test them. The alternative explanations of those against whom claims are made are not provided and so both reports become an accumulation of testimonies in which those stepping forward to testify against outweigh others and are the only matters recorded. Nor do the reports examine the process of academy sponsorship and, thus, the involvement of the DfE in promoting PVET as a means of improving the performance of other schools, notwithstanding that the Clarke Report, at least, interviewed a central figure from the DfE academies programme, as would emerge from the NCTL hearings. Specifically that individual was the officer involved in discussions (both with PVET and Birmingham officials from the schools improvement programme) of the sponsorship of Nansen and Golden Hillock and the abandoned sponsorship of Al-Furqan schools.

We have not yet set out precisely what the purported 'plot' amounted to and we will now provide the version that is common to both reports (the Clarke Report presents a condensed version, the Kershaw Report a lengthier version, but they are in all essentials the same and each report begins with the 'five step plan').[320]

The 'Five Step' Plan set out in the Trojan Horse letter and accompanying document:
- identify your schools;
- select a group of Salafi parents;
- put our [sic] own governor in;
- identify key staff to disrupt the school from within; and
- anonymous letter and PR campaign.

The Trojan Horse document makes claims about leadership change at four schools: Adderley Primary, Saltley School, Springfield School and Regents Park Community Primary, which although included in the 21 schools investigated by Ofsted do not come to be central. The Kershaw Report investigated 14 non-faith schools – Adderley Primary, Anderton Park School, Golden Hillock School, Highfield School, Ladypool Primary, Lozells Primary School, Marlborough Junior

---

[320] See Clarke Report, page 5; Kershaw Report, page 6.

School, Moseley School, Nansen Primary, Oldknow Academy, Park View Academy, Regents Park Primary, Saltley School and Washwood Heath Academy – and also heard evidence about two faith schools, Al-Hijrah and Al-Furqan, which were not part of the 21. The Clarke Report does not include Lozells and Marlborough, but does include two others, Springfield and Shaw Hill. The Clarke Report's reasons for not including Al-Hijrah are revealing: it is 'a Muslim faith designated voluntary-aided school and therefore it is able, where appropriate, to introduce elements of faith'.[321] The implication is that other schools are not able appropriately to introduce 'elements of faith'. This is a fundamental misunderstanding that shapes the investigation.

In each report, the schools are addressed in terms of evidence of each of the steps, although, as we have seen, the status of the 'evidence' is in the form of 'we were informed that …'. However, the Kershaw investigation does not appear to have been informed that PVET was in the process of incorporating Al-Furqan in September 2013, but withdrew because it was unwilling to adhere to the stricter practices allowed for a faith school. The Kershaw investigation was also unaware that the DfE was closely involved in Park View's prospective takeover of Al-Furqan, with a DfE representative participating in meetings who could have provided a counter to how the Kershaw investigation was otherwise 'informed'. In contrast, the Clarke Report had as an educational adviser, Ann Connor, one of the inspectors involved in the EFA Review of PVET, who would have known about the DfE's encouragement of this takeover but, apparently, did not believe it be a relevant matter, as it did not form part of the EFA Review of PVET of which she was a part. The DfE official involved in the academies programme in Birmingham, who was in detailed discussions with PVET, was interviewed, but his views were unreported. The transcript of that interview was among the documents that the NCTL was severely censured for withholding and which led to the collapse of the professional misconduct hearings against the senior teachers.[322]

---

[321] Clarke Report, page 116.

[322] 354 NCTL, May 2017, 'Professional conduct panel outcome', paragraph 122.

The Kershaw Report presents a table of findings where the evidence is presented that at least four of the five steps are found at seven schools, Adderley Primary, Golden Hillock, Lozells Primary, Moseley, Nansen Primary School, Park View Academy and Saltley School. The Clarke Report has a seven-point map of 'observed' behaviours (though, in truth it is, at best, a map of 'reported' behaviours). All seven features are found at Park View and Golden Hillock, with Saltley, Oldknow, Anderton Park and Adderley showing six of the features. Clarke also has a lengthy opening chapter about events at Saltley School and the process by which its newly appointed (in September 2012) head teacher left in January 2014 under a compromise agreement with Birmingham City Council, but no connections are made with individuals associated with PVET and no actions are subsequently taken against anyone at Saltley School.

Both reports include Regents Park community primary school. This is another school which had received an outstanding Ofsted report. However, its female head teacher, a non-Muslim, had resigned in October 2013. This episode appears in the original Trojan Horse document, where it is stated: 'we had to plant the seed of her cheating in order to get the results she has. This put her whole performance under scrutiny and once you scrutinize you will always find something, however small it may be and, by that time the damage is done and as such most people will resign before they are pushed'.[323] It is curious that neither Clarke nor Kershaw make any comments about the case, since it constituted one of the only examples of a seemingly 'successful head teacher' being hounded out. The case was in the public domain prior to the Trojan Horse letter and document being received by Birmingham City Council on 27 November 2013, since the resignations of the head teacher and deputy head teacher had been reported in the *Birmingham Mail* on 4 October 2013.[324] Perhaps the

---

[323] Clarke Report, Annex 2, page 110 'Trojan Horse' letter.

[324] See the report by Mike Lockley, 'Birmingham headteacher and deputy quit in SATs results probe', *Birmingham Mail,* 3 October 2013,. Available at: www.birminghammail.co.uk/news/local-news/small-heath-headteacher-deputy-quit-6135405.

two reports regarded the case as *sub judice*, since it had been referred to the NCTL for a professional misconduct hearing which took place in July 2014.[325] The head teacher was found guilty of dishonesty in altering the SATs papers of pupils. Nonetheless, without comment, the school appears in the charts provided by each report where the indicators of the '5 steps' are either left blank, or stated as 'No', but with no explanation given.

As we have seen, the Trojan Horse affair comes to focus primarily on four schools, Park View Academy, Golden Hillock, Nansen Primary (all of which came to be part of PVET) and Oldknow. This association with PVET, and the accompanying timeline, are highly significant because 'accusations' are recorded as applying back to 1998/99 at Park View, where Birmingham City Council, 'failed to deal with problematic [redacted] at Park View, because it was "frightened of upsetting local communities", and that due to this failure it is now "dealing with 21 schools"'.[326] It is also stated that:

in or around 1998 the Governing Body became hypercritical of the senior leadership … We were also informed that BCC seriously considered withdrawing the delegated powers of the Governing Body due to governors' behaviour … One witness stated that in subsequent years the teaching staff passed a vote of no confidence in the Governing Body following irregularities [redacted] BCC's response was to state that whilst the process was flawed, it did not want to exchange one set of problems with another.[327]

---

[325] She was prohibited from teaching for five years, but allowed then to reapply because it was accepted as a 'moment of madness' and because of her 'previous good history'. See NCTL, July 2014, 'Tina Ireland: Professional Conduct Panel outcome panel decision and reasons on behalf of the Secretary of State for Education'. Available at: www.gov.uk/government/publications/teacher-misconduct-panel-outcome-ms-tina-ireland.

[326] Kershaw Report, page 60.

[327] Ibid, page 51.

The Clarke Report presents a similar account of problems at Park View, 'under the Chairmanship of Tahir Alam'.[328] Yet, as we have seen, these apparent problems occur across the period in which Park View, under the chairmanship of Tahir Alam (and, after 2001, with Lindsey Clarke as head teacher), moves from being in 'special measures' in 1996 to being 'outstanding' in 2012. We have also seen that leadership and management of the school are strongly endorsed in Ofsted reports up to, and including, the 2012 report. The Kershaw Report identifies that there are 'key individuals' involved and noted 'a pattern of these individuals moving between schools in the area. These individuals include those in roles such as governors, deputy head teachers, acting head teachers or other teaching staff, trustees (in relation to academy schools) and parents, and often these individuals move between these roles and/ or hold a number of different posts across schools'.[329] These moves are, however, what might be expected from the 'heterarchal' and networked governance associated with the academies programme, with which Birmingham City Council cooperates. Washwood Heath School is mentioned in both reports as having problems in the late 1990s and going into special measures in 2002, when Tahir Alam is appointed to the Interim Executive Board, serving as governor until 2014.[330] No problems are reported during his tenure.

The Kershaw Report argues that the behaviours that are regarded as problematic go beyond holding the head teacher to account for educational performance, but concedes that, 'often there is evidence to show that underperformance of the school can be, but is not always, an issue'.[331] However, no timeline in relation to performance is presented in any of the cases, not even where there is reference to significant issues – for example, where an Interim Executive Board has been appointed at a school and where there would be an expectation both of new appointments and also that the interim board would be

---

[328] Clarke Report, page 119.
[329] Kershaw Report, page 9.
[330] Clarke Report, page 121; Kershaw Report, page 34.
[331] Kershaw Report, page 9.

replaced at some point, creating anxieties for staff in 'acting' positions, which might colour their testimony.

Similar problems are evident in the treatment of Nansen and Golden Hillock schools. On the one hand, difficulties with their respective governing bodies are associated with a period when each school is reported to be underperforming. Park View is identified as a sponsoring academy to 'take over' the schools and this is then taken as evidence of a long-term strategy on the part of governors and teachers linked to Park View. The Kershaw Report, for example, comments, 'we were informed that once Nansen became part of PVET, [redacted] were informed that the school would be restructured to [Park View's] model and there was no room for discussion'. For Golden Hillock, there is reference to an Academy Broker from the DfE taking part in a meeting in order to understand better a potential sponsored academy solution. The notes of the meeting are reported as stating that the Governing Body was 'driven by personal agendas' and that the governors were 'like a bunch of animals'.[332] However, this description is allowed to include the incorporation of the school into PVET, as if the problematic behaviours were continuous and uncontested. PVET, however, was the DfE's sponsored academy solution, supported by Birmingham City Council, precisely because it had confidence in its leadership and governance (and the appropriateness of its faith ethos).

Nor does either report properly consider the nature of the obligations on schools to teach religious education and have a daily act of collective worship. We saw at the end of the last chapter that the Kershaw Report misrepresents the statement by SACRE that the determination for Islamic collective worship expired for a number of schools, including Park View, shortly after they became academies. The determinations should have been renewed by the DfE, or the strict legal position would be that they should revert to Christian worship. We can leave aside, for the moment (it comes up again in the NCTL hearings in the next chapter), the question of reversion, simply to say that the failure to reflect upon this is symptomatic of the report's failure to

---

[332] Ibid, page 29, page 42.

address the fact that the schools had pupil intakes that were 98–99% Muslim, especially the schools that came to be the focus of concern. As we have seen, the examples of the introduction of 'Islamic faith' which are regarded in each report as problematic also take place when the schools did have determinations.

The Kershaw Report praises the due diligence of the local SACRE, but then resorts to a general point, that:

> an agreement by Birmingham SACRE or the Secretary of State (in respect of a free school or academy) to a determination not to provide a daily act of Christian worship does not mean that permission has been granted to offer an alternative Islamic, Sikh, Buddhist or any other form of worship in its place every day. This is an area of the law which is unclear and there is no obligation on SACRE when it decides that a daily act of worship is not appropriate, to specify what form (if any) the act of worship should take.[333]

In fact, the law is clear. Once a determination is granted it is up to the head teacher to do what is appropriate given the pupil body, with the proviso that it should not be 'denominational' though it may reflect the broad traditions of another faith.[334] Indeed, the purpose of a determination is to allow collective worship of a non-Christian kind and an application is accompanied by specification of what is intended.

We have already seen that at Park View space constraints meant that collective worship could only be available to groups of pupils on a weekly basis. However, evidence provided by Birmingham SACRE to the NCTL shows that schools did provide a detailed schedule of the form of alternative worship that was being proposed along with their applications for determinations and their renewal, including a

---

[333] Ibid, page 16.

[334] This is set out in the DfE Circular 1/94 'Religious education and collective worship', 31 January 1994. Available at: www.gov.uk/government/uploads/system/uploads/attachment_data/file/281929/Collective_worship_in_schools.pdf.

schedule of assembly topics.[335] The approval was also given in the context of the locally agreed curriculum on religious education, which Park View continued to teach, notwithstanding that the regulations for academies meant that it need not. For its part, the Clarke Report does not mention the SACRE or the locally agreed religious education curriculum (it arises just twice in the report, mentioned by a witness, but only briefly and in passing). Once again, this is something that arises as an issue in the NCTL hearings when it emerges that Simone Whitehouse, Religious Education Adviser to Birmingham SACRE, had provided evidence to the Clarke Report that was supportive of PVET and confirmed that its practices were agreed with Birmingham SACRE.[336]

Both reports seem to find that the schools are 'too Muslim' – after all, the context is the charge of 'Islamification' – but they do not reflect on what an appropriate Muslim ethos would be. Reference is made to the schools being not faith designated, but as we have seen, this does not mean they cannot have a religious ethos. Indeed, without a determination, they are required to at least have Christian assemblies. All instances of Muslim practice – such as provision of space and time for private prayer (including the call to prayer, which the Clarke Report explicitly refers to as 'coercive'[337]), Muslim assemblies, provision of Halal food, separate provision for girls and boys in physical education – are gathered under the idea that they represent an undue emphasis on Islam or the following of 'strict Muslim principles'. Yet they are practices which appear in the Ofsted reports prior to 2014 as unremarkable, except to state that they serve the pupils well and are contributing to their confidence and integration.

On the latter point, the Kershaw Report is directly contradictory, especially when considering the role of Birmingham City Council. On the one hand, it suggests that the 'proper commitment of BCC to community cohesion has, at times, and disastrously, overridden

[335] The National College for Teaching and Leadership and Birmingham Schools. Witness Statement of Simone Whitehouse.
[336] "NCTL, May 2017, 'Panel decisions and reasons', paragraph 125.
[337] Clarke Report, page 16.

the even more important commitment to doing what is right'. Barely two paragraphs later it states that 'there is no alignment of the schooling system in Birmingham with regeneration or community cohesion strategies (including Prevent), each of which is crucially dependent upon the delivery of the highest quality provision to improve standards of learning and outcomes'.[338] They relate this to a lack of an overarching council policy or document that sets out its approach to improving education and challenging schools on delivery of high quality education. Yet, as we have already indicated, schools in Birmingham were above the national average in terms of pupil performance and in terms of the proportion of schools with outstanding Ofsted ratings.

The Clarke Report also fails to consider the guidance to schools about community cohesion and, indeed, seems to interpret the latter in a manner that is similar to media reporting where a concern with community cohesion is seen as a potential constraint on authorities in acting in relation to complaints for fear of community tension or being charged with 'racism'. The interview transcript with a senior officer within the Children's and People's Directorate is more revealing because the phrase 'community tension' is replaced by 'community cohesion' in a question directly asked by Peter Clarke: 'Did you ever feel under any pressure not to ask for or suggest firmer action because of the concerns about community cohesion?'[339] While it may be legitimate to point to fears of community tension as a possible constraint on action, there is a clear conflation of tension with the policy objectives of community cohesion. It is a concern that there is no discussion of how practices at the schools might, in fact, relate to the requirements by schools (and other authorities) to promote community cohesion, with the latter widely understood as integral to the Prevent strategy, rather than in conflict with it.

As we have seen, the school at the heart of the affair – Park View – had produced exactly that alignment of community cohesion and

---

[338] Kershaw Report, page 13.
[339] Clarke Report, pages 6, 84.

the improvement of standards of learning and outcomes which is the long-term aim of government policy. It was commended in just these terms by successive Ofsted reports between 2001 and 2012, as we saw in the last chapter. But, for the Kershaw Report, there was 'a determined effort to change schools, often by unacceptable practices, in order to influence educational and religious provision for the students served'.[340] This is a view shared with the Clarke Report. They seem unable to countenance that the alignment they endorse, in principle, could be produced in schools with a Muslim religious ethos.

Pointing the finger?

The focus of the Clarke Report is a little different from that of the Kershaw Report and this difference is part of the reason why Park View comes to be at the centre of attention. The report finds an individual, namely Tahir Alam, to be the instigator of the 'plot'. In part, this derived from the poorly photocopied document included with the Trojan Horse letter. It is reproduced as annex 2 of the Clarke Report and it begins: '[illegible] the bigger agenda. It was Tahir Alam who wrote the Meeting the [needs of Muslim] pupils in state schools' publication and he fully believes that without [illegible] faith of Muslim pupils will break down, there will be disaffection, drugs [illegible] sexually-transmitted diseases amongst our children'.

The Clarke Report refers to being informed about specific events at schools – especially Oldknow, Park View, Golden Hillock and Nansen, but also Adderley Park – involving restriction on the teaching of personal and relationship education, displays of Islamic posters, provision of facilities for private prayer, anti-Western assemblies, lesson work sheets at Park View which stated that a wife must consent to sex with her husband, the recording of 'what appeared to be Al Qaeda terrorist videos into a DVD format'. These are presented in chapter 4 of the report, together with a list of specific egregious instances at PVET in chapter 6, alongside the comment, 'it is only fair to point out the

---

[340] Kershaw Report, page 4.

Trust disputed most, if not all, of the following allegations'.[341] We will see in the next section that the first occasion when they could do so, in fact, would be the NCTL hearings over a year after the publication of the Clarke Report and, in the context of media reporting, with those examples having come to be regarded as the 'facts'.

As we have seen, neither the Kershaw Report nor the Clarke Report define what an acceptable Muslim ethos for a school would be, notwithstanding that, as we have seen, all schools are supposed to have daily acts of collective worship and religious education. Neither referred to the locally agreed curriculum on religious education, notwithstanding that it was required for all schools, except academies and free schools. As we have also said, Park View continued to teach the curriculum after it became an academy, as well as having submitted its plans for assemblies at its last determination from the SACRE in 2007, plans which were not different from those subsequently criticised as too Islamic.

Yet the Clarke Report describes 'a sustained and coordinated agenda to impose upon children … the segregationist attitudes and practices of a hardline and politicised strand of Sunni Islam … In the context of schooling, it manifests itself as the imposition of an aggressively separatist and intolerant agenda, incompatible with full participation in a plural, secular democracy'. The report goes on to state that 'it goes beyond the kind of social conservatism practiced in some faith schools which may be consistent with universal human rights and respectful of other communities. It appears to be a deliberate attempt to convert secular state schools into exclusive faith schools in all but name'.[342] The reference to 'a social conservatism of some faith schools which *may be consistent with universal human rights*' is telling. The European Convention on Human Rights (ECHR) carries a different emphasis where religious faith is a protected human right and not seen as something potentially in conflict with human rights.

---

[341] Clarke Report, page 52.
[342] Ibid, page 48.

For example, protocol 1, article 2 gives parents the right to have their children schooled in their own faith or philosophical convictions.[343]

The further problem lies with the report's reference to a 'secular state school', which, as we have seen, is at odds with the legal requirement on all schools to have religious education and collective worship. But it also neglects the fact that guidelines on schools also advise them to be sensitive to the cultural and religious needs of their pupils, which can be expressed in separate teaching of some topics, and in physical education. Indeed, we have also seen that Park View had National Healthy School status during the very period it was operating under an apparently hardline agenda. In this context, the Clarke Report cites a document co-authored by Tahir Alam and published by the Muslim Council of Britain, *Meeting the Needs of Muslim Pupils in State Schools*.[344] Perhaps significantly, the Clarke Report misses out that the title given is the document's subtitle and the full title is *Towards Greater Understanding: Meeting the Needs of Muslim Pupils in State Schools.* This document provides guidance for maintained schools with Muslim pupils. It was discussed by Birmingham SACRE and was part of their reflections on religious education and collective worship in multi-faith Birmingham. Yet the Clarke Report treats it as part of a project of Islamification, writing that 'although such publications often address Muslim schools specifically, the movement aspires to promote Islam more widely within secular and other faith schools'.[345] We have also seen, in Chapter Six, that SACREs and LEAs with significant numbers of Muslim pupils offer similar guidance.

The Clarke Report goes on immediately to a chapter on PVET, where 'a central figure is Tahir Alam, who has extensive contacts within the education field in Birmingham', and has been 'closely involved with the running of Park View School for many years, having been

[343] See European Court of Human Rights (2015) Guide on Article 2 of Protocol No. 1 to the European Convention on Human Rights. Available at: www.echr.coe.int/ Documents/Guide_Art_2_Protocol_1_ENG.pdf.

[344] This document is summarised in annex 6 of the Clarke Report and published in full as an annex to the Kershaw Report.

[345] Clarke Report, page 48.

a governor since the 1990s. He has also exerted influence at other schools as a member of several governing bodies, and more recently at schools that have become part of Park View Education Trust'.[346] The report provides a hub-and-spoke diagram of his connections and different roles – from Birmingham Central Mosque, to Birmingham City Council, Birmingham Governors Association, Birmingham SACRE, Muslim Council of Britain and specific schools. This network provided ample opportunity to influence at 'policy level' and also 'to bring about change through delivering training and membership of governing bodies'.

What is missing is any understanding of the 'heterarchical' governance arrangements that followed the introduction of the academies programme and the way in which this encouraged networks of training and support to disseminate good practices. In this context, it is not unusual to find highly networked individuals in key nodal positions in local institutions. Moreover, by 2006 Park View school had been identified as the most improved school in Birmingham and the joint 15th most improved school in England. In these circumstances, it is likely that schools with a high proportion of Muslim pupils would be interested in how Park View had achieved its success. It was also the case that Birmingham City Council, as part of its schools improvement plans, would be equally keen to engage with the school and seek its influence elsewhere.

In Chapter Six, we suggested that academic success for ethnic minority children is frequently associated with the development of confidence in their own background and that this is not in conflict with the values of the majority culture. In fact, as we have seen, the combination of pride and confidence with tolerance and openness is precisely what Ofsted inspectors described at Park View, as well as noting how this was facilitated by the school's Islamic ethos. Nor do they describe this ethos as entailing a narrow curriculum. However, the Clarke Report takes the view that any accommodation of the needs

---

[346] Ibid, here, and following quotations, from page 50.

of Muslim pupils is tantamount to a problematic 'Islamification' and must involve a 'narrowing'. Thus, it comments that:

> Tahir Alam promoted the concept that schools can (and should) be changed to accommodate the faith needs of Muslim pupils by increasing Muslim representation on governing bodies and then insisting on changes to the ethos, policies and processes of the school ... Mr Alam was the key person determining the policies and activities at Park View School. Most of these appear to be recommendations from the Muslim Council of Britain Report he co-authored in 2007.

Finally, it is declared that 'Park View sought to export its Islamising blueprint'.

The Clarke Report seeks to establish that this blueprint is 'extremist' as defined by the Prevent agenda. In itself, failure by schools to engage with that agenda could not be regarded as a problem because there is no statutory requirement to do so. In any case, we have also seen that the DfE's own commissioned research showed that most schools conflate the duty to promote community cohesion, for which there was at the time a statutory requirement, with the Prevent agenda.[347] In this context, any failure to engage with Prevent shifts to the idea that schools with a high proportion of Muslim pupils should do so as part of more generic 'safeguarding concerns'. This looks like a specific focus on Muslims, but, in any case, the evidence from the same research was that schools with a high proportion of ethnic minority pupils were more likely to be familiar with Prevent and to be putting on specific activities. We saw in the last chapter that Park View *was* engaged in Prevent activities. However, in the absence of a 'benchmark' stating what should be done, and what is done elsewhere, provision can always be said to be insufficient, even where it is greater than at other schools.

The Clarke Report also suggests that there is active opposition to 'British values' evident in the Trojan Horse schools, and Park View

---

[347] See Phillips et al (2011) 'Community cohesion and Prevent'.

in particular. Again, evidence of religious conservatism is insufficient (although an Islamic ethos in a school is not evidence of religious conservatism) and the government's counter-extremism strategy is clear on that point. The Clarke Report cites as evidence of extremism a WhatsApp social media group that operated among male Muslim teachers at PVET between April 2013 and March 2014. It was called the 'Park View Brotherhood' and the Clarke Report devotes a separate chapter to it. Tahir Alam is not a member of the group, though the report clearly believes that some of those who are members are under his influence.

At the outset, it needs to be stated that WhatsApp is a 'private' social media facility, different from public social media like Facebook or Twitter. The messages are only seen by members of the group. There were 3235 separate postings and, as with any such postings, contributors vary in their degree of activity. The Clarke Report states that 'the majority of the postings are innocuous and often mundane'. However, it also suggests that some fall under the definition of extremism as provided by Prevent.[348]

However, the examples from the transcripts that are provided do not meet this definition. For example, there is a discussion of the advantages of gender segregation that refers to the practices of the best private schools, but the teachers involved are divided on the issue, although in principle, they are sympathetic. Another example is a discussion of pro-European bias in accounts of world history, where the value of pupils knowing about the 14th century North African Arab scholar Ibn Khaldoun is put forward. Ibn Khaldoun is widely regarded as one of the most important philosophers of history and politics in the Middle Ages. There is also a brief conversation between two teachers about soliciting support from the pupils for a petition that sought the

---

[348] Clarke Report, page 58. The definition from the 2011 Prevent Strategy is rehearsed prior to the discussion of the evidence: 'Extremism is vocal or active opposition to fundamental British values, including democracy, the rule of law, individual liberty and mutual respect and tolerance of different faiths and beliefs. We also include in our definition calls for the deaths of our armed forces, whether in this country or overseas'.

proscription of the English Defence League, a single post vehemently condemning gay marriage, and posts expressing abhorrence at a report of the use of a shrine in Pakistan as a meeting place for gay men.

There is a presentation about postings after the Boston bombings and the execution of Lee Rigby in which it is suggested that these are hoaxes. However, these responses are in the immediacy of the news, before their status as events is fully corroborated. The Clarke Report states that 'there are other postings which state quite clearly that what happened in Woolwich "*has no place in Islam*", and also a press release from Green Lane Masjid and Community Centre'.[349] There were negative posts about a Mosque holding a fundraising event for 'Help for Heroes', and two posts on a news article on the 'Troops to Teachers scheme'. There were also two images posted of the Israeli flag on lavatory paper.

The Clarke Report does not comment on the private nature of the conversations, but suggests it was significant that they were not 'challenged'. However, many of the exchanges are short and involve few participants and, of course, many of those on the list will not be reading the messages. Notwithstanding the earlier comment that the 'majority' of postings are 'innocuous' and 'mundane', the report concludes that 'the contributions, in terms of links to both news items and images, are overwhelmingly anti-Western, anti-American and anti-Israeli. There are numerous references to the politics of conflicts in Syria, the Middle East and south Asia'.[350] However, it is far from clear that the views are antagonistic to 'British values', even in the Prevent definition. Criticism of Western policy in the Middle East and elsewhere is not, as such, antidemocratic, nor is the repudiation of homosexuality and gay marriage (notwithstanding our own secular liberal commitments on such matters, or the responsibilities of schools to ensure equal opportunities for all its pupils, including protection from discrimination on the grounds of sexuality).

---

[349] Ibid, page 66.
[350] Ibid, page 72.

The What's App messages are treated by the Clarke Report as indications of intolerant attitudes on the part of the teachers involved. However, even if that were to be accepted, which is not straightforward, they would not establish that intolerant attitudes were expressed in the classroom, still less that the Islamic ethos of PVET was intolerant of other religions. That would need to be demonstrated separately. Significantly, in a blog written by the presenting officer of the NCTL case against the senior teachers, Andrew Colman, this distinction seems clear. He discusses another case where a teacher was successfully prosecuted for religious intolerance, and he makes a distinction between views expressed outside at a political meeting (providing they are within the law – the teacher involved was a supporter of the British National Party) and the same views expressed within the school. Mr Colman states that when the teacher 'crossed the boundary of the classroom and shared those views with his pupils, telling them that they were correct in his role as a teacher, he failed to demonstrate the respect for the British values of tolerance and respect for the faiths and beliefs of others that the Teachers' Standards demand'. He went on to state that 'parallel issues are likely to feature in the cases arising out of the Trojan Horse enquiry into Birmingham schools'.[351] It was not until the Counter-Terrorism and Security Act of 2015 published just after Mr Colman's post that teachers were required to promote British values inside and outside of school.[352]

---

[351] Andrew Colman, 'Religion, tolerance & freedom – what private views can a teacher express?', 10 July 2015. Available at: www.2harecourt.com/training-and-knowledge/religion-tolerance-and-freedom-what-private-views-can-a-teacher-express/.

[352] See HM Government (2015) *Revised Prevent Duty Guidance: for England and Wales*, version 2, revised 16 July 2015. Available at: www.gov.uk/government/uploads/system/uploads/attachment_data/file/445977/3799_Revised_Prevent_Duty_Guidance__England_Wales_V2-Interactive.pdf.

Conclusion

In each report, much stands or falls on the idea that an 'Islamic ethos' is, in itself, problematic. We have suggested that this is a misunderstanding, one that is allowed to arise because neither report systematically addresses the issue of the nature of the religious requirements on schools. Indeed, notwithstanding that educational advisers from the Department of Education were part of the Clarke Report, it repeatedly refers to schools without a faith designation as 'secular'. There is a further assumption in each report, too, that an 'Islamic ethos' would be 'intolerant', with the Clarke Report describing the Muslim Council of Britain's guidance on meeting the needs of Muslim pupils in state schools as a document about 'Islamification', although it is, in fact, a document designed to facilitate integration.

Each report addresses 'community cohesion', but they shift between two aspects. One is the idea that authorities were unwilling to act in relation to concerns expressed about governors at some schools because of fear of upsetting 'community cohesion'. Each begins from the assumption that it was potentially inappropriate (putting on 'unreasonable pressure') for there to be concerted action by community members and governors to raise standards in their local schools. However, raising standards in schools is explicitly represented in guidance to them as helping to contribute to long-term community cohesion. In fact, the justification of the academy schools programme was precisely that it would empower local communities to encourage an improvement in standards.

In this context, too, the different requirements on maintained and academy schools are significant and relevant to the evidence of individual complaints. It is not that we wish to diminish perceived harassment and other conflicts, but the process of introducing academies has also been one that has created conflict and opposition within schools. Yet this is not addressed when evaluating the status of any complaint. The reports indicate that many of the claims are 'contested' but do not attempt to reconcile them, or allow a voice to any alternative explanation.

In Chapter One, we set out how multiculturalism facilitated strong Muslim identification with British values based upon respect for plurality and the freedom to express religious practices. Indeed, as we shall see in our conclusion, there is good reason to believe that it is precisely the inculcation of confidence and pride in a pupil's cultural or religious heritage that is one of the means of achieving academic success for ethnic minority pupils of Muslim background and, therefore, one of the means of securing integration in a plural, multicultural Britain.

The reports try to square the circle by suggesting that the behaviours that they criticise are those of Muslims who are a minority in their own communities. The Clarke Report, for example, comments that:

> although good academic results can be achieved through a narrowing of the curriculum and a focus on core subjects, it comes at a cost. That is that young people, instead of enjoying a broadening and enriching experience in school, are having their horizons narrowed. They are not being equipped to flourish in the inevitably diverse environments of further education, the workplace or indeed any environment outside predominantly Muslim communities. They are thus potentially denied the opportunity to enjoy and exploit to the full the opportunities of modern multicultural Britain.[353]

It is well to recall that the reports trace the problems they believe they have identified back into the period when Park View school was in special measures. They do not believe that they arise with its conversion to an academy in 2012, but are longstanding. The creation of the PVET in 2012 merely enabled it to directly export its 'Islamising blueprint' to two other schools. Yet throughout this long period, Ofsted reports described the pupils as tolerant, well-adjusted and well equipped for life in multicultural Britain, including success in further education following on from their academic achievements. The school no longer

---

[353] Clarke Report, page 13.

has above average academic achievements whilst the experiences and culture of many of its pupils have been roundly vilified.

Taken together, the two reports set out to investigate allegations arising from the Trojan Horse letter, but they reproduce an account of 'circles of influence', extremist ideology and the introduction of Islamic practices in schools which is precisely the narrative of the original letter. Most seriously, however, as we shall see, evidence was presented to the Clarke Report that was directly exculpatory of PVET from Birmingham SACRE and from an official at the Department for Education responsible for the academies programme, yet this evidence is not discussed in the report. This evidence was available to the Kershaw Report, since it did not fall into the class of statements given to Clarke under conditions of strict confidentiality, yet it is not discussed in that report either.

NINE

The NCTL hearings and their collapse

In a short space of time – from early March to June 2014 – a particular narrative of the Trojan Horse affair became firmly established. This was that a small group of individuals, associated with PVET and operating with a hardline and conservative religious agenda, had taken over control of a number of local community (that is non-faith) schools in East Birmingham and had sought to establish an Islamic curriculum. In doing so, head teachers and other teaching staff had either been bullied into line or had been forced out. This narrative was given particular emphasis by the Clarke Report, which proposed that this conservative religious agenda was also extremist (as defined under Prevent) involving active hostility to 'British values'.

The nature of the evidence put forward was largely statements by witnesses involved in changes in local schools in the context of the government's academies programme. There was little opportunity for those at the centre of the charges to provide their own account. Although Ofsted inspections allow some involvement by a school, there is no formal opportunity to engage with a draft report and have inspectors reflect upon and modify their judgement (though we have seen suggestions that the 2014 Ofsted report on Park View Academy was modified at the instigation of Ofsted or the DfE).[354]

---

[354] See Adams, 'Ofsted inspectors make U-turn', *The Guardian*, 30 May 2014.

Inspections are simply a description of what is said to be found at the time of the visit. Nor is there an obligation upon the inspectors to reflect on those findings in the light of previous reports. Equally, the Clarke and Kershaw Reports took witness statements from many individuals, but did not seek to test whether the events described had, in fact, taken place, or were as described to them. Indeed, the Clarke Report provides a list of 20 serious incidents at PVET, about which it comments, somewhat laconically, 'it is only fair to point out that the Trust disputed most, if not all, of the allegations'.[355] This comment is itself misleading, since, as we shall see, exculpatory evidence was provided not only by the Trust, but also by an official at the DfE responsible for the academies programme and by the religious education adviser at Birmingham SACRE, but those views are not presented in the Clarke Report.[356]

Yet the 'serious incidents' were widely reported in the press as illustrations of the problems in the schools. For example, it was reported – among other claims – that teachers at PVET mixed religious views into the teaching of science, taught that wives had to consent to sex with their husbands and that there was no rape within marriage, coerced children into prayer (including during lessons), had invited an extremist speaker to address an assembly, and had banned Christmas celebrations. Most significantly – because it was the one incident that the House of Commons select committee that considered the reports in March 2015 accepted as a serious example of extremism[357] – there was a report that IT technicians at Park View had recorded onto a DVD a terrorist video believed to be from Al Qaeda. In fact, although this

---

[355] Clarke Report, page 52.

[356] These were statements whose existence became known as part of the challenge over the non-disclosure of documents at the NCTL Panel Hearing against the senior teachers. NCTL, May 2017, 'Professional conduct panel outcome', paragraph 125.

[357] Education Select Committee (2015) 'Extremism in schools', paragraph 8. The Select Committee concluded: 'we note once again that no evidence of extremism or radicalisation, apart from a single isolated incident, was found and that there is no evidence of a sustained plot nor of a similar situation pertaining elsewhere in the country' (paragraph 80).

allegation was initially brought forward as part of the NCTL schedule of charges against teachers at PVET, it was dropped before the hearings began (there was a first Case Management Hearing on 27 July 2015 and a second on 27 August 2015 which altered the charges). It had emerged that the recording was made at the request of West Midlands Counter Terrorism Unit to use as illustrative material in a session for pupils at the school on the risks of radicalisation. In other words, it was an example of the very opposite of what had been stated in the Clarke Report and reported in the press; it was an example of the school's engagement with the Prevent agenda.

We saw in Chapter Seven that the EFA Review had also accused PVET of financial irregularities and poor procedures. External accountants were commissioned to examine these irregularities in June 2014 and do a full audit. They reported in February 2015, having found only minor irregularities, mainly associated with lack of clarity over procedures.[358] They are not part of the charges made by the NCTL against the teachers, in contrast to high profile cases against other academy trusts, indicating that they were judged to be of a low level and they were not pursued as instances of misconduct.[359]

Possibly Peter Clarke, as a former serving policemen, felt that the place to test allegations was in something equivalent to a court of law. He recommended that professional misconduct hearings should be convened. In the public mind, however, the narrative was firmly established through regular statements to the press which referred back to the Trojan Horse affair as part of the framing for other stories. For example, reports on government policies to extend Prevent to include

---

[358] Education Funding Agency, *Park View Educational Trust Investigation Report*, February 2015. Available at: www.gov.uk/government/uploads/system/uploads/attachment_data/file/401897/Investigation_report_Park_View_Educational_Trust.pdf.

[359] See for example, NCTL, May 2017, 'Professional conduct panel outcome', chapter 3. See also the discussion of the NCTL's different handling of clams of serious financial irregularities at other academies compared with the Trojan Horse affair by John Dickens in 'The inside story of the Trojan Horse trial collapse', *Schools Week*, 7 June 2017. Available at: http://schoolsweek.co.uk/long-read-is-the-nctl-fit-for-purpose-after-trojan-horse-collapse/.

extremist ideology and measures to tackle extremist 'entryism'[360] used the case, as did reports on a renewed emphasis on the promotion of shared values (now called 'fundamental British values') in schools.[361] In each case, the government used the Trojan Horse affair as an example of what could go wrong, and the media faithfully reported in those terms.

Similarly, having once endorsed Park View Academy as exemplary, Sir Michael Wilshaw regularly referred to the Trojan Horse affair and claimed that there were continuing problems in Birmingham schools (and elsewhere) in speeches throughout his term of office. He warned that a repeat of the so-called Trojan Horse scandal, which saw a radical Islamic ethos introduced to schools in the city, was likely unless the government acted.[362]

The NCTL hearings, problems of procedure

The NCTL is the body responsible for teaching standards. Previously, that function was carried out by the General Teaching Council for England, established by the Teaching and Higher Education Act of 1998 which set up separate bodies for England, Wales and Scotland. Michael Gove, as Secretary of State for Education, announced its closure in 2010 as part of the government's 'bonfire of quangos', directed against non-departmental independent advisory or regulatory bodies. It was replaced by the Teaching Standards Agency in 2012 and renamed the National College for Teaching and Leadership in 2013. It is an executive agency within the DfE.

The NCTL hearings represented the first opportunity for the individuals who had been named in the investigation reports and in the media as part of a plot to Islamicise schools to respond, yet they had to do so in the context of widespread assumptions of their guilt. In April 2015, Richard Kerbaj and Sian Griffiths reported in the *Sunday*

[360] Home Office (2015) *Counter-Extremism Strategy*.
[361] Department for Education (2014) 'Promoting fundamental British values'.
[362] Report by Sian Griffiths, 'Children at risk in "rotten borough" Birmingham', *Sunday Times*, 11 December 2016. Available at: www.thetimes.co.uk/article/children-at-risk-in-rotten-borough-birmingham-fl5f00pkb.

Times that the NCTL was 'currently looking at about 30 teachers, but in total there are about 100 who will be targeted'.[363] This served to create the idea of the scale of the problem and the expectations of what was to come, yet no other cases were brought forward.

In the event, cases were brought against just 12 teachers (15 in some newspaper reports), mostly associated with PVET (one hearing, concerning three teachers, subsequently reduced to two, involved teachers at Oldknow primary). The teachers were divided among four hearings, which all began at around the same time in early October 2015. The hearings took place before a lay panel (of three members) supported by legal advisers, with a barrister and solicitor representing NCTL and barristers and solicitors representing those charged with misconduct. The hearings took place under court rules and procedures.

The hearings did not begin until October 2015, with a schedule for conclusion before Christmas of that year. In fact, they were to go on for another 18 months (the hearings were not continuous, and, if they ran over schedule, new dates had to be found when the Panel members and lawyers were available). One hearing was set up to address the senior leadership team at PVET, which included some who had previously held senior positions at Park View school. Thus, Lindsey Clarke, former head teacher at Park View and subsequently executive head teacher at the Trust was one, as was Monzoor Hussain, acting head teacher at Park View Academy, Hardeep Saini, acting principal at Golden Hillock and formerly at Park View, Arshad Hussain (no relation to Monzoor Hussain), assistant principal at Park View Academy, and Razwan Faraz, formerly a teacher at Park View and vice-principal at Nansen Primary (Hearing 1). The other hearings involved two junior teachers at Park View, one of whom had also been seconded to Oldknow and Golden Hillock (Hearing 2), and three teachers from Park View at a different hearing (Hearing 3), with the case against a fourth teacher from Park View at this hearing dropped. This hearing

---

[363] Richard Kerbaj and Sian Griffiths, '100 Islamist teachers face ban', *Sunday Times*, 5 April 2015. Available at: www.thesundaytimes.co.uk/sto/news/uk_news/Education/article1540185.ece.

was scheduled to finish after Hearing 1. Another hearing involved the former acting head teacher and another teacher at Oldknow (Hearing 4). The teachers at Hearing 3 were separated, with one teacher found not guilty in September 2016. A third teacher was initially included in Hearing 2, but the case against him was postponed because of serious ill health. A separate case was brought against a teacher at Park View and Golden Hillock in an individual hearing which concluded with a guilty verdict, but no ban, in February 2016. It is clear that Hearing 1 is the most important of the hearings since it involved the senior leadership team at PVET (the chair of the Board of Governors, Tahir Alam, was not under the jurisdiction of NCTL, but was separately banned from involvement in school management).[364]

We set out in the introduction to the book how one case (Hearing 2) that had concluded in February 2016 went to the High Court on appeal and, in October 2016, its findings were quashed on grounds of procedural irregularities involving failures to disclose evidence that had been presented in Hearing 1 (although the NCTL was subsequently allowed to convene a new hearing). However, this raised the question that there might be broader issues of the disclosure of evidence relevant to Hearing 1. There began a process of reviewing areas in which there might be documents for disclosure – including, but not only, statements provided to the Clarke Report. The High Court Appeal judgement had generated hostile media reports, which repeated the allegations against the teachers.[365] Now hostility was directed at the possible disclosure of evidence statements that had been provided to the Clarke Report under conditions of anonymity.[366] This gave rise

[364] He brought an appeal against his ban from involvement in school management in March 2017.

[365] See 'Two teachers in "Trojan horse" school who fed pupils a "diet of Islam", segregated assemblies and ignored sex education are allowed BACK into classrooms by a High Court judge', *Daily Mail*, 13 October 2016. Available at: www.dailymail.co.uk/news/article-3836622/Two-teachers-Trojan-horse-school-allowed-classrooms.html.

[366] See, for example, Turner, 'Alarm at move to reveal identity of whistleblowers who exposed Trojan Horse scandal', *The Telegraph*, 4 January 2017. See also Martin Robinson, 'Dozens of anonymous whistleblowers whose evidence helped expose

to further legal representations (including on behalf of some of those witnesses) in February 2017, and, finally, the identification of some 1600 pages of documents to be considered for their relevance to the defence. This all took place after the main evidence for prosecution and defence had been presented and witnesses questioned.

In fact, the evidence that was most at issue was not provided under conditions of anonymity, although some witnesses were doing so (as Witness A, Witness B, etc). There was an interest in their statements to the Clarke Report and the extent to which claims had subsequently been modified, but this need not have involved any breach of anonymity. However, as we will see when we consider the evidence in the next section, the key issues of disclosure concerned witnesses who had made more extended statements to the Clarke Report that included material that was favourable to the defence and yet had not been included either in the Clarke Report or in the witness statements elicited by NCTL. There was also an issue of disclosure of material outside the Clarke Report; for example material associated with preparations for the EFA Review visit to PVET.

These later developments were symptomatic of a larger problem created by the delays in hearings. There was intermittent media reporting about the hearings, especially during the period that the NCTL presented its evidence. The latter was completed by December 2015. The evidence for the teachers was completed by June 2016, with little media reporting of their detailed rebuttal (together with documentary evidence and supporting witnesses) of the claims against them, which took place after December 2015 when media interest had waned. The Panel had already put back the date at which it would make its judgements from 18 December 2015 to 29 July 2016, then to 14 October 2016 and, then again, to 23 December 2016, a date that

the Trojan Horse plot in Birmingham schools have been told their identities will be revealed to the ringleaders', *Daily Mail*, 4 January 2014. Available at: www.dailymail.co.uk/news/article-4087404/Dozens-anonymous-whistleblowers-evidence-helped-expose-Trojan-Horse-plot-Birmingham-schools-told-identities-revealed-ringleaders.html.

was itself postponed while consideration was given to the disclosure of documents following the High Court ruling on Hearing 2.

Hearing 1 itself finally collapsed in May 2017 on grounds of irregularities so grave that, in the Panel's view, they represented 'an abuse of the process which is of such seriousness that it offends the Panel's sense of justice and propriety. What has happened has brought the integrity of the process into disrepute'.[367] The NCTL could have applied for a judicial review of the decision, but decided to drop all outstanding cases. In the event, just one teacher was sanctioned (a five-year ban – the case against the other teacher was dismissed) as the outcome of a hearing (Hearing 4) that had already concluded, where that teacher had not had the benefit of the undisclosed documents whose potential relevance had led to the findings in Hearing 2 being quashed.[368]

The reasons for the Panel decision to discontinue the main hearing against the senior teachers make up 28 pages of text and are not restricted to discussion of the NCTL misleading the Panel about the use of transcripts of statements given to the Clarke Report in the preparation of witness statements for the NCTL hearing. At different points in the hearing, lawyers for the defence had made applications for the case to be dismissed – for example, immediately following the completion of the presentation of the prosecution case in June 2016 and at other times, up to and including on 3 May 2017, when there was the submission of a Note from the solicitors representing the NCTL (although the responsible partner failed to attend, as requested by the Panel, and the presenting officer for the NCTL case was also unavailable to respond to questions). This Note, the Panel concluded, contained an admission that they and the defence lawyers had been *deliberately misled*. The Panel decision sets out the reasons for the discontinuation, but it also rehearsed reasons why it had not previously stopped the case in the light of other claimed problems with procedures.

---

[367] NCTL, May 2017, 'Professional conduct panel outcome', paragraph 174.

[368] See, Richard Adam, 'Trojan Horse affair: remaining disciplinary proceedings dropped, *The Guardian*, 28 July 2017,. Available at: https://amp.theguardian.com/education/2017/jul/28/trojan-horse-affair-remaining-disciplinary-proceedings-dropped-teachers-birmingham-schools.

The Panel considered the claims in the light of article 6 of the European Convention on Human Rights concerning the right to a fair trial.[369] The Crown Prosecution Service also provides guidance on fair process.[370] It does so under four headings: delay; adverse media publicity; non-disclosure by prosecutor; and inability of the defence to examine evidence or to question prosecution witnesses. The NCTL Hearings potentially failed under all four categories.[371] For example, the hearings were still underway nearly three years after the allegations were first raised in the Kershaw and Clarke Reports. In the meantime, the media had reported those allegations as fact, with the government citing the Trojan Horse affair in justification of its counter-extremism strategy in October 2015 just as the substantive hearings were starting. The delays allowed adverse publicity to build and continue uncontested for a very significant length of time.

Indeed, the then Secretary for State for Education, Nicky Morgan, gave a major speech in January 2016 at Bethnal Green Academy where she stated:

> what defines every extremist organisation throughout history is that more than anything else their mission is to close and narrow young minds – to indoctrinate, instruct and inspire hatred. That's what we saw in the Birmingham schools at the heart of the Trojan Horse Affair: a concerted attempt to limit young people's world view and spread poisonous views which had no place in our education system.[372]

---

[369] European Court of Human Rights (2013) *Rights to a Fair Trial*. Available at: www.echr.coe.int/Documents/Guide_Art_6_ENG.pdf.

[370] See Crown Prosecution Service, *Legal Guidance: Abuse of Process*. Available at: www.cps.gov.uk/legal/a_to_c/abuse_of_process/.

[371] We should note here that the guidance is designed for criminal prosecutions, but can be regarded as applying to all cases subject to court rules.

[372] Nicky Morgan speaks about tackling extremism, 19 January 2016. Available at: https://www.gov.uk/government/speeches/nicky-morgan-speaks-about-tackling-extremism.

This is significant since the NCTL hearings report to the Secretary for State to decide on the nature of the sanction to be applied in the light of any findings of misconduct, findings and sanction which she seemed to have presumed in her speech and in advance of the conclusion of the hearings. Nicky Morgan went on to declare, 'that's why we are taking action to remove those responsible from our classrooms'.

The Panel's reasoning addresses each issue singly, without, however, considering how they are mutually compounded. The Panel found precedents where the dates of hearings were taking place over a number of months, and also proposed that judgements by a Panel of three members when compared with a decision by a judge sitting alone would be likely to take up more time.[373] Of course, the latter suggests that more time should have been scheduled, it does not explain the fact that the times set aside for the hearings were fragmented. It is not unusual for insufficient time to have been scheduled in the light of the nature of arguments that emerge *in the course of the consideration of evidence*. What is most unusual is for a hearing to *begin in the knowledge that it is going to take place over fragmented sessions.*

Were the hearing to have continued, the Panel would have been basing its decision on its recollection of witness statements going back 18 months. However, it was argued that the production of transcripts facilitated recall: 'the Panel was able to maintain a clear recollection of the witnesses who gave evidence but, even had this been an issue, it would not have been ameliorated to any extent by the hearing taking place in one block of time taking account of the fact that it took place over 34 days.'[374] They also cited a judgement in another case to the effect that, 'the balance must always be struck between the public interest in ensuring that those who are accused of serious crimes should be tried and the competing public interest in ensuring

[373] NCTL, May 2017, 'Professional conduct panel outcome', paragraphs 33, 36.
[374] Ibid, paragraph 36. We might note here that, under CPS Guidance, delay would normally refer to the time taken to bring a case to court, but would also apply to the delays of proceedings once underway, insofar as those delays had an impact upon the process of arriving at a judgement – for example, memory recall of witnesses and their demeanour under cross-examination.

that executive misconduct does not undermine public confidence in the criminal justice system and bring it into disrepute'.[375] As we shall see, the Panel seems to be extraordinarily willing to regard 'executive misconduct' as a singular event and not something that is evident from the special Ofsted reports onwards. In its view, failures of process are contingent rather than systematic. In addition, the Panel was not considering a 'serious crime', but a charge of 'professional misconduct' where the consequences were grave for those concerned but where the public interest would be best served by a judicious consideration of the evidence, rather than one where the rights of those accused were breached.

Lawyers for the defence in Hearing 1 had raised a number of fundamental issues with how the NCTL was conducting the case(s). These were associated with the separation of the different hearings and the problem of late disclosure. These were issues that followed the quashing of the judgement in Hearing 2 and arose as a concern when the Panel appeared minded to consider late disclosure as a 'misunderstanding' rather than deliberate. The Panel had convened on 3 May to consider this matter, before being presented with the Note from the NCTL solicitors. The defence lawyers were also concerned about the 'framing' of the charges against the teachers by the NCTL. We will discuss the latter in the next section.

The hearings were not only fragmented in terms of hearing evidence, they were also separated. It is not clear why this was done. NCTL probably thought it was relatively unproblematic, with all cases initially due to conclude at more or less the same time – 18 December 2015 for Hearing 1 and 18 November for the other hearings. However, even this gap might be taken to be prejudicial for judgements in any later case. This is especially so given that the charges against all the teachers were, in effect, that they were involved in a conspiracy (as the Clarke Report had alleged). Guilty outcomes in the earlier hearings of junior teachers would potentially put pressure upon Panel members in the later hearing, since it would not be comprehensible that the junior

---

[375] Ibid, paragraph 18.

teachers could be found guilty of something for which their seniors were not also guilty. In the case of a conspiracy, it would be usual for all those party to it to be heard together, even if their defences might be different and relate to their degree of seniority.

The evidence presented in the hearings, especially that presented for the defence, was different at each hearing. Clearly, there was a risk that the same instances of alleged illegitimate practices would be presented in the different hearings, with counter-evidence unavailable to some of those hearings. This would offer the possibility of contrary findings on matters supposedly of 'fact'. This became a reality when the findings in Hearing 2 were quashed in the light of the failure to disclose evidence. The judge did not rule on whether the new evidence would have led to a different conclusion, since that evidence was currently under determination in Hearing 1. Nor did the judge state that the separation of hearings *could not lead to a fair outcome*, as the appeal had proposed; that was a matter that would also need to be considered in the light of what happened at those other hearings, possibly as the basis of separate appeals to the High Court.

The issues of concern are broad in that, where witnesses appear across different hearings, their responses to questioning can become 'rehearsed', especially if not challenged because the evidence to do so was not available. This compounds the problem that earlier media reporting might also be regarded by witnesses as having corroborated their own understandings, for example regarding the status of Islamic practices in a supposedly 'secular' school.[376]

These concerns arose in Hearing 1, when, following limited disclosure of the Clarke transcripts for the purpose of determining their relevance and, therefore, admissibility, one of the lawyers for the defence noticed similarities between their content and statements given in written evidence submitted to the hearing. She inferred that this suggested that the witnesses to the hearing had their testimony to the Clarke Report to hand when preparing their statements. She was severely criticised for the impropriety of her inference, with the

---

[376] This is touched upon in paragraphs 118–120 of the Panel's reasons. Ibid.

view expressed by the presenting officer for the NCTL case that 'it was not surprising that there should be such similarity because it just means that the witnesses' accounts are consistent'.[377]

The Panel was further confronted by the fact that late disclosure occurred after witnesses had already appeared and they could not be cross-examined about their evidence. However, following a lengthy discussion across four pages, the Panel concluded that allowing the submission of new evidence (arising from some of the Clarke transcripts, but also of other documents, amounting to some 1600 pages) would enable the defence to challenge the credibility and reliability of some evidence without the need for cross-examination.[378] Indeed, in the view of the Panel some statements directly supported the defence case, so cross-examination was not necessary. In other instances, it was the presenting officer for NCTL that might wish to cross examine, but 'it is very unlikely that such an application from NCTL would find any favour with the Panel'. It had already been confirmed that the NCTL presenting officer 'did not intend to apply for leave to submit any further evidence'. None of these difficulties, in the Panel's view, made it impossible for the teachers to receive a fair hearing, notwithstanding that it was a 'wholly unsatisfactory situation'.[379]

The Panel summed up:

> Clearly, what should have happened is that the NCTL, with the assistance of its lawyers, should have fulfilled its responsibilities with regard to disclosure before the hearing commenced. The material disclosed since November 2016 which, by the NCTL's own admission, is capable of assisting the teachers' case or damaging that of the NCTL, should have been available to the teachers when preparing their defences to the allegations

---

[377] Ibid, paragraph 83.

[378] See, for example, the discussion at paragraph 124. Ibid.

[379] Ibid, paragraphs 125, 122, 126.

prior to the commencement of the hearing in October 2015. It should also have been available when testing the evidence of the NCTL's witnesses.[380]

No doubt the Panel was moved in its opinion by the 'genuine public interest and importance in knowing the findings of the Panel in respect of the allegations which have been made'. In the end, it emerged that the Panel had been misled and it judged that, 'there has been a lack of candour and openness with regard to the underlying reasons for those failures and a lack of cooperation in assisting the Panel to get to the bottom of what has happened'. Even at this point it regarded it as 'an extraordinarily serious error of judgement as opposed to bad faith'. However, the case was discontinued because it was, 'of such seriousness that it offends the Panel's sense of justice and propriety'.[381]

What, we might ask, of the sense of justice of the teachers? The case was discontinued without clearing them of the charges against them and alongside continued publicity of claims that were rebutted at the hearings. It is to this we now turn: the nature of the charges and the evidence associated with them.

… as charged

In this section, we will consider the charges against the teachers, for which they were to be judged by the Panels at the different hearings. We will consider Hearing 1 in detail, since that is where the core of the case against all the teachers was to be made.

As we have seen, what lies behind all the cases are the various reports on the Trojan Horse affair, but especially the Clarke Report, which recommended that misconduct cases be brought against teachers for their involvement in a 'plot' that it claimed to have uncovered. The Clarke Report (but not the Kershaw Report) was provided as evidence by the NCTL in presenting its case. However, it was offered only as

---

[380] Ibid, paragraph 26.
[381] Ibid, paragraphs 26, 173, 169, 174.

the 'background' against which the case was being brought. In the light of the failure to disclose evidence from the report, it would seem that this ambiguity of status was designed precisely to avoid directly addressing witness statements made to the Clarke team. In the Opening Note of the NCTL case (which documents and explains the charges), it is stated:

the case has attracted considerable publicity but you will set that all aside and decide the matter judiciously according to the evidence. It has also generated a number of enquiries and you have the Clarke report within your papers. That report is not, though, the primary evidence on which you should decide this case. Whereas it contains useful background information, the primary evidence comes from the witnesses from whom you will hear.[382]

Of course, the publicity associated with the Clarke Report was very significant. However, while the report was to be regarded as a source of 'information', it was not something that could be tested at the hearing, except indirectly.[383] At the outset, then, the intention was that some of the witnesses who had provided evidence to the Clarke (and Kershaw) investigations would present their testimony separately

---

[382] NCTL Opening Note NCTL v Monzoor Hussain, Arshad Hussain, Razwan Faraz, Hardeep Saini and Lindsey Clark, paragraph 9.

[383] We indicated in the preface to the book that one of the authors was an expert witness called by the defence in Hearing 1. Part of the remit was to comment on the Clarke Report. Once the proceedings were underway, lawyers for the DfE made an application to the Speaker's Office for a ruling that the witness report should be set aside as a breach of Parliamentary privilege. This was a claim that the Clarke Report was made to the House of Commons and, therefore, should not be subject to criticism in a court process. In the event, legal advice to the Speaker's Office ruled against such an interpretation. Significantly, a similar claim has been made in the ongoing court process in the Mau Mau rebellion reparations case. See report by Owen Bowcott, 'Claim that MP lied about Kenya massacre "may be in contempt of parliament"', *The Guardian*, 21 March 2017. Available at: www.theguardian.com/world/2017/mar/21/kenya-mau-mau-case-lawyers-contempt-parliament-foreign-office.

to the NCTL hearing. It would only be this evidence that would be tested, though it would be treated as evidence of the conspiracy that was outlined in the Clarke Report. It was this approach by NCTL which was in disarray once it was admitted that the witness statements provided as evidence to the NCTL hearing had been drawn up in the light of earlier statements to the Clarke team – in other words, they were basing their evidence to the NCTL on transcripts previously supplied to the Clarke enquiry.[384]

The Opening Note does, however, contain a very significant variation from the Clarke Report, at the same time as upholding that report's narrative of a conspiracy. According to the NCTL, the case was not about *extremism*. Instead, the case was about:

> the failure to respect diversity. The education of children in a number of schools in Birmingham was altered at the instigation of a group of like-minded individuals who all shared deeply-held religious beliefs. They were not malicious or ill-willed but they believed that the best way to educate the children of their community was to make them mirror their vision of good Muslims.[385]

This approach was somewhat compromised by the fact that one of their key witnesses was an education adviser to the Clarke Report, Ann Connor, who had also been a member of the EFA Review of PVET. She did believe that the case was one of extremism, as defined under Prevent, although, under cross-examination, she was unable to

---

[384] In the words of the NCTL lawyer explaining this situation, 'someone took the decision to put what they considered to be relevant material into a witness statement. Mainly without revealing the fact that that person had given evidence and that there was a transcript of that evidence to the Clarke Enquiry'. NCTL, May 2017, 'Professional conduct panel outcome', paragraph 106. The Panel comments: 'it was then admitted that such a decision would have to have been made when the person taking the statement was in possession of the Clarke transcript'. Ibid.

[385] NCTL Opening Note, paragraph 10.

THE NCTL HEARINGS AND THEIR COLLAPSE

provide any details of guidance to schools, other than the July 2015 guidance, which post-dated the period in question.[386]

Indeed, the Panel in Hearing 2 made its initial judgement of findings in line with that set out in the Opening Note for Hearing 1, that the case was *not about extremism*. However, it was asked by the DfE to amend this aspect of its judgement. Thus, Mr Justice Phillips, in his High Court judgement, states:

> The Panel expressly stated in each decision, when pronounced on 9 February 2016, that the allegations were 'in no way concerned with extremism'. It appears that this wording troubled the Head of the Department for Education's Due Diligence and Counter Extremism Group, Hardip Begol. He asked for publication to be delayed pending 'clarification'. With the apparent agreement of the chair of the Panel, the decisions were amended prior to publication so as to state that the allegations against Mr Anwar and Mr Ahmed were 'in no way concerned with *violent* extremism'.[387]

The nature of the EFA Review's attitude to the PVET was also a matter of concern for the lawyers representing the teachers in Hearing 1. Ann Connor, for example, declared that she had limited knowledge of discussions at the DfE that might have taken place as part of the preparations for the EFA Review of the Trust and which may have

---

[386] Transcript of Proceedings, PVLT Day 15, 8 December 2015, page 106 and following.

[387] In *the High Court of Justice, Queen's Bench Division Administrative Court*,13 October 2016, paragraph 37. Available here: *http://www.bailii.org/ew/cases/ EWHC/Admin/2016/2507.html*. The 'clarification' directly mirrors the Clarke Report conclusion that, 'I neither specifically looked for, nor found, evidence of terrorism, radicalisation or violent extremism in the schools of concern … [However] I found clear evidence that there are a number of people, associated with each other and in positions of influence in schools and governing bodies, who espouse, sympathise with or fail to challenge extremist views'. Clarke Report, page 95.

guided it in terms of what it was looking for.[388] This was so, she claimed, notwithstanding that individuals from the Department's Due Diligence and Counter Extremism Division were involved in the visits. However, subsequent disclosure of evidence revealed email exchanges at the DfE that indicated the pressures brought to bear upon officials. The Panel commented that 'no doubt it would be argued that this further undermined her credibility and the reliability of her evidence'.[389]

The idea of a conspiracy between individuals and across schools, which was such a significant part of the Clarke Report, is also evident in the Opening Note. The evidence, it states, is focused:

> on two secondary schools, Park View and Golden Hillock, and one primary school, Nansen, but the pattern of behaviour, and the network of contacts, extended beyond those schools to others in the same local area ... The similar changes wrought in different schools were not co-incidental. There was agreement between the teachers in this case, in concert with other teachers and Governors, to increase the religious content of education to a level more like that provided in faith schools.[390]

The Opening Note is also accompanied by charges against each teacher. One of the features of a court case is that the charges need to be 'particularised'; that is, they need to identify and differentiate charges against individuals, as well as identify the nature of the evidence that is associated with those charges. This is to enable the defence to prepare its case. The Panel accepted that this was not properly done and that this had been a concern of the defence team from the start. The Panel writes, 'concerns with regard to the difficulty experienced by the teachers and their representatives in understanding the NCTL's case in respect of the allegations and their particulars have been expressed

---

[388] See Transcript of Proceedings, day 14, 1 December 2015, page 108 and following.

[389] NCTL, May 2017, 'Professional conduct panel outcome', paragraph 124.

[390] NCTL, Opening Note, paragraphs 11 and 12.

from the outset'. The Panel goes on to state that cross-referencing of evidence to the allegations in the Opening Note under discussion at the case management hearing on 27 August 2015 'did not happen to the extent that it should have'. However, the Panel judged that the fact that the defence had presented arguments and evidence against the allegations provided effective particularisation, notwithstanding that the onus of particularisation properly fell on the NCTL! Thus, 'the Panel's assessment of the cross-examination of the NCTL's witnesses by those representing the teachers is that it was focussed and relevant to the issues to be determined by the Panel'.[391]

A glaring example of the problem of the particularisation is evident in the first of the (three) charges, which is the one involving conspiracy associated with undue religious influence (where particularisation is especially important). Thus, a typical set of charges reads:

> 1. … you agreed with others to the inclusion of an undue amount of religious influence in the education of the pupils at … School and/or … School … by: 2. a. appointing members of staff who might assist with that aim, b. reforming the … School's curriculum to exclude the proper teaching of Sex and Relationship education, c. organising and/or delivering assemblies and/or meetings of an overly religious nature and/or with inappropriate content; 3. Your conduct as described in paragraph 1 above tended to undermine tolerance and/or respect for the faith and beliefs of others.[392]

The charges are not particularised with regard to time or with regard to what constitutes undue religious influence. The charges cover the period from 2001 through to March 2014, yet the teachers were appointed at different times and with different (and changing) roles. As we have seen, this time period also covers the period when Park

---

[391] NCTL, May 2017, 'Professional conduct panel outcome', paragraphs 42, 43, 44.

[392] From the statement of allegations put to all teachers in the case.

View was improving and before and after it became an academy. With regard to the second issue, the very reference to *undue* religious influence supposes the possibility of an appropriate amount of religious influence (as, indeed, follows from the legal requirements of religious education and collective worship). In these circumstances, then, it is necessary for a line to be drawn, where practices can be identified as falling on one or other side of that line. The NCTL called upon no expert witness to establish a benchmark for their claim about undue religious influence and seemed to approach the matter through itemising specific instances.

It is necessary to reproduce the Panel's comment at length about this approach:

> The Panel considers that the teachers understood what the case was primarily about, namely the allegation of the existence of an agreement to the inclusion of an undue amount of religious influence in the education of pupils at one or more of three schools. However, the way in which the allegations were particularised meant that there had to be a careful and close scrutiny of the evidence to determine whether, in respect of allegation 1 for example, any of the particulars had been found proved in order then to determine whether the overarching allegation contained in allegation 1 was proved. There is the added complexity that, within certain of the particulars themselves, alleged conduct and alleged events and alleged characteristics were pleaded in the alternative. *For example, in respect of particular 1(d), the Panel calculated that, in respect of this particular alone, it is necessary to reach 64 separate decisions.*[393]

It may be noted that this degree of complexity should also be understood in the context of the failure to join the different hearings and delays, as well as the issue of the disclosure of new evidence bearing upon those manifold decisions.

---

[393] NCTL, May 2017, 'Professional conduct panel outcome', paragraph 46 (our emphasis).

But let us now turn to what some of that evidence might be. As we noted in Chapter Seven, recruitment practices (for example, the failure to advertise the 'acting' positions that were a consequence of the movement of staff across the schools as part of putting in place a programme of improvement) were also part of the process associated with the stalled takeover of Al-Furqan primary school and involved the DfE's approval. The NCTL did not provide any context or evidence relating to 'interactions' between teachers at Park View and Golden Hillock and Nansen, for example, involving Park View Academy as a sponsoring academy as part of an intervention in the other two schools at the behest of the DfE in discussion with Birmingham LEA officials. The intervention is implied as seeking to bring about undue religious influence, rather than to improve academic performance. Indeed, evidence provided by an adviser on academy sponsorship at the DfE and given to the Clarke Report, but not discussed there, confirmed the DfE's positive engagement with PVET and that there was no concern about extremism or problematic religious influence.

Moreover, failure to establish a clear timeline meant that there was no clear distinction made between recruitment practices under the auspices of the LEA (prior to 2012) and those undertaken after the formation of PVET when appointments were made by the governing body of the Trust. In addition, witnesses were recalling events that were also reported in the press, which may have influenced their testimony. This is an issue addressed by the Panel when discussing the disclosure of documents that were withheld.[394] A similar problem arises with regard to the government modification of the Prevent strategy after 2015 to include the ending of partnerships with Muslim organisations. While Peter Clarke is clearly sympathetic to this development – after all, he regards the Muslim Council of Britain as a problematic organisation – it means that such judgements are applied retrospectively. Thus, Sheikh Shady Alsuleiman is regarded as an 'extremist' speaker, who gave a talk at the school in 2013, yet he was widely consulted by schools

---

[394] NCTL, May 2017, 'Professional conduct panel outcome', paragraph 118 and following.

and educational authorities in Australia and had not at the time been subject to any sanction.[395]

Of course, the issue of religion and academic performance need not be seen as mutually exclusive, as we saw in Chapter Six. However, the practices associated with PVET are understood by NCTL to involve a 'religious monoculture' in so far as they failed to respect diversity. However, as we saw, while a religious or cultural 'monoculture' is not correlated with academic success, confidence in one's own religious or cultural background on the part of ethnic minority pupils is associated with success.

The core of the case against the teachers was that of an 'inclusion of an undue amount of religious influence in the education of pupils' and that this entailed a 'failure to respect diversity'. Yet we have seen that there is a requirement on all schools to provide religious education and collective worship. We have also seen that the latter need not be Christian and a 'determination' can specify other forms of collective worship. The NCTL case makes a surprising admission that 'many schools do not teach according to an agreed religious education syllabus or provide a daily act of collective worship despite the legal requirements'. The argument goes on:

> you may think that it would be ludicrous, or offensive, in a school with a 98% or higher Muslim intake to require the children to undergo an act of Christian worship. *We do not, therefore, criticise these teachers for failing to do so, nor for not specifically teaching the Birmingham Agreed Syllabus for Religious Education* (although it remains a useful benchmark for what broad and balanced religious education should look like). Rather, it is what they did instead that is the basis of the allegations.[396]

---

[395] Transcript of Proceedings, Day 21, 16 December 2015. See discussion at page 63 and following.

[396] Opening Note, paragraph 5 (our emphasis).

We have already presented the key features of the Birmingham agreed syllabus, in particular that it is based on the idea of common 'dispositions' which are exemplified across different religious traditions. It is a syllabus that is particularly well suited to the circumstances of multi-faith and multicultural communities such as Birmingham. It is also effective in promoting children's understanding of, and respect for, diversity. While secularism is not part of the syllabus, as we saw, secular values – for example, democracy and the rule of law – would be part of a curriculum on citizenship education, such as that taught at Park View.

The NCTL was not referring specifically to the Birmingham syllabus. It was basing its case on what would be entailed by *any* locally agreed syllabus; such a syllabus, *in principle*, would be a 'useful benchmark for what a broad and balanced religious education should look like'. Because Park View Academy, as an academy, did not have to teach such a syllabus, there is an assumption that it did not. This is not the case. The NCTL's very benchmark, against which Park View might be judged, was precisely what was being taught at the school. Notice, though, that the syllabus for religious education is not particularised in the charges set out above, and nor was evidence provided about the religious education curriculum; for example, no evidence was provided of lesson plans deemed to be problematic. So what, then, is the evidence of 'undue religious influence'?

We have already seen in Chapter Four that the locally agreed syllabus for religious education was controversial even though it was arrived at through a consensual process. In a similar manner, not all witnesses against the teachers believed that Islamic collective worship is appropriate in a school, even where there is a determination, and certainly not after the determination has lapsed (notwithstanding the failure of the DfE to put in place measures for renewal). The NCTL claims not to take this view. Instead, the Opening Note suggests that the problem is that the assemblies are potentially 'too denominational' in their approach to Islam (an interpretation of the fact that Christian collective worship is not supposed to be denominational, though the NCTL Opening Note accepts that Islam does not have 'denominations' as such). However, this seems to derive from their understanding that, of the five senior teachers under scrutiny, the three who are Muslims share a Sunni religious affiliation (as does Tahir Alam).

Nonetheless, the Department of Education's adviser to the Clarke Report and member of the EFA Review of PVET, Ann Connor, testified that when the 'determination' lapsed in 2012, Park View Academy should have reverted to Christian worship. When asked about the possible impact on children at the school (98.9% of whom were Muslim), her response was that 'there isn't any reason why the, um, the nature of the worship shouldn't have prepared the children, and there's also a possibility for, um, the teaching of Islam in other, in other aspects of school life in religious education'.[397] In other words, while Christian collective worship would be unproblematic ('preparing children for life in modern Britain'), notwithstanding the background of the pupils, Islamic collective worship is suggested to be *problematic in itself*. It also rather misses the point that collective *worship* is supposed to afford pupils a moment of spiritual reflection on values, not information about Britain's religious heritage.

Moreover, much of what was taking place at Park View school was subject to scrutiny and review by Birmingham SACRE. According to evidence from Simone Whitehouse, Religious Education Adviser to Birmingham Schools and Birmingham SACRE, Nansen Primary had a determination which ran until September 2016, while that of Park View Academy was due for renewal in April 2013. Golden Hillock had a determination for 'multi-faith assemblies' which expired in November 1998 (but of course, it did not enter under PVET's remit until 2012). The most recent submission from Park View was from September 2008 and it provided a description of what an assembly would involve, as well as an explanation that space constraints made it impossible to have 'whole school' assemblies:

> Prior to starting, a Qur'anic recitation is played to create atmosphere for worship. The format for Collective Worship

---

[397] Transcript of Proceedings, Day 15, pages 45, 46.

that is adhered to is as follows: Greeting (Assalaam Al-Alaikum); Recitation from Qur'an in Arabic and English; Delivery of theme which may be using a story, poetry, audio or visual aids; Opportunity to reflect on what has been said; Prayer (Du'a) in Arabic and English.[398]

The application also explains that private prayer facilities are available to students.

Simone Whitehouse's evidence to the Clarke Report was more extensive, bearing directly upon the claim by witnesses put forward by NCTL that there should not have been collective worship that was wholly Islamic even where there was a determination. The Panel commented on the disclosure of this evidence that:

> in her interview for the purposes of the Clarke Report, SW goes into considerably more detail about SACRE and her role within it. In particular, it is suggested by Ms Langdon that the account SW gave to Peter Clarke conflicts with the evidence of NCTL witnesses who had been saying that it was wrong for collective worship to be solely about Islam when a school had a determination but SW, who had been with SACRE for 9 years, said it was acceptable.[399]

It seems that not only was religious education provided to the 'benchmark' of Birmingham SACRE's locally agreed syllabus, its provision of collective worship and other provision for Muslim pupils was also approved by them (and, of course, commended by Ofsted prior to March 2014). Despite the idea that announcing the time for prayer, or displaying posters, was regarded as coercive by some witnesses, only about 20% of pupils made use of the facility of private prayer, with around 80% of girls wearing the 'hijab'. Indeed, girls at the school

---

[398] The National College for Teaching and Leadership and Birmingham Schools. Witness Statement of Simone Whitehouse, page 53.

[399] NCTL, May 2017, 'Professional conduct panel outcome', paragraph 125.

complained about being asked by the EFA inspection team, 'who forced you to wear a headscarf?',[400] as if it could not be understood as a voluntary expression of religious commitment.[401]

In failing to set out how Park View 'deviated' from what had been subject to scrutiny and review, 'undue religious influence' for NCTL became a matter of specific instances claimed by witnesses as not right, but subject to cross-examination as to their real substance. Let us take several of them, in turn. A number arise from the visit to the schools as part of the EFA Review which refers to their 'Islamic focus'. We have already had occasion to refer to Ann Connor's views (once again, she was a member of the EFA Review of PVET and adviser to the Clarke Report). She also seemed to believe that the curriculum should be 'compartmentalised' – that is, that it would be inappropriate if reference to Islam arose in lessons other than religious education. This included classes in PSHE, where she commented that 'I could see no reason in a, a non-faith lesson for the word "Muslim" to be in the books'.[402] Of course, as we saw in Chapter Three, meeting the cultural and religious sensitivities of children and their parents is precisely what is recommended in guidance provided to schools. In other parts of her evidence, Ann Connor revealed herself also to be unaware of guidance on collective worship and religious education, as well as on promoting community cohesion, and did not see it as part of her role as education adviser to the Clarke Report to draw such guidance to the attention of the team.[403] Nor was she aware of guidance about how to improve the academic performance of boys

---

[400] Transcript of Proceedings, Day 15, pages 23 and following, and page 58.

[401] This reflects a common misconception that covering is a practice that is not actively chosen by Muslim women – notwithstanding that Muslim women frequently challenge this misconception, and a substantial body of research indicating the multiple reasons why women in the West choose to veil. See, for example, Joan Wallach Scott (2010) *The Politics of the Veil*, Princeton, NJ: Princeton University Press; Sara F. Farris (2017) *In the Name of Women's Rights: The Rise of Femonationalism*, Durham, NC: Duke University Press.

[402] Transcript of Proceedings, Day 15, page 12.

[403] Ibid, page 80.

from Bangladeshi and Pakistani backgrounds, which included the use of examples from Islamic traditions within lessons.[404]

The cross-examination also shows that she interpreted the presence of posters of prayers in Arabic on some classroom walls – for example, in the maths classrooms – as an indication that pupils were encouraged to pray in classes, and perhaps end each lesson with a prayer. The children she spoke to on visits are presented as being nonplussed by her questions on this, but the posters are nonetheless cited by her as a problematic indication of an 'Islamic focus'. The simple explanation was that, for reasons of space constraints (in part, deriving from building work), Park View held 'group assemblies' in form rooms. The posters she observed were related to the provision of collective worship and not an indication that prayer was part of all classes that took place in the room. Other kinds of displays were not recorded in reports or evidence statements, yet were described in notebooks of the EFA visit that were subsequently disclosed to the Hearing – one instance is the note: 'walls covered with British history'.[405]

One of the main concerns for the lawyers acting for the teachers is that the EFA inspection team members seemed to have prior information about the context of their visit. This visit took place on 21 March, three days after the final day of the Ofsted inspection on 18 March. Both members of the inspection team who appeared before the NCTL Panel – Ann Connor and Anthony Dunne – deny that they were aware of the Trojan Horse affair, either from the media or from briefings from the DfE, although each accepted that the visit was focused on safeguarding and leadership and management rather than academic performance.[406] Their cross-examination addresses

---

[404] For example, the Birmingham Local Education Authority project on 'Raising Achievement of Pakistani and Bangladeshi Boys: Good Practice Guide for Schools', Nargis Rashid, Iram Naz and Mohammed Hussain. School Effectiveness Division, 2005.

[405] Transcript of Proceedings. Day 15, pages 48, 65.

[406] We have seen that disclosed emails circulating at the Department for Education casts doubt on their statements. See NCTL, May 2017, 'Professional conduct panel outcome', para 124.

statements made about observations of classes (lasting 10 to 15 minutes) and what appeared to the defence lawyers to be a lack of follow-up to clarify them. For example, Anthony Dunne described a music room in which he saw no evidence of musical instruments (although there were computers with musical keyboards attached and a large keyboard). Yet evidence provided by the head of music at Park View was that:

> the curriculum covered topics such as blues, the history of pop music, in media and song writing. The students were all taught how to play the keyboard, compose their own music, learned how to work with music technology, whilst many also learned to play the guitar and steel bands. All students were also taught how to play the African drums and were encouraged to sing a wide variety of songs.

She goes on to say that she 'ran music clubs every lunch hour. These clubs included the school choir. On average there were 40 members. There were ensemble groups, solo singing, steel bands, drumming and keyboard'.[407]

There were similar concerns about the lack of follow-up associated with Anthony Dunne's account of a class for the lowest ability group in GCSE maths, in which he understood the class to be performing at the level of grade D and suggested that they could be encouraged to achieve grade C. A girl followed him out of the class and said she is not allowed to attend a supplementary class provided on Sunday mornings for pupils who might achieve a grade C with extra support. Anthony Dunne observed that the pupil was not wearing a hijab and therefore deduced that she is either not a Muslim, or is not devout. He met with the acting head teacher Monzoor Hussain, who expressed his consternation at what is described to him. This is taken as him being found out as having failed properly to monitor how pupils were selected for the supplementary class. However, it will be recalled that the school

---

[407] Evidence cited in Transcript of Proceedings, Day 14, PVLT, 1 December 2014, page 46.

has particularly good achievements in maths, partly because of their interventions. Monzoor Hussain's response reflected his perplexity about the situation being described to him. It transpired that the class was, in fact, at a level well below that surmised by Anthony Dunne (in fact, it was for grades E–G) and that the supplementary class was not available for the girl because it was not suitable for her level of ability.[408]

Another claim associated with other witnesses – staff at the school – was that a teacher issued a handout in a sex education class in which it was stated that wives must consent to sex with their husbands. The incident is described as taking place sometime in 2011 and a witness also reports arranging for the handout to be sent to the British Humanist Association.[409] The witness also alleges failures of senior teachers to act when informed about the matter. However, it was accepted on cross-examination that the incident involved a printout from an internet source distributed by some boys and not a teacher. It was also accepted that when brought to the attention of the senior teacher with responsibility in the area, it was made a topic in the next assembly when it was clearly repudiated with the statement that consent was required under English law and by Islamic teaching.[410]

There were also allegations about gender segregation, although, as we have seen, it is something that is allowed for in PE and sensitive topics in PSHE. We have also seen that a preference among pupils for same-sex socialising during meals and breaks, as well when sitting in classes, is well documented and is independent of religious orientation.[411] Park View was also involved in major building works between 2011 and 2013, which meant that there were constraints on space, something we have already noted with regard to holding assemblies. However, having separate classes for PE meant that there needed to be separate classes for the subject scheduled at the same time (for example, for boys, when girls were at PE). This was the case

---

[408] The cross-examination on this episode is at ibid, pages 9–14.

[409] Transcript of Proceedings, Day 5, 26 October 2015, page 81.

[410] Transcript of Proceedings, Day 4, 22 October 2015, page 89 following.

[411] For a discussion, see Maccoby (2002) 'Gender and group process'.

for some religious education classes, but follows from the inability to schedule separate PE classes at the same time.[412]

Allegations were also made that the 'celebration of Christmas' was banned at Nansen Primary. It should be recalled that the main concern within the Trust was how to raise academic performance at the schools they were asked to sponsor. They were concerned that preparing for Christmas was taking up too much time, with children being shown videos and doing other activities that were a distraction from the improvement that was being sought. In this context, it was proposed that celebration of Christmas should be restricted to the last week of term and activities should also have a substantive aim. Documentary evidence was provided to show what was suggested – for example, in literacy/religious education it was proposed that children could listen to, and retell, 'The Story of the Nativity'; in art/design technology pupils could make moving Christmas cards; while in mathematics there could be an identification of symmetry within churches. The final afternoon of the term involved a party where pupils brought and shared food and had a celebration before leaving for the Christmas break.

If it is made to appear by the nature of the charges that the experience of pupils at PVET was 'joyless', and perhaps overly committed to academic success, we should recall the warm commendations that are otherwise found in Ofsted reports prior to the Trojan Horse affair. However, there is one area where Park View's approach comes under particular scrutiny. This concerns the alleged role of prefects in monitoring relationships among pupils. It is alleged that the school forbade physical relationships among pupils – for example, hand holding or kissing. It was school policy that pupils should conduct themselves professionally; but relationships were not, as such, forbidden, only their physical expression on school premises.[413] Prefects were not asked to report on personal relationships.

Indeed, in a different context, the school's rules might have been regarded as 'feminist', rather than Islamic, and indicative of a proper

---

[412] Transcript of Proceedings, Day 6, 28 October, page 89 following.

[413] Transcript of Proceedings, Day 29, 27 May 2016, page 83 following.

safeguarding approach in seeking to protect pupils from harassment and sexual bullying. Indeed, in September 2016 the House of Commons Women and Equalities Committee published a report on the topic, including concern about behaviour that tended to be accepted as 'low level banter', which was widely reported.[414] In fact, Sir Michael Wilshaw adopted similar policies when he was headmaster of Mossbourne Academy. Thus, in an interview with the *Guardian* in 2010, it is reported that 'hugging has been ruled unacceptable lest, as Wilshaw coyly puts it, "boys use it as an opportunity to do things they shouldn't do"'.[415]

Conclusion

At the heart of our argument is that there have been fundamental flaws in the NCTL case and of the investigations leading up to it. The first is associated with a failure properly to consider the context of the affair. Nowhere in the Clarke and Kershaw Reports, and nowhere in the NCTL hearings, is it acknowledged that Park View was a highly successful school and that the DfE and Birmingham City Council each believed that its sponsorship of Golden Hillock and Nansen schools would solve problems identified at each of those schools. This is most egregious when the criticism of academic achievement at those schools, and the subsequent resignation of the head teacher at Golden Hillock, are presented as having been instigated by teachers and governors at Park View. Their involvement comes afterwards, when their intervention is promoted as the solution to such problems.

---

[414] See for example, 'Editorial: The Guardian view on sexual harassment in schools: action is needed', *The Guardian,* 13 September 2016. Available at: https://www.theguardian.com/commentisfree/2016/sep/13/the-guardian-view-on-sexual-harassment-in-schools-action-is-needed. The House of Commons Committee Report is available at: https://publications.parliament.uk/pa/cm201617/cmselect/cmwomeq/91/9102.htm.

[415] See Peter Wilby, 'Is Mossbourne Academy's success down to its traditionalist headteacher?', *The Guardian*, 5 January 2011. Available at: www.theguardian.com/education/2010/jan/05/mossbourne-academy-wilby-profile.

PVET was accused of introducing an Islamic curriculum and practices. However, there is no evidence that this was outside the (non-statutory) guidance provided by many local authorities and other bodies. The simple and deeply worrying fact is that the authors and advisers associated with the Kershaw and Clarke Reports, as well as the NCTL itself, seemed unaware of practices in this area. This is most evident in their comparison of non-faith with faith schools and the claim that 'undue religious influence' meant the introduction of practices appropriate in a faith-designated school into a non-faith school. It seemed to be enough that some of the practices at the school(s) were Islamic, without there being any attempt to consider how that related to the nature of their pupil intake, the expectations of their local community and statutory requirements and guidelines on good practice.

CONCLUSION

Lessons from the Trojan Horse affair

We have had two aims in this book. One has been to expose a glaring injustice in the treatment of teachers and governors associated with PVET and the Trojan Horse affair. The disciplinary proceedings undertaken by the NCTL against the senior teachers were discontinued in May 2017, some three years after the allegations first hit the headlines. The reason was 'an abuse of the process which is of such seriousness that it offends the Panel's sense of justice and propriety'.[416] No doubt the teachers are relieved, but they have been denied the opportunity to clear their names.

As should be clear from the evidence we have presented throughout this book, we have no confidence that the Panel was on the way to a correct decision. In each of the different steps of the unfolding of the affair, the various investigations and how they have been reported have been stacked against those involved. As we have shown, the Ofsted reports on the school found 'evidence' of Islamic influence and failures of safeguarding, but they were not conducted in an independent manner and with regard to the very different findings of earlier Ofsted reports. In the latter reports, the same practices were praised by Ofsted inspectors as contributing to Park View's success.

---

[416] Education Select Committee (2015) 'Extremism in schools'.

In a similar manner, it became clear that the EFA Review of PVET was also conducted with a view to finding any evidence that might justify action against the Trust, based upon direction from the DfE's Due Diligence and Counter Extremism Division. For their part, the Kershaw and Clarke Reports were also deeply flawed, not least because they failed to address the nature of the requirements for religious education and collective worship and the role of the DfE in supporting PVET and its incorporation of other schools as a sponsoring academy. Throughout the process the DfE has been exempt from any scrutiny and yet officials at the department and the Secretary of State did their best to exert their influence, first by influencing the EFA Review and then by setting up an investigation under Peter Clarke, former head of counterterrorism at the Metropolitan Police, and, finally, by influencing proceedings at the NCTL hearings.

These circumstances demand a separate Inquiry, as has been suggested by Peter Oborne and supported by Baroness Sayeeda Warsi, former cabinet minister and chair of the Conservative Party.[417] In our view, as we have already argued in Chapter Six, the case has parallels to that of the Hillsborough football match disaster (albeit with no loss of life), where, as part of a cover-up of police failings, the behaviour of fans was misrepresented and vilified in the press. A similar narrative of vilification has occurred in the Trojan Horse affair. In the aftermath of the collapse of the NCTL hearings, the narrative has softened a little, with some suggesting that it might have been a mistake to represent the case as involving 'extremism', but it was, nonetheless about people pursuing an unrepresentative hardline conservative religious agenda reflecting an isolated and self-segregated community (with the added wrinkle that it was proposed that mainstream Muslims did not agree with the agenda and, therefore, it was not a problem of Muslims as such).

---

[417] Peter Oborne, 'The "Trojan Horse" plot? A figment of neo-Conservative imagination', *Middle East Eye*, 2 June 2017. Available at: www.middleeasteye.net/columns/trojan-horse-plot-figment-neo-conservative-imagination-1295765958.

For example, Christopher de Bellaigue, writing in a review of James Fergusson's book *Al-Britannia, My Country: A Journey Through Muslim Britain* a few days after the discontinuation of the NCTL case, comments 'what there was, undoubtedly, was a very conservative ethos, heavily informed by Islam and coloured by rebarbative views on homosexuality and women'.[418] This was also a version proffered by Baroness Warsi herself, prior to the discontinuation, in an otherwise excellent book that documents the baleful effects of 'neoconservative' ideology and Islamophobia over government policy, especially associated with Prevent. She deconstructs the Trojan Horse affair thus: 'in a nutshell, a bunch of blokes with pretty misogynistic, conservative and intolerant views had decided they were right and everyone else was wrong, that their vision of the world was going to trump others and through the brown boys network had managed to keep power in the hands of themselves and their mates'.[419]

The reality of the school and those involved in it was quite different. The qualities of the school and its teachers were enthusiastically endorsed by Ofsted reports up until 2012 and its achievements were exceptional. Government intervention in the wake of the Trojan Horse affair destroyed those achievements and the reputations of those who had brought them about. The pupils at the school were very well served by their teachers and the nature of government intervention has seriously harmed their interests.

Our second aim has been to explore how the Trojan Horse affair is indicative of issues and problems of multicultural Britain, or, more properly, the problems of a mainstream Britain that repudiates multiculturalism. It was not accidental that the Trojan Horse affair was associated with schools in a poor part of East Birmingham with a very high proportion of Muslims. In general terms, the circumstances that the school was addressing are those that are usually associated

---

[418] Christopher de Bellaige, 'Al-Britannia, My Country by James Fergusson review – a compelling survey of British Islam', *The Guardian*, I June 2017. Available at: www.theguardian.com/books/2017/jun/01/al-britannia-my-country-james-fergusson-review-british-islam-minority-population.

[419] Warsi (2017) *The Enemy Within*, page 150.

with poor pupil performance – for example, we have seen that the school at the centre, Park View, had a pupil intake that was 98.9% Muslim, 72.7% of its pupils received free school meals, and just 7.5% had English as a first language. Yet the academic performance of its pupils was above the national average. This made the school an example for others concerned with improving pupil performance, especially in communities with a high proportion of ethnic minority and Muslim pupils.

It is hard to avoid the conclusion that it also made the school a target. Notwithstanding the fact that policy across several governments had made improving school performance a major objective, when those who were challenging existing governing bodies and senior teachers were Muslims then the nature of their engagement was understood differently. Pupil achievement and equal opportunities are a major part of what has been presented as 'British values' and they are seen as contributing to long-term community cohesion, as we have shown. Yet the involvement of Muslim parents and governors in pressing for school improvement was believed to derive from their cultural particularism and failure to integrate or endorse shared values.

The narrative of the Trojan Horse affair included the argument that 'successful' head teachers were targeted. Sir Michael Wilshaw, in declaring the outcomes of the Ofsted inspections he had ordered in the wake of the first media reports of a 'plot', stated that 'some headteachers, including those with a proud record of raising standards, said that they have been marginalised or forced out of their jobs. As a result, some schools previously judged to be good or outstanding have experienced high levels of staff turbulence, low staff morale and a rapid decline in their overall effectiveness'.[420] We have seen that the opposite is the case. It was schools that were outstanding that were put at the centre of the plot, and their governors, head teachers and other teachers who were responsible for that success were marginalised and forced out of their jobs, with hearings undertaken by NCTL with

---

[420] Michael Wilshaw, 9 June 2014. 'Advice note'.

the intention of handing down lifetime bans on their pursuit of their vocations.

Neither the Clarke Report nor the Kershaw Report addressed the issue of school performance. Nor did they address the role of the DfE and Birmingham's local education services in promoting Park View's sponsorship of underperforming schools, a sponsorship that gave rise to charges of their (Islamic) takeover of schools. Both reports were constructed around the '5 step strategy' outlined in the original Trojan Horse document and neither felt it necessary to consider whether the document was a hoax and what may have motivated it. They declared that they were only concerned with 'evidence'. However, they failed to disclose information about one of the 'outstanding' schools – Regents Park Community Primary School – where a 'successful' female, non-Muslim head teacher was ostensibly a target of the supposed plot. She had resigned in October 2013 and was subsequently barred from teaching in July 2014 at an NCTL hearing in which she admitted dishonestly changing SATs exam papers of pupils.

We have also seen a deep equivocation around whether the Trojan Horse affair involved extremism. This is argued in the Clarke Report, but it is not alleged in the NCTL hearings. However, in prejudgement of those hearings where evidence could finally be tested, the government has used the affair as an example of 'extremist entryism'. This first occurred in its outline of a new strategy directed against extremist ideology opposed to British values immediately after the Trojan Horse affair broke. Thus, it is stated that there is 'evidence that our institutions are increasingly targeted by extremists, who look to use them to spread their ideology'. It goes on to provide a summary of the Clarke Report that includes claims which were not in it, stating that the report 'described extremists gaining positions on governing bodies and joining the staff, unequal treatment and segregation of boys and girls, extremist speakers making presentations to pupils, and bullying and intimidation of staff who refused to support extremist views'.[421]

---

[421] Home Office (2015) *Counter-Extremism Strategy*, paragraphs 21, 22.

In making these claims, the government prejudged the NCTL hearings, while also levelling accusations of 'bullying and intimidating staff who refused to support extremist views'. It also raised the stakes for the Panels in terms of the significance of their findings, lending the weight of government pressure for them to find in support of the NCTL case. This is most clearly illustrated in the fact that the NCTL outline of charges against the teachers did not involve any claims of extremism, yet the Panel at Hearing 2 came under pressure from the DfE to modify their findings to state that they did not involve *violent* extremism, a formulation that was intended to imply ideological extremism.

Throughout the period since the Kershaw and Clarke Reports were published in July 2014, actions have been taken on the basis of lessons supposedly learned from the affair. As we argued in the introduction of the book, this is why the case matters beyond the injustice done to those at the heart of the Trojan Horse affair. It matters for all of us, because it is indicative of a wider populist attack on multiculturalism that scapegoats fellow citizens who are Muslims and promotes a disregard for due process and rights. In other words, it is a betrayal of the very values that the teachers in the Trojan Horse affair are held to have disavowed. However, it has also shaped a change in the nature of what is meant by 'British' values and has also shaped debates about the proper role of religion in public life (including schooling). We will argue that it is illustrative of wider problems in British politics where a particular kind of authoritarianism has been facilitated by the hollowing out of local responsibilities and their appropriation by central government. This is something that is evident in the developing governance arrangements for schools, arrangements which have been taken further in Birmingham in the wake of the Trojan Horse affair.

We will outline a different set of lessons, but first let us set out what has otherwise emerged. One consequence has already been identified, namely the government's argument on the need to extend Prevent to include extremist ideology and not simply violent extremism. A second is the need to 'promote British values' in schools, notwithstanding that promoting 'shared values' has been part of a statutory duty to promote social cohesion since 2008.[422] It was also a duty that the DfE's own commissioned research showed was well understood by teachers and with which schools were fully compliant, including Park View school.[423] The Select Committee on Education that reviewed the Trojan Horse affair in 2015 also raised the issue of the efficacy of the Ofsted inspection regime. It had, apparently, previously 'missed' what was then picked up in the 2014 inspections. It stated that 'Ofsted now inspects the active promotion of British values as part of its judgement on leadership. Although Sir Michael Wilshaw previously suggested that there should be an additional separate judgement on the curriculum to include preparation for life in modern Britain, this has not been pursued'.[424] Once again, we saw in Chapter Seven that Ofsted had inspected these matters under the duty to promote community cohesion and had commented explicitly on Park View in these terms. While it is true that the government itself changed the inspection criteria in the Education Act of 2011, we also saw that the statutory obligations remained and the government stated that the new criteria incorporated them and they would be covered by the new inspection regime. There is no warrant for the view that there was something untoward taking place that the inspection regime missed and was unable to uncover because of its own failings. The problem is not a failure of Ofsted inspections prior to 2014, but what the inspections in 2014 purported to find.

In our view, the lessons that have been drawn from the Trojan Horse affair are the wrong ones, and they are building up serious problems for the future. We now set out some alternative lessons.

---

[422] Department for Education, 'Promoting fundamental British values as part of SMSC in schools', November 2015. Available at: www.gov.uk/government/publications/promoting-fundamental-british-values-through-smsc.

[423] Phillips et al (2010) 'Community cohesion and Prevent'.

[424] Education Select Committee (2015) 'Extremism in schools', paragraphs 41, 70.

Lesson 1: The problem of Prevent

Key to the judgements about the problem of 'extremism' in the Birmingham schools was the purported failure of the schools to implement the government's Prevent strategy. As we set out in Chapters Two and Three, this led in several cases to schools being severely downgraded by Ofsted – notwithstanding their continued successes in relation to pupil attainments. We saw that these judgements were made at a time when the Prevent strategy itself was in flux – it was not a statutory requirement for schools, there was relatively little reference to extremism in the Ofsted inspection criteria at the time, and little guidance to schools on implementing Prevent. Consequently, the understanding and implementation of Prevent across the sector was relatively low – or schools tended to consider that they were discharging any responsibilities under Prevent through their implementation of their statutory duty to promote community cohesion.

Although the schools were penalised for their failures to implement Prevent, the various reports into the Trojan Horse affair did not find any evidence of radicalisation within the schools. As we saw, the Kershaw Report concluded that 'There is no evidence of a conspiracy to promote an anti-British agenda, violent extremism or radicalisation in schools in East Birmingham',[425] whilst the Clarke Report found no evidence of 'terrorism, radicalisation or violent extremism' in the schools – rather religious conservatism or a 'hardline strand of Sunni Islam'.

The charges that were brought against the teachers by the NCTL were not of extremism, but a 'failure to respect diversity' and of seeking to bring about 'an undue amount of religious influence in the education of the pupils'. In the Panel 2 Hearing, seemingly under the direction of the DfE's Due Diligence and Counter Extremism Division, the assertion by the DfE's lawyers that the cases were not about extremism was amended to not being about '*violent* extremism' – a shift that clearly sought to maintain a very open interpretation

[425] KershawReport, page 4.

of extremism. As we have shown in Chapters Six to Nine in Part Two of this book, the allegations of 'undue religious influence', or attempts at Islamification, rest on erroneous assumptions about the schools as otherwise properly 'secular' as well as seeming ignorance of the guidance to and requirements on schools to reflect the religious identities of their pupils in their curriculum and daily practices. In any case, the various allegations against the schools and teachers in the NCTL hearings were ultimately dropped, not substantiated or rebutted.

Nonetheless, as we showed, the purported facts of the Trojan Horse affair have been cited by government as evidence for the need to take further action – they were explicitly referred to in the 2015 Counter-Extremism Strategy to justify the proposal to introduce further specific measures to prevent 'extremist entryism' in public institutions, and other related measures. As this book has highlighted, however, the Trojan Horse affair does not in fact provide evidence of 'extremist entryism'.

Indeed, a hallmark of the reports and investigations into the affair has been the uncertainty and inconsistencies about what constitutes 'extremism' – as revealed by the denials by the lawyers presenting the cases against the teachers in the NCTL hearings that the cases were about 'extremism', and the requested correction of the NCTL's Opening Note in Hearing 2 by the DfE's Due Diligence and Counter Extremism Division to include reference to 'violent' extremism. It is perhaps unsurprising that what constitutes 'extremism' throughout this affair has proven so slippery and elusive. In fact, this is a problem that has been noted elsewhere – including subsequently by the House of Commons Joint Select Committee on Human Rights, which in 2016 argued that the government's definitions of extremism:

> are couched in such general terms that they would be likely to prove unworkable as a legislative definition … It is difficult to arrive at a more focused definition of extremism and it does not appear that the Government so far has been successful in arriving at one. It is far from clear that there is an accepted definition of

what constitutes extremism, let alone what legal powers there should be, if any, to combat it.[426]

Perhaps unsurprisingly, then, the promised legislation that was signalled in the 2015 Counter-Extremism Strategy has reportedly been held up by the Home Office's failure to frame a legally acceptable definition of extremism.[427]

The government's proposed expansion of its Counter-Extremism Strategy – promised by the Conservatives in the 2017 General Election manifesto and referred to in the 2017 Queen's Speech – brings counter-extremism policy ever more in tension with civil liberties and indeed in tension with the very elements of the government's definition of 'fundamental British values' that it draws on to define extremist attitudes. Thus, it is in tension with the values of democracy and the right to hold different, even extreme or religiously or socially conservative views. The criticisms of the DfE's handling of the NCTL processes by the NCTL Panel do not sit well with a government approach that purports to be about tackling those who oppose the rule of law. The evolution of Prevent into an agenda that has become focused on tackling those who hold the 'wrong' kinds of values is at odds with the principles of mutual respect and tolerance of diversity.

And yet in shifting towards a focus on tackling values, Prevent seems to be moving further away from being an effective approach to interrupting or preventing terrorism. Following the recent terrorist attacks in Manchester and London in June 2017, it emerged that in both cases those involved in perpetrating the attacks had been reported to the security services – and by members of their communities – but these were seemingly not followed up. As Yahya Birt points out,

---

[426] House of Commons Joint Select Committee on Human Rights, 21 July 2016. Available at: www.publications.parliament.uk/pa/jt201617/jtselect/jtrights/105/10503.htm.

[427] See 'Theresa May's counter-terrorism bill close to "sinking without trace"', *The Guardian*, 29 January 2017. Available at: www.theguardian.com/politics/2017/jan/29/theresa-may-counter-terrorism-bill-sinking-without-trace-extremism-british-values.

subsequently 'the government has only promised to review powers but not resources, the latter having been flagged as serious issues by Labour and the Mayor of London'.[428]

A less discussed aspect of the government's evolving counter-extremism agenda is that the definition of extremism on which it is founded, and the powers that it has accrued to tackle extremism, are theoretically applicable to a *very* wide range of political and social positions – and not just those associated with conservative Islamic positions. If the focus and effectiveness of Prevent in tackling terrorism is becoming increasingly tenuous, the features and fallout from the Trojan Horse affair show that the expansive and coercive application of Prevent may undermine the British values government claims it is seeking to defend.

Lesson 2: Multiculturalism works

We saw in Chapter One that the government's emphasis on 'shared values' became increasingly associated with claims that multiculturalism had 'failed'. Failure was ascribed to self-segregation among some ethnic minority communities, especially Muslims. It was also suggested that they were either indifferent, or hostile, to 'British values' of democracy, the rule of law and religious tolerance. However, we showed that British Muslims typically show a higher commitment to those values than do other minority groups and that segregation derived from a failure on the part of others to include them, rather than a lack of willingness on the part of British Muslims to participate in wider aspects of public life.

We suggested that one of the problems in the debate on the 'Britishness' of 'British values' has been a failure to distinguish between particularistic aspects of identity and the universalistic aspects of values. Most recently, these two have been confused by David Goodhart in

[428] Yahya Birt (2017) 'After Finsbury Park: tackling Islamophobia as "extremism" will compound Prevent's failures'. Available at: https://medium.com/insurge-intelligence/after-finsbury-park-the-proposed-commission-for-countering-extremism-and-the-securitization-of-a5d85b5ad2d8.

his distinction between those who are from 'somewhere' and those who are from 'anywhere'.[429] We can use his coinage to specify just what is at issue. He treats each as if it were an 'identity'. However, we are all from 'somewhere', just different 'somewheres'. 'Anywhere', by contrast, describes universalistic values that facilitate interaction among people with different identities. Goodhart's conflation of the two endorses 'ethno-nationalism', that some 'somewheres' should be allowed to trump the different 'somewheres' of others; that is, that there are some members of the political community that have a special claim to belonging. We propose that all 'somewheres' have their place in the public sphere and to argue differently is a form of nativism.

In this context, multiculturalism should not be seen as an endorsement of multiple and separate differences, but an expression of how difference can be lived and respected through civic values, as previously argued in the Parekh Report.[430] In other words, multiculturalism depends on 'universalist' civic values and is in no way in contradiction to them. As we have suggested, British Muslims understand this connection very well. The point is that all 'somewhere' identities refer to lived identities. The Trojan Horse affair has been, in part, about the lived identities of Muslims and their expression within schools. There has been a problem of educational achievement of ethnic minorities within British schools, perhaps especially involving boys from Pakistani and Bangladeshi backgrounds, something that Birmingham has done much to overcome. Park View school was a prime example of this success.

As we have seen, pupils from minority ethnic backgrounds do badly if their culture is denigrated, or if they see themselves as subject to discrimination. Park View school achieved its success by combining a commitment to the universalistic values of equal opportunities and educational achievement with respect for the cultural and religious commitments of its pupils. In this way, it brought about the synthesis of multicultural and civic values that educators regard as necessary to

---

[429] Goodhart (2017) *The Road to Somewhere*.
[430] Runnymede Trust (2000) *The Parekh Report*.

achievement by ethnic minority pupils. Multiculturalism does not mean endorsing a separate 'mono-culture', and nor could academic achievement be produced within one. The only exception to the latter rule is where the mono-culture in question is that of the dominant culture, which, in inscribing the experiences of a middle class majority, can secure their success to the disadvantage of minorities (including those with different class-based experiences). The academic success of Park View school is prima facie evidence that it was preparing pupils for life in a diverse modern Britain. Indeed, as we have seen, educational disadvantage is widely understood as one of the main issues of integration in contemporary Britain. Worryingly, what the Trojan Horse affair reveals is that a school that successfully equipped its pupils for integration was denigrated and undermined.

In this context, then, the issue for schools is not one of teaching pupils *about* differences in order to promote life in multicultural Britain, it is about *allowing those differences to be expressed* within schools. The successor school to Park View, Rockwood Academy, has a special focus on 'British values', including multiculturalism, but without a significant exemplification of the religious tradition of their pupils. In October 2016, Defence Secretary Michael Fallon launched a plan for 150 new Army Cadet Units in state schools, while praising the army as an 'engine of social mobility' for those with poor school achievements. The first Army Cadet Unit would be at Rockwood School, which was described as 'a phoenix from the ashes of a Trojan horse school that is now instilling British values, instead of promoting religious segregation'.[431]

Sir Michael Wilshaw was asked by the House of Commons Select Committee on Education in 2015 if he thought that children, communities and schools in Birmingham had benefited from Ofsted's intervention. He replied: 'they have benefited in some sense, because they are not the subject of the sort of policies that would be pursued

[431] Michael Fallon, Speech at Tory Party Conference, 4 October 2016. Available at: https://blogs.spectator.co.uk/2016/10/full-text-michael-fallons-tory-party-conference-speech/#.

by these governors with a very particular view of how schools should be run. They are free of that. But those schools have been through an enormous amount of turmoil'.[432] We have seen in Chapter Seven that academic achievement at Rockwood is currently well below that of its predecessor school, Park View Academy. In other words, its pupils have been 'freed' from the supposed constraints of their own cultural expression, while not being provided with the academic achievements that would ensure social mobility. In the meantime, they are offered access to the British Army as an alternative route.

Lesson 3: Religion is not a problem

We indicated in Chapter Four that both authors of this book are secular in orientation. We had not expected that one of our conclusions would also be that 'religion works'. Nonetheless, to argue that multiculturalism works necessarily means arguing for acceptance of the expression of religion in public life, including the public life of schools. However, one of the conclusions of the Report of the Commission on Religion and Belief in Public Life, published in 2015 in the wake of the Trojan Horse affair, was to recommend that the requirement for compulsory collective worship be repealed and that it should be replaced by 'inclusive' assemblies with time for reflection. It also recommended that there was a 'need for greater religion and belief literacy', in a curriculum that had the same status as other humanities; that is, that pupils should be taught *about* religions.[433]

These conclusions reflect the observations of the Commission about declining religiosity and increasing secular orientations of the wider British population. However, as we saw in Chapter Four, the Commission also recognised that this was taking place alongside continuing religiosity and commitment to religious values among the ethnic minority population. In addition, demographic factors

---

[432] Education Select Committee (2015) 'Extremism in schools', paragraph 76.

[433] Report of the Commission on Religion and Belief in British Public Life (2015) *Living with Difference*, pages 82, 36.

meant that an increasing proportion of school pupils are from such backgrounds. In this context, its call for greater religious and belief literacy is perhaps directed at the wrong population, while the recommendation that collective worship be repealed is a concession to the secular majority, albeit one with an indirect stake in schooling.

The problem with the Commission's report is that it does not really address how section 78 of the 2002 Education Act would be met otherwise, and how it would be met equally for all pupils regardless of their cultural tradition. Section 78 calls for a broadly based and balanced curriculum that 'promotes the spiritual, moral, cultural, mental and physical development of pupils at the school and of society; and prepares pupils at the school for the opportunities, responsibilities and experiences of later life'.[434] This is important because it makes the development of the character of pupils paramount, in a wider context otherwise of targets and attainment at SATs and GCSEs, and so on, and broader worries about the reduction of education to instrumental purposes. Character is about the development of the whole person, and it does not take place by learning *about* other religions and beliefs, but in taking care of the self and its interdependencies with others.

We saw in Chapter Six that schools with a high proportion of ethnic minority pupils also do well when they encourage religious *expression*. For pupils from religious backgrounds, this enables them to bring their 'whole selves' to school. Overcoming the tensions of religious minority children being schooled in a Christian or secular context is not facilitated by the displacement of the religious selves of those pupils. We repeat again the statement from Harrow SACRE:

> within the curriculum there are subjects and aspects which explore how belonging to a religious community influences the moral and ethical decisions of individuals and which requires self-discipline in lifestyles. When there are pupils, and perhaps staff, modelling those choices regularly and independently, this

---

[434] Education Act (2002) Section 78. Available at: www.legislation.gov.uk/ukpga/2002/32/section/78.

allows both adults and children to learn about and from religions as observers, whose integrity and own backgrounds and beliefs are protected and respected … It also demonstrates that for many within religious communities, observance of religious obligations is about more than what people eat and wear and is about daily disciplines not just festival celebrations![435]

These should be matters for public debate and consideration – a continuing conversation as the Commission put it – but it needs to be a debate in which the rights of minorities and the conditions of educational achievement are fully understood. However, those debates are increasingly conducted at national, rather than local level, with local communities displaced from involvement in their schools, as a consequence of new governance arrangements. We have seen, for example, that the academies programme has also diminished the place of local SACREs in developing this conversation. Yet, as Birmingham SACRE put to the Secretary of State for Education, Michael Gove, SACREs necessarily play a moderating role. Their displacement represents a fundamental change in local engagement with schools, equivalent to changes in how governing bodies are constituted, which are themselves increasingly detached from the local communities in which their schools are located. The conversation has also been distorted by false claims about the Trojan Horse affair. There was no 'undue influence of religion' in the curriculum at Park View school. Rather, there was just that amount of influence that current legislation allows, and there is no evidence that it did anything other than serve the pupils well and prepare them for life in modern (multicultural) Britain.

Lesson 4: Local governance of schools works

We set out in Chapter Five how a new regime of 'heterarchical' governance has been replacing an older regime of 'hierarchical'

---

[435] Harrow SACRE Guidance on Offering Space for Prayer and Reflection in School, page 4.

governance through LEAs. This is a consequence of the expansion of the academies programme pursued by successive governments. As we have seen, heterarchical governance is represented as 'flat' and composed of a network of different bodies, including schools, trusts, consultancies, for-profit companies and the like. On this model, local authorities become commissioners of services rather than providers of services. At the same time, governing bodies of schools and trusts are increasingly established to be more like corporate boards than bodies representing those with interests in a school, such as parents and local communities. For the advocates of 'heterarchical' governance, the new model facilitates innovation and overcomes what were understood to be bureaucratic limitations of LEAs.

In September 2014, the Secretary of State for Education appointed a new Commissioner for Education for Birmingham, Sir Mike Tomlinson (a former Chief Inspector of Schools from 2000 to 2002), to review provision of educational services in the city. He recommended the completion of the transition from provider to commissioner of services, and the replacement of some functions of the city's Education Department with a new Trust, Birmingham Education Partnership, which would deliver its schools improvement programme. Birmingham Education Partnership is a charitable trust and business formed of head teachers in the city. There are no other 'stakeholders' than the commissioning city council. The new 'flat' networked system, then, is very limited in the range of interests represented by its partners.

In the light of the Trojan Horse affair, a mixed system of governance in Birmingham has been moved further toward a fully 'heterarchical' system with no investigation of the role of 'heterarchical' governance itself in the affair. Few were willing to defend PVET against the onslaught of criticism. Local politicians swung into line in a damage limitation exercise to support Birmingham City Council while condemning the teachers and governors.[436] Yet the Trojan Horse

---

[436] See for example, Rowena Mason, 'Birmingham schools "feel like the Balkans" say Labour', *The Guardian*, 22 July 2014. Available at: www.theguardian.com/education/2014/jul/22/birmingham-schools-balkans-liam-byrne-trojan-horse-islamism; Jonathan Walker, 'Stop pretending Trojan Horse plot is fake, urges

affair was a 'moral panic' without substance. The failure properly to examine the evidence against PVET made Birmingham City Council more, rather than less, vulnerable to criticism.

For example, the Trojan Horse Review Group, which had been given the job of reviewing the findings of the Kershaw Report (or Report of the Independent Chief Adviser) for the leader of Birmingham City Council, were concerned at the reputational effects. There is something plaintive about their response. They endorsed the report's findings, but said, 'at the same time, we endorse the ICA's conclusion that these issues relate to risks of small groups of activists seeking to subvert a small number of schools, and the ICA's recognition that many of the 437 schools in the city are successful in meeting the educational and social needs of our children'.[437] The final judgement is a correct one – as we shall see, Birmingham's schools were (and are) successful – but it is a judgement that should include Park View and Oldknow, which were, at the time, two of Birmingham's outstanding schools.

In part, the response of politicians and council leaders in Birmingham was because the city was caught up in wider problems of which its educational services were too readily seen to be a part. In July 2014, former Cabinet Secretary Sir Bob Kerslake was asked by the Secretary of State for Communities and Local Government and Sir Albert Bore, Leader of Birmingham City Council, to conduct an independent review of corporate governance of Birmingham City Council. This review added the Trojan Horse affair to others, such as those associated with services for looked after children, waste management and a failure to put in place measures to secure equal pay, which alongside reductions in the central government's financial allocation to the council were putting services at risk.

The Kerslake Report does not say very much about schooling since that was to be considered by Sir Mike Tomlinson. However,

Labour MP', *Birmingham Mail*, 21 July 2014. Available at: www.birminghammail.co.uk/news/midlands-news/stop-pretending-trojan-horse-plot-7467609.

[437] Trojan Horse Review Group, *Report to Leader of Birmingham City Council*, 18 July 2014, paragraph 2.6.

a separate document provided supporting analysis for the report. It sets out data for Birmingham and comparator cities (for example, Leeds, Sheffield, Manchester and Liverpool) and for Great Britain as a whole. The remarkable aspect of the data is that on most indicators the city is performing less well than other cities (with the exception of Liverpool) and much less well than Great Britain as a whole. The one area where this situation is reversed is that of schooling. A higher proportion of pupils in Birmingham achieve at least five A*–C GCSEs than comparator cities and the city has been outperforming them, and performing above the national average, since 2008/9. Birmingham also has a higher proportion of local authority run schools which received an 'outstanding' Ofsted rating – nearly 25% compared to 18% nationally.[438] This is in the context of indicators of social deprivation, unemployment and low skills in the adult population – the areas in which Sir Bob Kerslake judged the city to be failing – that are all higher than the national average and are typically associated with worse school performance.

Lesson 5: The problem of the 'news'

The possibility of a national conversation about religion, multiculturalism and schools is also diminished by the role of the media. Since the election of Donald Trump as President of the United States, and the disparagement of experts in the Brexit campaign – significantly, by the former Secretary of State for Education Michael Gove – we have become used to the idea of 'fake' news. This involves the repetition of 'facts' which have little corroborating evidence, but a high degree of emotional salience among the publics for which they are designed. In truth, this is not a lot different to the form of a 'moral panic', as described in Chapter Six, where a scapegoating of marginalised groups in the context of a public anxiety is amplified by the press. Terrorist

---

[438] Supporting Analysis. Available at: www.gov.uk/government/publications/birmingham-city-councils-governance-and-organisational-capabilities-an-independent-review, slide 14.

threats, and especially those from 'homegrown terrorists', created heightened concerns about the integration of Muslims. However, there are some new twists in contemporary moral panics that are reflected in the idea of 'fake news'. The growth of social media has made stories available for recycling without the mediation of more authoritative sources. Competitive pressures on news media also mean that media that previously had an authoritative role are now part of the process of recycling of stories. Newspaper sales have declined and most are operating with reduced journalistic staff to cover stories and, especially, to cover them in depth.

We have seen that the Trojan Horse affair initially came into the press via 'investigative' reports in the *Sunday Times* and the *Sunday Telegraph*, with subsequent reporting in other newspapers including the *Guardian*. However, as Sara Cannizzaro and Reza Gholami have observed, the majority of reports were focused on 'Islamic extremism', with a minority on problems of governance that had allowed different practices to emerge.[439] None of the reporting examined the underlying 'facts', and none exposed the most obvious anomaly, namely that the affair was not about successful head teachers being subjected to harassment, but about successful schools being criticised at the moment of their 'sponsorship' of underperforming schools. The latter meant that the DfE was necessarily implicated, yet no reporter sought to uncover its role. The 'facts' presented by the Clarke and Kershaw Reports became the basis of news stories, notwithstanding the serious flaws of those reports, especially concerning the role of religion in schools and their failure to understand the requirements on non-faith schools.

However, there is also the aspect of public figures using the Trojan Horse agenda to pursue personal agendas by providing media stories. This was particularly significant for the way in which the media repeated 'false' stories without any attempt to counter the claims being made, simply because of the position of the person making the comment. There are a number of examples associated with the

---

[439] Cannizzaro and Gholami (2016) 'The devil is not in the detail'.

precipitate manner in which the various investigations were set up and the lack of coordination among them. However, perhaps the most egregious example is from Sir Michael Wilshaw in his interview with the *Sunday Times*, on leaving office in December 2016. The report outlined that Birmingham city council is 'a rotten borough ... beyond redemption', whose powers to run schools and social services should be overhauled because children are at risk, according to the Chief Inspector of Schools. In his final interview before stepping down, Sir Michael Wilshaw said that 'the "appalling children's services" and "awful schools" in Britain's second largest city had been his greatest cause of concern during his five years in office. He warned that a repeat of the so-called Trojan Horse scandal, which saw a radical Islamic ethos introduced to schools in the city, was likely unless the government acted'.[440]

The report is particularly significant because it takes Sir Michael's opinions on trust, precisely because they fit the newspaper's own preferred narrative. However, we have seen that Ofsted data shows Birmingham schools not to be 'awful', but above average. Moreover, the schools at the centre of the Trojan Horse affair were 'outstanding'. If 'awful' schools put children at risk of falling prey to extremism, then the way in which Ofsted and the DfE acted increased that risk and undermined the very schools where children were protected from it.

Just as we were finishing the book, a media story emerged of a 'Trojan Horse plot' in Oldham. Once again, it was written by Andrew Gilligan and appeared in the *Sunday Times* and later in the *Sunday Telegraph*.[441] The story had been based on what was referred to as a 'confidential' report for Oldham City Council from the previous

---

[440] Report by Griffiths, 'Children at risk in "rotten borough" Birmingham', *Sunday Times*, 11 December 2016.

[441] Andrew Gilligan, 'Revealed: new "Trojan Horse plot". Head teacher fears for her safety', *Sunday Times*, 19 February 2017. Available at: www.thetimes.co.uk/article/revealed-new-trojan-horse-plot-9hbknhmc8. See also Henry Bodkin, 'Second Islamist "Trojan Horse" scandal feared after Oldham headteacher reports death threats', *Sunday Telegraph*, 19 February 2017. www.telegraph.co.uk/news/2017/02/19/second-islamist-trojan-horse-scandal-feared-oldham-headteacher/.

December, which the newspaper had seen. However, this report had found no evidence, and the claims had also been repudiated by the DfE and its Due Diligence and Counter Extremism Division, as well as by Manchester Police's counterterrorism unit. The story was accompanied by a subsidiary headline, 'Head teacher fears for her safety'. This, of course, describes a subjective state reported by a head teacher, so can be presented as 'fact', notwithstanding that the city council report found no basis for her fears.

The story was framed by a statement from the National Association of Head Teachers, saying it was 'supporting a number of members in the Oldham area with a variety of apparent Trojan Horse issues', followed by a statement by 'a senior national figure in counter-extremism', who said there was a 'significant problem of Islamist infiltration in Oldham' and that 'it is an absolute model of entryism'. The story set out allegations against two individuals, and went on to suggest similar 'problems' at two other schools. However, it downplayed the council report and did not mention that the charges had been repudiated by the DfE, which also investigated them. It concluded with a 'timeline' of the Birmingham Trojan Horse affair.

The story was repeated again a week later in the *Mail Online*, extending the claim to another school, also citing the Birmingham Trojan Horse affair.[442] Commentator Yasmin Alibhai-Brown also recycled the 'fake news', associating it with her own knowledge of the Trojan Horse affair:

is this really happening? Was it happening three years ago? Yes, my journalistic investigations confirm that in the Midlands and northern towns, there have indeed been conspiracies and entryism by Salafis. I don't doubt Salafis are still at it. It enrages and scares me, the extent to which such people and

---

[442] Richard Spillett, '"He said not wearing a hijab would turn women into whores": SECOND headteacher claims there's a "Trojan Horse-style plot" at Oldham school with Muslim governors, *Mail Online*, 26 February 2017. Available at: www.dailymail.co.uk/news/article-4260986/Second-Oldham-headteacherclaims-Trojan-Horse-bullying.html.

their reactionary ideas, are accommodated by educators and politicians.[443]

Her article makes no reference to the repudiation of her claims by Oldham City Council or the DfE.

Lesson Six: The problem of leadership

We have already discussed the 'heterarchical' nature of governance embodied in the academies programme. We have seen it described as facilitating innovation, in contrast to hierarchical modes of governance. However, the multiplicity of agents – the different entities involved in a network, from schools to consultancies, bodies designed to communicate good practice, for-profit providers of services, to lobbying organisations, to agencies of the DfE – and the loose arrangements among them represents a considerable increase in complexity. Stephen Ball argues that they often also involve considerable 'stumbling and blundering', before going on to say, in the perspective of its advocates, that too may be positive, insofar as such arrangements are 'more likely to give bad decisions a second chance to be rectified'.[444] This does not seem to capture the nature of the situation, especially where anything that is perceived to be a bad decision takes place under the gaze of the press. In those circumstances, it becomes an object of peremptory and arbitrary power.

What is missing in the account of governance is that a heterarchical system in the area of public services also operates as an 'autocracy'. It is organised from a centre, specifically, in the case at hand, that of the DfE and its Secretary of State. In part this is because regulatory

---

[443] Yasmin Alibhai-Brown, 'Islamists won't give up trying to take over British schools because nobody is willing to stop them', *International Business Times,* 21 February 2017. Available at: www.ibtimes.co.uk/islamists-wont-give-trying-take-over-british-schools-because-nobody-willing-stop-them-1607790. The Trojan Horse letter refers to Salafis, but the Clarke Report makes it an issue of Sunnis.

[444] See Ball (2011) 'Academies, policy networks, and governance', page 148. Ball is citing arguments from Nigel Thrift (2005) *Knowing Capitalism*, Sage: London.

bodies such as Ofsted or NCTL are established as agencies within the DfE itself and, therefore, potentially subject to direct influence. In this way, the centre of power is able to set itself outside the regulatory constraints set up for the other bodies. Thus, one of the striking features of the investigations into the Trojan Horse affair is that none of them have had the role of the DfE as part of their terms of reference. Neither the Ofsted inspections, nor the EFA Review of PVET, nor the Kershaw and Clarke Reports considered how the DfE sought to have Park View Academy become PVET and develop an improvement programme for other schools. The Kershaw Report does recommend that Birmingham City Council, 'in consultation with the DFE, should review the process of due diligence in determining the suitability and capacity of a multi academy trust as a sponsor of a maintained school converting to academy status'.[445] However, it does not ask about the nature of due diligence at the DfE, or address how it involves issues of school performance and judgements about suitability of a sponsor's management and leadership team. Nor does it discuss the fact that the DfE was not at arm's length but actively involved in the process of determining sponsorship.

We have seen that Michael Gove, when Secretary of State for Education, precipitated an investigation under Peter Clarke, strongly shaped by the Prevent agenda; and he did so without consultation with Birmingham City Council. The latter set up a review into its own responsibilities, but could not put the role of the DfE into its terms of reference. Its investigation was conducted under the auspices of Northern Education, an academy trust which was itself part of the new 'heterarchy', in the sense that it, too, was outside local authority control. It did not make the new arrangements part of its concern; rather it was focused entirely on those aspects under Birmingham City Council's responsibility. It did not apparently think it worth addressing the programme for school improvement in Birmingham and how it was both implicated in the Trojan Horse affair *and* successful. Indeed, as we have seen, it seemed to believe that there was no programme for school

[445] Kershaw Report, page 21.

improvement. Here was another potential conflict of interest on the part of the Kershaw Report in so far as the shift toward heterarchical arrangements is sanctioned in the name of school improvement, yet Birmingham's comparative success was produced under the pre-existing arrangements.

Michael Gove did set up an inquiry within the DfE. It was not carried out independently, but under the department's own Permanent Secretary.[446] Its terms of reference were extremely limited and concerned merely with the question of whether the department had been informed of any of the concerns associated with the Trojan Horse letter prior to November 2013 when it was sent to Birmingham City Council. The review recommended the need for robust vigilance, but found no instances of any warnings having been ignored. It did not address the processes through which the DfE exercised its responsibilities for academies and free schools.[447] Instead, its recommendations were all associated with Prevent. Thus, it recommended increasing the size of the Due Diligence and Counter Extremism Division (DDCED), and strengthening the academy conversion process, including 'for schools in Prevent priority areas, open source checks on key members in of the Academy governance structure and detailed checks by colleagues in DDCED where any issues are identified'.[448]

Wider processes of governance were not addressed and nor were they by the Parliamentary Select Committee on Education's own consideration of the Trojan Horse affair. This was the only body with the possibility of holding the DfE to account. The committee did, however, state that there was no evidence of the extremism that had

---

[446] Wormald (2015) *Review into Possible Warnings to DfE*.

[447] One, after the election in 2010, describes two meetings between officials and a minister at the Department for Education with a Birmingham head teacher about the challenges political Islam posed for schools in Birmingham. This individual was Tim Boyes, who would go on to become Chief Executive Officer of Birmingham Education Partnership. However, his expressed concerns were about the governance of academy schools. Park View was not an academy until 2012. Annex 3 of the report gives a transcript of a BBC news report on 28 May 2014 describing these meetings.

[448] Wormald (2015) *Review into Possible Warnings to DfE*, page 13.

led to changes in the counter-extremism agenda and tightening of scrutiny of schools and those involved with them in Prevent priority areas. For this it was roundly attacked by the Secretary of State for 'undermining efforts to tackle extremism'.[449] In this way, Michael Gove, the signatory of the authorisation of the incorporation of a faith school – Al-Furqan primary – into PVET on the basis of the latter's 'faith ethos', evaded all personal scrutiny of the conduct of the DfE. This would have included conduct that would have been exculpatory for PVET.

We began this chapter with reference to problems of authoritarianism. We see this as associated with these changes to governance. In effect, there is an expansion of bodies operating under a corporate style of governance with responsibility only for supplying services on a 'contract' basis. For example, Birmingham Education Partnership is a partnership of head teachers 'supplying' school improvement to the city council, but without obligations outside the terms of the contract. These developments place increasing emphasis on the Chief Executive Officer as a business 'leader' supported by a professional governing body. In a similar way, the head teacher as 'charismatic' leader is made responsible for school improvement and is to be challenged only by a governing body which they dominate, or by a Trust partnership of head teacher peers. Sir Michael Wilshaw, in the role of the Chief Inspector of Schools, also understood that role as one of charismatic leadership to drive up standards.

It is this 'noisy', high salaried version of charismatic leadership that is strongly associated with the ability to capture a media presence. It helps to create the conditions for authoritarianism by undermining local capacities for engagement and holding to account. It drowns out the 'quiet' charisma of teachers committed to the school improvement by their persuasive presence in front of pupils and unpaid governors acting to improve schools for their communities.

---

[449] See Richard Adams, 'Education department hits back at MPs over Trojan horse criticisms', *The Guardian*, 26 June 2015. Available at: www.theguardian.com/education/2015/jun/26/education-department-hits-back-at-mps-over-trojan-horse-criticisms.

Implications

In this book, we have sought to explain how a successful school could become the focus of public anxiety and denigration. Part of the explanation lies in the complexity of governance arrangements. This is not to say that there were gaps through which the school avoided proper scrutiny. Rather their complexity was such that those asked to investigate the circumstances seemed unaware of the nature of the obligations schools were under, whether these referred to the Prevent agenda, community cohesion, or collective worship and religious education. The investigations – from special Ofsted inspections through the EFA and the Kershaw and Clarke Reports were conducted precipitately – and in many cases under direct pressure from the DfE and its Secretary of State(s). The inquiries that might have contributed to a national conversation instead led to a distortion of that debate.

We have seen that British Muslims *are* committed to 'British values'. Yet it is frequently declared that they are self-segregated and intolerant of religious pluralism while it is their own religious expression that is viewed with suspicion. In Chapter One we cited research by Hiranthi Jayaweera and Tufyal Choudhury showing that ethnic minorities in Britain do want greater participation in civic and political life. However, the new governance arrangements of schools reduce the number of governors from ethnic minority backgrounds precisely because they follow a corporate model. Thus, no trustee or member of the executive board at Birmingham Education Partnership is from an ethnic minority, despite the fact that school pupils in Birmingham are majority ethnic minority. Equally, the body set up under the aegis of the DfE from which it takes advice – the Headteacher Board for the West Midlands – has no ethnic minority members. Moreover, if those wishing greater involvement live in a Prevent priority area, as many Muslims do, their participation will be subject to special scrutiny.

Jayaweera and Choudhury conducted their interviews with local policy makers and practitioners before the Trojan Horse affair: 'Many interviewees argued that efforts on improving cohesion issues at the local level can be undermined by national policy and political rhetoric, and by media discourse, particularly around issues of asylum and terrorism.'[450] Indeed, following the Trojan Horse affair, if Muslim parents or community members dare to question a head teacher over school performance, or if they wish to have provision of prayer facilities or other arrangements for their children, they will be subject to accusations of Islamification, as occurred most recently in Oldham.

The former Chief Inspector of Schools, Sir Michael Wilshaw, as we saw, erroneously and gratuitously described Birmingham's schools as 'awful', with the implication that a significant part of the problem was that they were too embedded in their local communities, a theme that was also echoed by Tim Boyes, CEO of Birmingham Education Partnership. Commentators such as Ted Cantle have also expressed the view that schools are more segregated than their local communities, notwithstanding that this is an artefact, in large part, of the different age structure of ethnic minority populations compared with the white British population.[451] Successful schools are necessarily part of the solution to any problem of community cohesion. Indeed, in Chapter One, we cited Yasmin Hussain and Paul Bagguley's argument that where disaffection among Muslim young people exists, it is not because of the attractions of radical Islam, but because of disappointment in the realisation of their *rights as British citizens*, especially in the context of unequal opportunities and material disadvantage.[452]

There are two tragedies bound up together in the Birmingham Trojan Horse affair. One is the disruption of the lives of teachers and governors in Birmingham, who made such a difference to the prospects of the pupils under their care, and were unjustly accused of placing them at risk. We have seen that the educational opportunities of pupils at the school were very significantly damaged because of the way in which the DfE intervened. The second tragedy is that it has made it more difficult to realise the rights to educational opportunities more generally of young people from Muslim backgrounds – opportunities

---

[450] Jayaweera and Choudhury (2008) 'Immigration, faith and cohesion', page 117.

[451] 'Understanding school segregation in England 2011–2016', SchoolDash, March 2017.

[452] Hussain and Bagguley (2005) 'Citizenship, ethnicity and identity'.

and rights that are theirs as British citizens and which, quite properly, are regarded as key to long term community cohesion. That is the failure of 'British values' that the Birmingham Trojan Horse case exposes and it is one that should be laid at the door of government.

Bibliography

Academic

Allen, Danielle S. (2004) 'Invisible citizens: on exclusion and domination in Ralph Ellison and Hannah Arendt', in M. Williams and S. Macedo (eds) *Nomos XLVI: Political Exclusion and Domination*, New York: NYU Press.

Archer, Toby (2009) 'Welcome to the *Umma*: the British state and its Muslim citizens since 9/11', *Cooperation and Conflict*, 44(3): 329-47.

Ball, Stephen (2011) 'Academies, policy networks, and governance', in Helen M. Gunter (ed) *The State and Education Policy: the Academies Programme*, London: Continuum.

Banfield, Paul and Kay, Rebecca (2012) *Introduction to Human Resource Management*, Oxford: Oxford University Press.

Baxter, Jacqueline (2016) *School Governance: Policy, Politics and Practices*, Bristol: Policy Press.

Bhambra, Gurminder K. (2017) 'Locating Brexit in the pragmatics of race, citizenship and empire', in William Outhwaite (ed) *Brexit: Sociological Responses*, London: Anthem Press.

Birt, Yahya (2009) 'Promoting virulent envy?', *The RUSI Journal*, 154(4): 52–58.

Birt, Yahya (2017) 'After Finsbury Park: tackling Islamophobia as "extremism" will compound Prevent's failures'. Available at: https://medium.com/insurge-intelligence/after-finsbury-park-the-proposed-commission-for-countering-extremism-and-the-securitization-of-a5d85b5ad2d8.

Blackwood, Leda (2015) 'What is wrong with the official "psychological" model of radicalisation?', *Public Spirit,* 23 October 2015. Available at: www.publicspirit.org.uk/what-is-wrong-with-the-official-psychological-model-of-radicalisation/.

British Humanist Association (2014) 'Birmingham schools findings reflect need for wider review of place of religion in schools', 9 June. Available at: https://humanism.org.uk/2014/06/09/34029/.

British Humanist Association (2014) 'Birmingham taxpayers' money used to urge systematic discrimination against non-religious in RE', 12 June. Available at: https://humanism.org.uk/2014/06/12/birmingham-taxpayers-money-used-council-urge-systematic-discrimination-non-religious-re/.

Brown, Andrew and Woodhead, Linda (2016) *That Was the Church That Was: How the Church of England Lost the English People,* London: Bloomsbury.

Cannizzaro, Sara and Gholami, Reza (2016) 'The devil is not in the detail: representational absence and stereotyping in the "Trojan Horse" news story', *Race, Ethnicity and Education.* First online, 19 July 2016. Available at: http://dx.doi.org/10.1080/13613324.2016.1195350.

Catney, Gemma and Sabater, Alfres (2015) 'Ethnic minority disadvantage in the labour market: participation, skills and geographical inequalities', Report for the Joseph Rowntree Foundation. Available at: https://livrepository.liverpool.ac.uk/2014190/1/ethnic-minority-disadvantage-full.pdf.

Cohen, Stanley (1972) *Folk Devils and Moral Panics*, London: MacGibbon and Kee Ltd.

Colman, Andrew (2015) 'Religion, tolerance & freedom – what private views can a teacher express?', 10 July. Available at: www.2harecourt.com/training-and-knowledge/religion-tolerance-and-freedom-what-private-views-can-a-teacher-express/.

Cumper, Peter, and Mawhinney, Alison (eds) (2015) *Collective Worship and Religious Observance in Schools: An Evaluation of Law and Policy in the UK.* AHRC Network report. Available at: http://collectiveschoolworship.com/documents/CollectiveWorshipReligiousObservanceAHRCNetworkReport13November2015.pdf.

Davies, Lynn, Limbada, Zubeda, McDonald, Laura Zahra, Spalek, Basia and Weeks, Doug (2015) *Formers and Families: Transitional Journeys in and out of Violent Extremisms in the UK*. Available at: www.connectjustice. org/admin/data/files/UK%20Formers%20&%20Families%20Final. pdf.

Dean, Charlotte, Dyson, Alan, Gallannaugh, Frances, Howe, Andy and Raffo Carlo (2007) *Schools, Governors and Disadvantage*, York: Joseph Rowntree Foundation.

Deem, Rosemary, Brehony, Kevin and Heath, Sue (1995) *Active Citizenship and the Governing of Schools*, Buckingham: Open University Press;

Farris, Sara F. (2017) *In the Name of Women's Rights: The Rise of Femonationalism*, Durham, NC: Duke University Press.

Finney, Nissa and Simpson, Ludi (2009) *Sleepwalking to Segregation? Challenging Myths about Race and Migration*, Bristol. Policy Press.

Foner, Nancy and Alba, Richard (2008) 'Immigrant religion in the US and Western Europe: bridge or barrier to inclusion?', *International Migration Review*, 42: 360–392.

Foucault, Michel (1991) 'Governmentality', in Graham Burchell, Colin Gordon and Peter Miller (eds), *The Foucault Effect: Studies in Governmentality*, Hemel Hempstead: Harvester Wheatsheaf, pages 87–104.

Full Fact (2016) 'Academies and maintained schools: what do we know?', April. Available at: https://fullfact.org/education/academies-and-maintained-schools-what-do-we-know/.

Gale, Richard T. (2013) 'Religious residential segregation and internal migration: the British Muslim case', *Environment and Planning A*, 45: 872–891.

Goodhart, David (2017) *The Road to Somewhere: The Populist Revolt and the Future of Politics*, London: Hurst and Company.

Goodhart, David (2017) '"Racial self-interest" is not racism', *Policy Exchange*, 3 March. Available at: https://policyexchange.org.uk/ publication/racial-self-interest-is-not-racism/.

Gove, Michael (2006) *Celsius 7/7: How the West's Policy of Appeasement Has Provoked Yet More Fundamentalist Terror – And What Needs to be Done About It Now*, London: Phoenix.

Gunter Helen M. (ed) (2011) *The State and Education Policy: The Academies Programme,* London: Continuum.

Guveli, Ayse and Platt, Lucinda (2011) 'Understanding the religious behaviour of Muslims in the Netherlands and the UK', *Sociology,* 45: 1008–1027.

Hatcher, Richard (2009) 'Setting up academies, campaigning against them: an analysis of a contested policy process', *Management in Education,* 23(3): 108-12.

Husband, Charles and Alam, Yunis (2011) *Social Cohesion and Counter-Terrorism: A Policy Contradiction?,* Bristol: Policy Press.

Hussain, Yasmin and Bagguley, Paul (2005) 'Citizenship, ethnicity and identity: British Pakistanis after the 2001 "Riots"', *Sociology,* 39: 407–425.

Jayaweera, Hiranthi and Choudhury, Tufyal (2008) 'Immigration, faith and cohesion: evidence from local areas with significant Muslim populations', York: Joseph Rowntree Foundation. Available at: www.compas.ox.ac.uk/2008/pr-2008-muslims_cohesion_final/.

Joppke, Christian (2008) 'Immigration and the identity of citizenship: the paradox of universalism', *Citizenship Studies,* 12(6): 533–546.

Jackson, Richard (2015) 'The epistemological crisis of counterterrorism', *Critical Studies on Terrorism,* 8(1): 33–54.

Karlsen, Saffron and Nazroo, James Y. (2015) 'Ethnic and religious differences in the attitudes of people towards being "British"', *Sociological Review,* 63(4): 774.

Karner, Christian and Parker, David (2011) 'Conviviality and conflict: pluralism, resilience and hope in inner-city Birmingham', *Journal of Ethnic and Migration Studies,* 37: 355-72.

Kay, William K. and Francis, Leslie J. (eds) (1998) *Religion in Education,* Leominister: Gracewing.

Khan, Omar and Weekes-Bernard, Debbie (2015) *This is Still About Us: Why Ethnic Minorities See Immigration Differently,* Runnymede Report on Race and Immigration. Available at: www.runnymedetrust.org/uploads/Race%20and%20Immigration%20Report%20v2.pdf.

Kundnani, Arun (2015) *A Decade Lost: Rethinking Radicalisation and Extremism*, London: Claystone. Available at: http://www.claystone. org.uk/wp-content/uploads/2015/01/Claystone-rethinking-radicalisation.pdf.

Kundnani, Arun (2009) *Spooked: How not to Prevent Violent Extremism*, London: Institute of Race Relations. Available at: http://www.irr.org. uk/news/spooked-how-not-to-prevent-violent-extremism/.

Maccoby, Eleonor E. (2002) 'Gender and group process: a developmental perspective', *Current Directions in Psychological Science*, 11(2): 54–58.

Manning, Alan and Roy, Sanchari (2010) 'Culture clash or culture club? National identity in Britain', *The Economics Journal*, 120(542): F72–F100.

Nalgra, Daljit (2007) 'The man who would be English', in Daljit Nagra *Look We Have Coming to Dover*, London: Faber and Faber.

NUT (2016) 'Prevent strategy motion'. 28 March. Available at: http:// schoolsweek.co.uk/nut-prevent-strategy-motion-what-it-actually-says/.

Open Society Justice Initiative (2016) *Eroding Trust: The UK's Prevent Counter-Extremism Strategy in Health and Education*, New York: Open Society Foundations. Available at: www.opensocietyfoundations. org/reports/eroding-trust-uk-s-prevent-counter-extremism-strategy-health-and-education.

O'Toole, Therese, Jones, Stephen H., Nilsson DeHanas, Daniel and Modood, Tariq (2013) 'Prevent after TERFOR: why local contexts still matter', *Public Spirit*, December 2013. Available at: www.publicspirit. org.uk/the-importance-of-local-context-for-preventing-extremism/.

O'Toole, Therese, Nilsson DeHanas, Daniel and Modood Tariq (2012) 'Balancing tolerance, security and Muslim engagement in the United Kingdom: the impact of the "Prevent" agenda', *Critical Studies on Terrorism*, 5: 373–389.

O'Toole, Therese, Nilsson DeHanas, Daniel, Modood, Tariq, Meer Nasar and Jones, Stephen H. (2013) *Taking Part: Muslim Participation in Contemporary Governance*, Bristol: University of Bristol. Available at: www.bristol.ac.uk/media-library/sites/ethnicity/migrated/ documents/mpcgreport.pdf.

O'Toole, Therese, Meer, Nassar, Nilsson DeHanas, Daniel, Jones, Stephen H. and Modood, Tariq (2016) 'Governing through Prevent? Regulation and contested practice in state-Muslim engagement', *Sociology*, 50(1): 160–177. Available at: http://journals.sagepub.com/doi/pdf/10.1177/0038038514564437.

Parker, Stephen G. and Freathy, Rob J.K. (2011) 'Context, complexity and contestation: Birmingham's Agreed Syllabuses for Religious Education since the 1970s', *Journal of Beliefs and Values*, 32(2): 247–263;

Parker, Stephen G. and Freathy, Rob J.K. (2012) 'Ethnic diversity, Christian hegemony and the emergence of multi-faith religious education in the 1970s'. *History of Education,* 41(3): 381-404.

Phillips, Chris, Tse, Daniel and Johnson, Fiona (2010) *Community Cohesion and PREVENT*, Ipsos Mori Research Report 0085 for the Department for Education. Available at: www.gov.uk/government/uploads/system/uploads/attachment_data/file/182300/DFE-RR085.pdf.

Power, Michael (1997) *The Audit Society*, Oxford: Oxford University Press.

Quilliam Foundation (2010) 'Preventing terrorism: where next For Britain?'. Available at: www.scribd.com/doc/34834977/Secret-Quilliam-Memo-to-government.

Ranson, Stewart and Crouch, Colin (2009) 'Towards a new governance of schools in the re-making of civil society', Research Paper, Institute of Education, University of Warwick. Available at: www.educationdevelopmenttrust.com/~/media/EDT/Reports/Research/2009/r-school-governors-and-the-partnership-arrangement-report-2009.pdf.

Report of the Commission on Religion and Belief in British Public Life (2015) *Living with Difference: Community, Diversity and the Common Good,* Cambridge: Woolf Institute. Available at: www.woolf.cam.ac.uk/uploads/Living%20with%20Difference.pdf.

Runnymede Trust (1997) *Islamaphobia: A Challenge for us All.* Available at: www.runnymedetrust.org/publications/17/74.html.

Runnymede Trust (2000) *The Future of Multi-Ethnic Britain. The Parekh Report*, London: Profile Books.

Salaman, Graeme (2001) *Understanding Business Organisations*, London: Routledge.

School Dash (2017) *Understanding School Segregation in England 2011–2016*, March. Published by SchoolDash, the Challenge and the iCoCo Foundation. Available at: www.schooldash.com/blog.html#20170322.

Scott, Joan Wallach (2010) *The Politics of the Veil*, Princeton, NJ: Princeton University Press.

Scraton, Phil (1999) *Hillsborough: The Truth*, Edinburgh: Mainstream Publishing.

Shain, Farzana (2011) *The New Folk Devils: Muslim Boys and Education in England*, Stoke-on-Trent: Trentham Books.

Simpson, Ludi (2012) 'More segregation or more mixing?', Manchester: Centre on Dynamics of Ethnicity. Available at: www.ethnicity.ac.uk/medialibrary/briefingsupdated/more-segregation-or-more-mixing.pdf;

Simpson, Ludi (2013) 'Has neigbourhood ethnic segregation decreased?', Manchester: Centre on Dynamics of Ethnicity. Available at: www.ethnicity.ac.uk/medialibrary/briefingsupdated/has-neighbourhood-ethnic-segregation-decreased.pdf.

Telles, Edward E. and Ortiz Vilma (2008) 'Finding America: creating educational opportunity for our newest citizens', in Brian D. Smedley and Alan Jenkins (eds) *All Things Being Equal: Instigating Opportunity in an Inequitable Time*, New York: The New Press.

Thomas, Paul (2010) 'Failed and friendless: the UK's "Preventing Violent Extremism" programme', *British Journal of Politics and International Relations*, 12(3): 442-58.

Thrift, Nigel (2005) *Knowing Capitalism*, Sage: London.

Uberoi, Varun and Modood, Tariq (2013) 'Inclusive Britishness: a multiculturalist advance', *Political Studies*, 61: 23–41.

Walford, Geoffrey (2000) *Policy and Politics in Education. Sponsored Grant-Maintained Schools and Religious Diversity*, Aldershot: Ashgate.

Walford, Geoffrey (2008) 'Faith-based schools in England after ten years of Tony Blair', *Oxford Review of Education*, 34(6): 689-99.

Warsi, Sayeeda (2017) *The Enemy Within: A Tale of Muslim Britain*, London: Allen Lane.

West, Ed (2013) *The Diversity Illusion: What we Got Wrong about Immigration and How to Set it Right*, London: Gibson Square.

Wise, Amanda and Velayutham, Selvaraj (eds) (2009) *Everyday Multiculturalism*, Basingstoke: Palgrave Macmillan.

Wong, Charlotte, Eccles, Jacquelynne, and Sameroff, Arnold (2003) 'The influence of ethnic discrimination and ethnic identification on African American adolescents' school and socioemotional adjustment', *Journal of Personality*, 71: 1197–1232.

Yasui, Miwa, Dorhan, Carole La Rue, and Fishion, Thomas J. (2004). 'Ethnic identity and psychological adjustment: a validity analysis for European American and African American adolescents', *Journal of Adolescent Research*, 19: 807–825.

Official Reports, Speeches, and other publications

Bell, David (2003) Speech to the Fabian Society, Access and achievement in urban education. Text, *the Guardian*, 20 November. Available at: www.theguardian.com/education/2003/nov/20/schools.uk3.

Birmingham City Council Education Service (2003) 'Asian heritage achievement action plan', 19 December. Birmingham.

Birmingham City Council (2010) 'Project Champion: scrutiny review into ANPR and CCTV cameras: a report from Overview & Scrutiny', 2 November. Available at: www.birmingham.gov.uk/downloads/file/460/project_champion_scrutiny_review_into_anpr_and_cctv_cameras_november_2010.

Birmingham Local Education Authority (2005) 'Raising Achievement of Pakistani and Bangladeshi Boys: Good Practice Guide for Schools', Nargis Rashid, Iram Naz and Mohammed Hussain. School Effectiveness Division.

Birmingham SACRE (n.d) 'The 24 dispositions', Faith Makes a Difference. RE in Birmingham. Available at: https://www.faithmakesadifference.co.uk/dispositions.

Birmingham SACRE (n.d 'The Basic Curriculum in Birmingham Summary of the 2007 Birmingham Religious Education Syllabus'. Available at: www.faithmakesadifference.co.uk/sites/faithmakesadifference.co.uk/files/Summary_2007_Birmingham_RE_Syllabus_2_0.pdf.

Brown, Gordon (2007) Speech at the Commonwealth Association. Full text, *The Guardian*, 27 February. Available at: www.theguardian.com/politics/2007/feb/27/immigrationpolicy.race.

Cameron, David (2011) PM's speech at Munich Security Conference, 5 February. Available at: www.gov.uk/government/speeches/pms-speech-at-munich-security-conference.

Cameron, David (2011) King James Bible Speech, 16 December. Available at: www.gov.uk/government/news/prime-ministers-king-james-bible-speech.

Cantle, Ted (2001) *Community Cohesion: A Report of the Independent Review Team*, London: Home Office. Available at: http://resources.cohesioninstitute.org.uk/Publications/Documents/Document/DownloadDocumentsFile.aspx?recordId=96&file=PDFversion.

Casey, Dame Louise (2016) *The Casey Review: a review into opportunity and integration*. An independent report for the Department of Communities and Local Government, 5 December. Available at: www.gov.uk/government/publications/the-casey-review-a-review-into-opportunity-and-integration.

Clarke Report (2014) *Report into Allegations concerning Birmingham Schools arising from the 'Trojan Horse' Letter*. London, House of Commons. HC 576. Available at: www.gov.uk/government/uploads/system/uploads/attachment_data/file/340526/HC_576_accessible_-.pdf.

Commission on Integration and Cohesion (2007) *Our Shared Future: Final Report of the Commission*, Wetherby: Crown Office, Available here: http://resources.cohesioninstitute.org.uk/Publications/Documents/Document/Default.aspx?recordId=18.

Denham, John (2001) *Building Cohesive Communities: A Report on the Ministerial Group on Public Order and Community Cohesion*, London: Home Office. Available at: www.tedcantle.co.uk/publications/005%20Building%20Cohesive%20Communities%20(The%20Denham%20Report)%202001.pdf.

Department for Communities and Local Government (2007) *Preventing Violent Extremism Guidance Note for Government Offices and Local Authorities in England*, London, DCLG.

Department for Communities and Local Government (2007) *Preventing Violent Extremism: Winning Hearts and Minds*, London: DCLG. Available at: http://webarchive.nationalarchives.gov.uk/20070701080545/http://www.communities.gov.uk/index.asp?id=1509398.

Department for Communities and Local Government (2008) *Delivering Prevent – Responding to Learning*. Available at: http://lx.iriss.org.uk/content/delivering-prevent-responding-learning.

Department for Communities and Local Government (2009) *Summary Report: Understanding Muslim Ethnic Communities*, London: DCLG. Available at: http://webarchive.nationalarchives.gov.uk/20120920001411/http://www.communities.gov.uk/documents/communities/pdf/1203896.pdf.

Department for Communities and Local Government (2011) Freedom of Information Request: Prevent Funding. 7 July. Available at: www.gov.uk/government/publications/prevent-funding.

Department for Education (1994) Circular 1/94 'Religious education and collective worship', 31 January. Available at: www.gov.uk/government/uploads/system/uploads/attachment_data/file/281929/Collective_worship_in_schools.pdf.

Department for Education (2011) Freedom of Information Release: Community Cohesion, 28 February. Available at: www.gov.uk/government/publications/community-cohesion/community-cohesion.

Department for Education (2014) 'Promoting fundamental British values as part of SMSC in schools. Departmental advice for maintained schools', London: Department for Education, November. Available at: www.gov.uk/government/uploads/system/uploads/attachment_data/file/380595/SMSC_Guidance_Maintained_Schools.pdf.

Department for Education (2015) *The Prevent Duty: For Schools and Childcare Providers*, 1 July. Available at: www.gov.uk/government/publications/protecting-children-from-radicalisation-the-prevent-duty#history.

Department for Education (2016) *Educational Excellence Everywhere*. March. Available at: www.gov.uk/government/uploads/system/uploads/attachment_data/file/508550/Educational_excellence_everywhere__print_ready_.pdf.

Department for Education (2016) *Schools that Work for Everyone*, Government Consultation. September 2016. Available at: https://consult.education.gov.uk/school-frameworks/schools-that-work-for-everyone/.

Department for Education and Employment (2000) 'Sex and Relationship Education Guidance', London: Department for Education and Employment. Available at: www.gov.uk/government/uploads/system/uploads/attachment_data/file/283599/sex_and_relationship_education_guidance.pdf.

Department for Education and Skills (2004) *What are Academies?* Available at: https://tinyurl.com/ybb754m3.

Department for Education and Skills (2005) *Higher Standards, Better Schools for All: More Choice for Parents and Pupils*, October. Available at: www.educationengland.org.uk/documents/pdfs/2005-white-paper-higher-standards.pdf.

Department for Schools, Children and the Families (2007) 'Guidance on the duty to promote community cohesion', London. Available at: http://webarchive.nationalarchives.gov.uk/20130401151715/http://www.education.gov.uk/publications/standard/publicationDetail/Page1/DCSF-00598-2007.

Department for Schools, Children and Families (2008) 'Learning together to be safe together: a toolkit to help schools contribute to the prevention of violent extremism', Nottingham: DCSF. Available at: http://dera.ioe.ac.uk/8396/1/DCSF-Learning%20Together_bkmk.pdf.

Education Select Committee (2015) 'Extremism in schools: the Trojan Horse affair'. Available at: www.publications.parliament.uk/pa/cm201415/cmselect/cmeduc/473/47302.htm.

Education Funding Agency (2014) *Review of Park View Education Trust*, 9 June. Available at:www.gov.uk/government/publications/review-of-park-view-educational-trust.

Fallon, Michael Sir (2016) Speech at Tory Party Conference, 4 October. Available at: https://blogs.spectator.co.uk/2016/10/full-text-michael-fallons-tory-party-conference-speech/#.

Gove, Michael (2012) Speech at Freedom and Autonomy for Schools National Association conference, 5 July. Available at: www.gov.uk/government/speeches/michael-gove-on-fasnas-first-twenty-years.

Hansard (1988) House of Commons Debate, 23 March, vol 130, cc398–426. Available at: http://hansard.millbanksystems.com/commons/1988/mar/23/the-national-curriculum.

Harrow SACRE (2013) Guidance on Offering Space for Prayer and Reflection in School. Available at: www.harrow.gov.uk/www2/documents/s108380/sacre.

HM Government (2013) *Tackling Extremism in the UK: Report from the Prime Minister's Task Force on Tackling Radicalisation and Extremism*, December 2013, London: Cabinet Office. Available at: www.gov.uk/government/uploads/system/uploads/attachment_data/file/263181/ETF_FINAL.pdf.

HM Government (2014) *A Report to the Secretary of State for Education and the Minister for Children and Families on Ways Forward for Children's Social Care Services in Birmingham*, chaired by Professor Julian Le Grand, February. Available at: https://www.gov.uk/government/uploads/system/uploads/attachment_data/file/297748/Birmingham_report_25.03.14.pdf.

HM Government (2014) *Governors' Handbook: for Governors in Maintained Schools, Academies and Free Schools*, January. Available at: www.gov.uk/government/uploads/system/uploads/attachment_data/file/270398/Governors-Handbook-January-2014.pdf.

HM Government (2015) *Revised Prevent Duty Guidance: for England and Wales*, version 2, revised 16 July. Available at: www.gov.uk/government/uploads/system/uploads/attachment_data/file/445977/3799_Revised_Prevent_Duty_Guidance__England_Wales_V2-Interactive.pdf

HM Government (2015) *Channel Duty Guidance*. Available at: www.gov.uk/government/uploads/system/uploads/attachment_data/file/425189/Channel_Duty_Guidance_April_2015.pdf.

HM Government (2015) The Queen's Speech. 27 May. Available at: www.gov.uk/government/uploads/system/uploads/attachment_data/file/430149/QS_lobby_pack_FINAL_NEW_2.pdf.

HM Government (2015) *Revised Prevent Duty Guidance: for England and Wales*, version 2, revised 16 July. Available at: www.gov.uk/government/uploads/system/uploads/attachment_data/file/445977/3799_Revised_Prevent_Duty_Guidance__England_Wales_V2-Interactive.pdf.

HM Government (2017) Queen's Speech, 21 June. Available at: www.gov.uk/government/speeches/queens-speech-2017.

Home Office (2011) *Prevent Strategy*. Presented to Parliament by the Secretary of State for the Home Department by Command of Her Majesty. London: Cm8092. Available at: www.gov.uk/government/uploads/system/uploads/attachment_data/file/97976/prevent-strategy-review.pdf.

Home Office (2015) *CONTEST: The United Kingdom's Strategy for Countering Terrorism: Annual Report for 2014,* March, London: Home Office. Available at: www.gov.uk/government/uploads/system/uploads/attachment_data/file/415708/contest_annual_report_for_2014.pdf.

Home Office (2015) *Counter-Extremism Strategy*, 19 October. Available at: www.gov.uk/government/publications/counter-extremism-strategy.

House of Commons (2010) *Preventing Violent Extremism: Sixth Report of Session 2009–10*, Communities and Local Government Committee, London: House of Commons. Available at: www.publications.parliament.uk/pa/cm200910/cmselect/cmcomloc/65/65.pdf.

House of Commons (2017) *Briefing Paper: Faith Schools in England; FAQs*. Briefing Paper Number 06972, 13 March. Authors Robert Long and Paul Bolton. Available at: http://researchbriefings.parliament.uk/ResearchBriefing/Summary/SN06972.

House of Commons Joint Select Committee on Human Rights, (2016) *Counter-Extremism Second Report of Session 2016–17.* 20 July. Available at: https://publications.parliament.uk/pa/jt201617/jtselect/jtrights/105/105.pdf.

House of Commons The Women and Equalities Committee (2013) *Sexual Harassment and Sexual Violence in Schools.* 8 September. Available at: https://publications.parliament.uk/pa/cm201617/cmselect/cmwomeq/91/9102.htm.

Kerslake Report (2014) *Report on Birmingham City Council's Governance and Organisational Capabilities: An Independent Review under Sir Bob Kerslake*, December. Available at: ,www.gov.uk/government/publications/birmingham-city-councils-governance-and-organisational-capabilities-an-independent-review.

Kerslake Report (2014) Supporting Analysis. Available at: www.gov.uk/government/publications/birmingham-city-councils-governance-and-organisational-capabilities-an-independent-review.

Kershaw Report (2014) *Investigation Report: Trojan Horse Letter.* Prepared for Birmingham City Council and published by Eversheds LlP, page 9. Available at: www.birmingham.gov.uk/downloads/file/1579/investigation_report_trojan_horse_letter_the_kershaw_report.

Macpherson Report (1999). *Report of the Stephen Lawrence Inquiry.* Report of an Inquiry by Sir William Macpherson Available at: www.gov.uk/government/publications/the-stephen-lawrence-inquiry.

Morgan. Nicky (2016) Speech about tackling extremism, 19 January. Available at: https://www.gov.uk/government/speeches/nicky-morgan-speaks-about-tackling-extremism.

Ofsted (2001) Ofsted Inspection Report Park View School, Inspection number 187797, 26 February to 2 March.

Ofsted (2007) Ofsted Inspection Report for Park View School, Inspection number 286688, 20–21.

Ofsted (2012) Ofsted Inspection Report, Park View Business and Enterprise School, Inspection number 376921, 11–12 January.

Ofsted (2013) Ofsted Inspection Report, Oldknow Academy, January. Available at: https://reports.ofsted.gov.uk/inspection-reports/find-inspection-report/provider/ELS/138052.

Ofsted 2014) Ofsted Inspection Report, Park View Academy of Mathematics and Science, 5‾6 March, 17–18 March. Available at: https://reports.ofsted.gov.uk/inspection-reports/find-inspection-report/provider/ELS/138059.

Ofsted (2014) Ofsted Inspection Report, Oldknow Academy, April.

Ofsted (2014) *School Inspection Handbook*, April.

Ofsted (2016) Ofsted School Inspection Report, Rockwood Academy, 16–17 March. Available at: https://reports.ofsted.gov.uk/inspection-reports/find-inspection-report/provider/ELS/138059.

Ofsted (2016) *School Inspection Handbook*, August.

Ofsted/Audit Commission (2002) Inspection of Birmingham Local Education Authority, April. Available at: https://reports.ofsted. gov.uk/sites/default/files/documents/local_authority_reports/ birmingham/012_Local Authority Inspection as pdf.pdf.

Phillips, Sir Trevor (2005) 'Sleep-walking to segregation'. to the Manchester Council for Community Relations, 22 April. The text of the speech is available at: https://www.jiscmail.ac.uk/cgi-bin/webadm in?A3=ind0509&L=CRONEM&E=quoted-printable&P=60513&B= %EF%BF%BD%E2%80%94_%3D_NextPart_001_01C5C28A.095017 83&T=text%2Fhtml;%20charset=iso-8859%E2%80%931&pending=.

Powell, Enoch (1968) Speech delivered to a Conservative association meeting in Birmingham on 20 April 1968 ('Rivers of Blood'). Available at: www.telegraph.co.uk/comment/3643823/Enoch-Powells-Rivers-of-Blood-speech.html.

Safer Birmingham Partnership (2009) *Building Resilience to Violent Extremism: Delivering the Prevent Strategy in Birmingham*, Birmingham: SBP. Available at: https://www.whatdotheyknow.com/request/18244/ response/50154/attach/html/3/BUILDING%20RESILIENCE%20 TO%20VIOLENT%20EXTREMISM%20Final%20Version%201. pdf.html.

Swann Report (1985) *Education For All. Report of the Committee of Enquiry into the Education of Children from Ethnic Minority Groups*. Available at: www.educationengland.org.uk/documents/swann/swann1985.html.

Thames Valley Police (2010) *Project Champion Review*, London: TVP. Available at: www.statewatch.org/news/2010/oct/uk-project-champion-police-report.pdf.

Trojan Horse Review Group (2014) Report to Leader of Birmingham City Council, 18 July. Available at: www.birmingham.gov.uk/ info/20179/news_and_media/984/trojan_horse_review

Wandsworth Borough Council (2015) *Guidance for Wandsworth Primary Schools with Muslim Pupils*. May. Available at: https://wandsworth-public.sharepoint.com/info4schools/Circulars/Wandsworth%20 Guidance%20for%20schools%20with%20Muslim%20pupils%20-%20 May%202015.pdf.

West Midlands Counter Terrorism Unit (2008) 'Memorandum: Report to Chief Constable and Chief Executive of Police Authority seeking delegated authority concerning element of Project Champion', 3 September. Available at: www.whatdotheyknow.com/request/36652/response/107429/attach/6/Champion%20Delegated%20Auth%20for%20Main%20Contract%20Award%206%20Oct%202009.pdf.

Wilshaw, Sir Michael (2011) Speech: Good schools for all – an impossible dream?, 28 November. Available at: http://arkreboot.bitmachine.co.uk/sites/default/files/111129_mw_speech_4pm_with_logo_final_0_0.pdf.

Wilshaw, Sir Michael (2014) Speech on Trojan Horse, 9 June. Available at:www.birminghammail.co.uk/news/midlands-news/trojan-horse-sir-michael-wilshaws-7240705.

Wilshaw, Michael Sir (2014) Letter to Michael Gove, 'Advice note provided on academies and maintained schools in Birmingham to the Secretary of State for Education, Rt Hon Michael Gove MP, as commissioned by letter dated 27 March 2014'. 9th June. Available at: www.gov.uk/government/publications/advice-note-on-academies-and-maintained-schools-in-birmingham.

Wormald, Chris (2015) *Review into Possible Warnings to DfE relating to Extremism in Birmingham School.* Report by the Permanent Secretary at the DfE, Chris Wormald, January. Available at: www.gov.uk/government/uploads/system/uploads/attachment_data/file/396211/Review_into_possible_warnings_to_DfE_relating_to_extremism_in_Birmingham_schools.pdf.

Legal documents and proceedings

Crown Prosecution Service (n.d.) *Legal Guidance: Abuse of Process.* Available at: www.cps.gov.uk/legal/a_to_c/abuse_of_process/.

Crown Prosecution Service (2014) 'Expert evidence'. Available at: www.cps.gov.uk/legal/assets/uploads/files/expert_evidence_first_edition_2014.pdf.

European Court of Human Rights (2013) *Rights to a Fair Trial.* Available at: www.echr.coe.int/Documents/Guide_Art_6_ENG.pdf.

European Court of Human Rights (2015) Guide on Article 2 of Protocol No. 1 to the European Convention on Human Rights. Available at: www.echr.coe.int/Documents/Guide_Art_2_Protocol_1_ENG.pdf.

In the High Court of Justice, Queen's Bench Division Administrative Court. In the Matter of an Appeal Under The Teachers' Disciplinary (England) Regulations 2012. Birmingham Civil Justice Centre, 13 October 2016. Neutral Citation Number: [2016] EWHC 2507 (Admin). Available at: www.bailii.org/ew/cases/EWHC/Admin/2016/2507.html.

R (Fox) v Secretary of State for Education (2015). Available at: www.judiciary.gov.uk/wp-content/uploads/2015/11/r-fox-v-ssfe.pdf.

NCTL (2014) 'Tina Ireland: Professional Conduct Panel outcome panel decision and reasons on behalf of the Secretary of State for Education'. March. Available at: www.gov.uk/government/publications/teacher-misconduct-panel-outcome-ms-tina-ireland.

NCTL Opening Note (2014) *NCTL v Monzoor Hussain, Arshad Hussain, Raswan Faraz, Hardeep Saini and Lindsey Clark.*

NCTL (2014) 'Witness Statement of Simone Whitehouse, before the Professional Conduct Panel Case No. 12139 (2014). In the matter of: The National College for Teaching and Leadership and Monzoor Hussain (and others)'.

NCTL (2014) 'Witness statement of Tim Brighouse, before the Professional Conduct Panel Case No. 12139 (2014). In the matter of: The National College for Teaching and Leadership and Monzoor Hussain (and others)'.

NCTL (2014) Expert Witness statement of Marius Felderhof (2015) *NCTL v Hussain, Saini, Clarke, Farwaz & Hussain.*

NCTL (2017) 'Monzoor Hussain, Hardeep Saini, Arshad Hussain, Razwan Faraz, Lyndsey Clark. Professional conduct panel outcome: Panel decision and reasons on behalf of the Secretary of State for Education in respect of applications for the proceedings to be discontinued'. May. Available at: www.gov.uk/government/publications/teacher-misconduct-panel-outcome-mr-monzoor-hussain-mr-hardeep-saini-mr-arshad-hussain-mr-razwan-faraz-ms-lyndsey-clark.

Transcript of Proceedings, PVLT Day 4, 22 October 2015.

Transcript of Proceedings, PVLT Day 5, 26 October 2015.

Transcript of Proceedings, PVLT Day 6, 28 October 2015.

Transcript of Proceedings, PVLT Day 14, 1 December 2015.
Transcript of Proceedings, PVLT Day 15, 8 December 2015.
Transcript of Proceedings, PVLT Day 21, 16 December 2015.
Transcript of Proceedings, PVLT Day 29, 27 May 2016.

Media Reports

Adams, Richard (2014) 'Ofsted inspectors make U-turn on "Trojan Horse" school, leak shows', *The Guardian*, 30 May. Available at: www.theguardian.com/education/2014/may/30/ofsted-u-turn-trojan-horse-park-view-school-leak.

Adams, Richard (2015) 'Education department hits back at MPs over Trojan horse criticisms', *The Guardian*, 26 June. Available at: www.theguardian.com/education/2015/jun/26/education-department-hits-back-at-mps-over-trojan-horse-criticisms.

Adams, Richard (2017) 'Trojan Horse affair: remaining proceedings dropped', the *Guardian,* 28 July. Available at: https://amp.theguardian.com/education/2017/jul/28/trojan-horse-affair-remaining-disciplinary-proceedings-dropped-teachers-birmingham-schools.

Adams, Richard (2017) 'Five teachers in Trojan Horse affair free to return to classroom', *The Guardian*, 30 April. Available at: www.theguardian.com/education/2017/may/30/trojan-horse-tribunal-five-birmingham-teachers-islam.

Adams, Richard (2017) 'Trojan Horse affair: remaining disciplinary proceedings dropped', *The Guardian*, 28 July. Available at: amp.theguardian.com/education/2017/jul/28/trojan-horse-affair-remaining-disciplinary-proceedings-dropped-teachers-birmingham-schools.

Alibhai-Brown, Yasmin (2017) 'Islamists won't give up trying to take over British schools because nobody is willing to stop them', *International Business Times,* 21 February. Available at: www.ibtimes.co.uk/islamists-wont-give-trying-take-over-british-schools-because-nobody-willing-stop-them-1607790.

Awford, Jenny (2016) 'Two teachers in "Trojan horse" school who fed pupils a "diet of Islam", segregated assemblies and ignored sex education are allowed BACK into classrooms by a High Court judge', *Daily Mail*, 13 October. Available at: www.dailymail.co.uk/news/article-3836622/ Two-teachers-Trojan-horse-school-allowed-classrooms.html.

Becket, Francis (2008) 'Too much power', *The Guardian*, 13 May. Available at: www.theguardian.com/education/2008/may/13/schools. newschools.

de Bellaige, Christopher (2017) 'Al-Britannia, My Country by James Fergusson review – a compelling survey of British Islam', *The Guardian*, 1 June. Available at: www.theguardian.com/books/2017/jun/01/al-britannia-my-country-james-fergusson-review-british-islam-minority-population.

Birmingham Mail (2010). 'Police apologise for Project Champion Birmingham spy camera scheme', 5 July. Available at: www. birminghammail.co.uk/news/local-news/police-apologise-for-birmingham-spy-camera-127653.

Birmingham Mail (2013) 'Birmingham headteacher and deputy quit in SATs results probe', 3 October. Available at: www. birminghammail.co.uk/news/local-news/small-heath-headteacher-deputy-quit-6135405.

Birmingham Mail (2014) '"We're sorry" Council leader admits staff ignored Trojan Horse issue for "fear of being accused of racism"', 18 July. Available at: www.birminghammail.co.uk/news/midlands-news/ birmingham-mail-trojan-horse-investigation-7456936.

Birmingham Mail (2014) 'Stop pretending Trojan Horse plot is fake, urges Labour MP', 21 July. Available at: www.birminghammail.co.uk/news/ midlands-news/stop-pretending-trojan-horse-plot-7467609.

Birmingham Mail (2015) 'Trojan Horse one year on: headteacher who warned the government five years ago reveals plans to create "families" of schools', 23 April. Available at: www.birminghammail.co.uk/news/ trojan-horse-one-year-on-9095037.

Bodkin, Henry (2017) 'Second Islamist "Trojan Horse" scandal feared after Oldham headteacher reports death threats', *Sunday Telegraph*, 19 February. www.telegraph.co.uk/news/2017/02/19/second-islamist-trojan-horse-scandal-feared-oldham-headteacher/.

Bowcott, Owen (2017) 'Claim that MP lied about Kenya massacre "may be in contempt of parliament"', *The Guardian*, 21 March. Available at: www.theguardian.com/world/2017/mar/21/kenya-mau-mau-case-lawyers-contempt-parliament-foreign-office.

Daily Mail (2016) 'Warning on 'UK Muslim ghettoes': Nation within a nation developing says former equalities watchdog', 11 April. Available at: www.dailymail.co.uk/news/article-3533041/Warning-UK-Muslim-ghettoes-Nation-nation-developing-says-former-equalities-watchdog.html.

Dickens, John (2017) 'The inside story of the Trojan Horse trial collapse', *Schools Week*, 7 June. Available at: http://schoolsweek.co.uk/long-read-is-the-nctl-fit-for-purpose-after-trojan-horse-collapse/.

Garner, Richard (2013) 'Teachers urge boycott of new Ofsted regime', *Independent*, 31 March. Available at: www.independent.co.uk/news/education/education-news/teachers-urge-boycott-of-new-ofsted-regime-8555233.html.

The Guardian (2016) 'Editorial: The Guardian view on sexual harassment in schools: action is needed', 13 September. Available at: www.theguardian.com/commentisfree/2016/sep/13/the-guardian-view-on-sexual-harassment-in-schools-action-is-needed.

Gilligan, Andrew (2014) 'Trojan Horse: how we revealed the truth behind the plot', *The Telegraph*, 15 June 2014. Available at: www.telegraph.co.uk/education/educationnews/10899804/Trojan-Horse-how-we-revealed-the-truth-behind-the-plot.html.

Gilligan, Andrew (2017) 'Revealed: new "Trojan Horse plot". Head teacher fears for her safety', *Sunday Times*, 19 February. Available at: www.thetimes.co.uk/article/revealed-new-trojan-horse-plot-9hbknhmc8.

Griffiths, Sian (2016) 'Children at risk in "rotten borough" Birmingham', *Sunday Times*, 11 December. Available at: www.thetimes.co.uk/article/children-at-risk-in-rotten-borough-birmingham-fl5f00pkb.

Hope, Christopher (2013) 'David Cameron: we will "drain the swamp" which allows Muslim extremists to flourish', *Telegraph*, 3 June. Available at: www.telegraph.co.uk/news/politics/10097006/David-Cameron-We-will-drain-the-swamp-which-allows-Muslim-extremists-to-flourish.html.

Howse, Patrick (2014) 'School governors "should be more business-like"', BBC 13 January. Available at: www.bbc.com/news/education-25713820.

Kerbaj, Richard and Griffiths, Sian (2012) 'Islamist plot to takeover schools', *Sunday Times*, 2 March. Available at:www.thesundaytimes.co.uk/sto/news/uk_news/Education/article1382105.ece.

Kerbaj, Richard, and Griffiths, Sian (2015) '100 Islamist teachers face ban', *Sunday Times*, 5 April. Available at: www.thesundaytimes.co.uk/sto/news/uk_news/Education/article1540185.ece.

Lepkowska, Dorothy (2012) 'First "outstanding" school of 2012 reveals all', *The Guardian*, 13 February. Available here: www.theguardian.com/education/2012/feb/13/outstanding-osted-for-birmingham-school.

Marr, Andrew (2012) 'Interview with Sir Michael Wilshaw, Ofsted's Chief Inspector', *The Andrew Marr Show*, 2 September. London: BBC. Transcript available at:http://news.bbc.co.uk/2/shared/bsp/hi/pdfs/0209122.pdf.

Mason, Rowena (2014) 'Birmingham schools "feel like the Balkans" say Labour', *The Guardian*, 22 July. Available at: www.theguardian.com/education/2014/jul/22/birmingham-schools-balkans-liam-byrne-trojan-horse-islamism.

Martin, Jamie (2017) 'Schools must be more vigilant on Islamism than ever', *Schoolweek*, 11 June. Available at: http://schoolsweek.co.uk/schools-must-be-more-vigilant-on-islamism-than-ever/.

Oborne, Peter (2011) 'Where's the divide?', *The Spectator*, 29 January. Available at: https://www.spectator.co.uk/2011/01/whereandx2019s-the-divide/.

Oborne, Peter (2017) 'The "Trojan Horse" plot? A figment of neo-Conservative imagination', *Middle East Eye*, 2 June 2017. Available at: www.middleeasteye.net/columns/trojan-horse-plot-figment-neo-conservative-imagination-1295765958.

Pells, Rachael (2016) 'Full academisation of schools still a reality, despite government U-turn, think tank confirms', *Independent*, 10 May. Available at: www.independent.co.uk/news/education/education-news/full-academisation-of-schools-still-reality-despite-government-u-turn-nicky-morgan-think-tank-a7023156.html.

Pidd, Helen and Dodd, Vikram (2014) 'Police chief condemns appointment of terror officer over "Islamic schools plot"', *The Guardian*, 15 May. Available at: www.theguardian.com/uk-news/2014/apr/15/police-chief-counter-terror-officer-islamic-schools-plot-birmingham.

Priestland, David, Reynolds, Margaret, Wentworth, Richard, Parker, Matt, Baker, Yvonne, Hamnett, Chris and Byrne, Nick. (2013) 'Michael Gove's new curriculum: what the experts say', *The Guardian*, 12 February. Available at: www.theguardian.com/commentisfree/2013/feb/12/round-table-draft-national-curriculum.

Robinson, Martin (2014) 'Dozens of anonymous whistleblowers whose evidence helped expose the Trojan Horse plot in Birmingham schools have been told their identities will be revealed to the ringleaders', *Daily Mail*, 4 January. Available at: www.dailymail.co.uk/news/article-4087404/Dozens-anonymous-whistleblowers-evidence-helped-expose-Trojan-Horse-plot-Birmingham-schools-told-identities-revealed-ringleaders.html.

Roy, Olivier (2017) 'Who are the new jihadis?', *The Guardian,* 13 April. Available at: www.theguardian.com/news/2017/apr/13/who-are-the-new-jihadis.

Sewell, Dennis (2010) 'Michael Gove vs the Blob', *The Spectator*, January 2010. Available at: www.spectator.co.uk/2010/01/michael-gove-vs-the-blob/.

Sparrow, Andrew (2014) 'Nigel Farage: Parts of Britain are like a foreign land', *The Guardian*, 28 February. Available at: www.theguardian.com/politics/2014/feb/28/nigel-farage-ukip-immigration-speech.

Sparrow, Andrew (2014) 'Ofsted finds "culture of fear and intimidation" in some schools', *The Guardian*, 9 June. Available at: www.theguardian.com/politics/blog/2014/jun/09/ofsted-publishing-trojan-horse-plot-reports-and-michael-goves-statement-politics-live-blog#block-5395e28ce4b0a6aad6394ac8.

Spillett, Richard (2017) '"He said not wearing a hijab would turn women into whores": SECOND headteacher claims there's a "Trojan Horse-style plot" at Oldham school with Muslim governors, *Mail Online*, 26 February. Available at: www.dailymail.co.uk/news/article-4260986/Second-Oldham-headteacherclaims-Trojan-Horse-bullying.html.

Stanford, Peter (2014) '30,000 volunteers wanted – but who'd be a school governor?', *The Telegraph*, 6 January. Available at: www.telegraph.co.uk/education/educationopinion/10553621/30000-volunteers-wanted-but-whod-be-a-school-governor.html.

Stewart, Heather and Walker, Peter (2016) 'Theresa May to end ban on new grammar schools', *The Guardian*, 9 September. Available at: www.theguardian.com/education/2016/sep/09/theresa-may-to-end-ban-on-new-grammar-schools.

Stuart, Hannah and Blake, John David (2017) 'Trojan Horse: "If anyone is still in any doubt that the practices uncovered were inappropriate, just listen to the pupils"', *TES*, 16 June. Available at: www.tes.com/news/school-news/breaking-views/trojan-horse-if-anyone-still-any-doubt-practices-uncovered-were?platform=hootsuite.

Travis, Alan (2012) 'Stark choice under new immigration rules: exile or family breakup', *The Guardian*, 8 June. Available at: www.theguardian.com/uk/2012/jun/08/immigration-rules-couples-stark-choice.

The Telegraph (2010) 'Editorial: Britain is no place for the white, working-class male', *The Telegraph*, 14 January. Available at: www.telegraph.co.uk/news/politics/labour/6990777/Britain-is-no-place-for-the-white-working-class-male.html.

The Times (2016) 'Muslims are not like us, race equality chief says', 27 January. Available at: www.thetimes.co.uk/tto/news/politics/article4675392.ece.

Townsend, Mark (2017) 'Theresa May's counter-terrorism bill close to "sinking without trace"', *The Guardian*, 29 January. Available at: www.theguardian.com/politics/2017/jan/29/theresa-may-counter-terrorism-bill-sinking-without-trace-extremism-british-values.

Travis, Alan (2008) 'MI5 report challenges views on terrorism in Britain', *The Guardian*, 20 August. Available at: www.theguardian.com/uk/2008/aug/20/uksecurity.terrorism1.

Turner, Camilla (2017) 'Alarm at move to reveal identity of whistleblowers who exposed Trojan Horse scandal', *The Telegraph*, 4 January. Available at: www.telegraph.co.uk/education/2017/01/04/alarm-move-reveal-identity-whistleblowers-exposed-trojan-horse/.

Wilby, Peter (2011) 'Is Mossbourne Academy's success down to its traditionalist headteacher?', *The Guardian*, 5 January. Available at: www.theguardian.com/education/2010/jan/05/mossbourne-academy-wilby-profile.

Wintour, Patrick (2014) 'Trojan horse inquiry: "A coordinated agenda to impose hardline Sunni Islam"', *The Guardian*, 17 July. Available at: www.theguardian.com/uk-news/2014/jul/17/birmingham-schools-inquiry-hardline-sunni-islam-trojan-horse.

Vasagar, Jeevan (2012) 'An Inspector calls: the day the Head of Ofsted visited one school', the *Guardian*, 27 March. Available at: www.theguardian.com/education/2012/mar/27/michael-wilshaw-ofsted-school-inspector.

Index